QUEER CHIVALRY

SOUTHERN LITERARY STUDIES

Fred Hobson, Series Editor

QUEER *Chivalry*

MEDIEVALISM AND THE MYTH OF WHITE MASCULINITY IN SOUTHERN LITERATURE

TISON PUGH

Louisiana State University Press *Baton Rouge*

Published by Louisiana State University Press

Manufactured in the United States of America
First printing

Designer: Michelle A. Neustrom
Typeface: Whitman
Printer and binder: Maple Press

Library of Congress Cataloging-in-Publication Data

Pugh, Tison.
Queer chivalry : medievalism and the myth of white masculinity in Southern literature / Tison Pugh.
pages cm. — (Southern literary studies)
Includes bibliographical references and index.
ISBN 978-0-8071-5184-6 (cloth : alk. paper) — ISBN 978-0-8071-5185-3 (pdf) — ISBN 978-0-8071-5186-0 (epub) — ISBN 978-0-8071-5187-7 (mobi) 1. American literature—Southern States—History and criticism. 2. Homosexuality in literature. 3. Middle Ages in literature. 4. Chivalry in literature. 5. Masculinity in literature. 6. Southern States—In literature. 7. Southern States—Intellectual life. I. Title.
PS261.P84 2013
810.9'975—dc23

2012048442

The paper in this book meets the guidelines for permanence and durability of the Committee on Production Guidelines for Book Longevity of the Council on Library Resources. ♾

In memory of my brother, Gordon Alexander Pugh Jr.
(April 29, 1967–June 18, 2008),

and my father, Gordon Alexander Pugh Sr.
(July 30, 1937–July 20, 2009)

Contents

Acknowledgments

My thanks to Dean José Fernández and the College of Arts and Humanities at the University of Central Florida for providing me with a sabbatical research leave in the spring semester of 2008 to develop this project. I am also grateful for funding this book received from the University of Central Florida's College of Arts and Humanities. In addition, I deeply appreciate the generous support of the team at Louisiana State University Press, particularly Margaret Lovecraft, John Easterly, Catherine Kadair, Lee Sioles, Lauren Tussing-White, Michelle Neustrom, and MaryKatherine Callaway, whose professionalism and steadfast backing of this project have been inspiring.

An earlier version of chapter 2 was published as "Dialectical History, White Indians, and Queer Anxiety in Mark Twain's *A Connecticut Yankee in King Arthur's Court*," *Essays in Arts and Sciences* 31 (2002): 83–102. An earlier version of chapter 4 was published as "'It's prolly fulla dirty stories': Masturbatory Allegory and Queer Medievalism in John Kennedy Toole's *A Confederacy of Dunces*," *Studies in Medievalism* 15 (2006): 77–100. I am grateful to David Sloane, editor of *Essays in Arts and Sciences*, and to Karl Fugelso and Caroline Palmer of *Studies in Medievalism*, published by Boydell & Brewer, for their support of this research and for their permission to republish it, in substantially revised form, in this monograph.

QUEER CHIVALRY

1

INTRODUCTION

Southern History, Mythic White Masculinity, and Queering the Medieval Chivalric Ideal

Chivalry is a historical myth, and a queer one at that. Because histories and myths are often little better than lies, the chivalric ideal of white southern masculinity cannot stand as a triumphant declaration of manhood and must confront its queer foundations. As Samuel Johnson famously observed, "All history, so far as it is not supported by contemporary evidence, is romance,"[1] and in positing the frequent overlap of history and romance, Johnson suggests the likelihood of a culture's factual foundations assuming fictional colorings. When romance, myths, and outright lies seep into and distort the history of a given culture, the odd commingling of fiction and fact renders both romance and history bereft of taxonomic clarity. History is often purported to record the factual foundations of a society, yet its ideological purpose of forming "proper" citizens cannot be divorced from its ostensibly impartial and archival position: in building the necessary cultural background from which a coherent society emerges, history constructs and contorts, creates and constricts. Hayden White observes that "[e]very historical narrative has as its latent or manifest purpose the desire to moralize the events of which it treats," and this remark captures the ways in which history promotes the ideological values of a culture through the interpretive praxis inherent in historiography.[2] Creating a functioning and cohesive culture necessitates a shared history, and often this shared history celebrates conceptions of normative gender and sexuality by idealizing particular persons and identities as praiseworthy and denigrating others as reprobate.

In a manner similar to the ideological and gendered function of history, societies depend upon their foundational myths to outline the parameters of membership and thereby to acculturate their citizens. Within semiotic, literary, sociological, and anthropological paradigms, myths are believed to structure thought through the iconic deployment of signs and narratives suggestive of deeper ideological tenets: "Myths are . . . imaginative patterns, networks of powerful symbols that suggest particular ways of interpreting the world," argues Mary Midgley.[3] In a similar vein, Claude Lévi-Strauss affirms: "I therefore claim to show, not how men think in myths, but how myths operate in men's minds without their being aware of the fact."[4] Myths bear the potential to garble history, and the resulting mixtures of myth and history create powerful cultural narratives that define a society and its people with little regard for those being so defined outside the parameters of the normative.

Such blurrings of history and myth run throughout narratives of the U.S. South, and these tensions invite deep questions about the historical foundations of southern identity. In his classic study *The Burden of Southern History*, C. Vann Woodward notes the friction between two camps of historians, whom he terms mythmakers and iconoclasts, and their quarrel over a defining myth of the U.S. South: the chivalry of its men. "While some Southern historians have contributed to the mythmaking, others have been among the leading iconoclasts, and their attacks have spared few of the South's cherished myths," Woodward avows. He then elegiacally identifies the myth of southern masculinity as a victim of iconoclasm: "The Cavalier Legend as the myth of origin was one of the earlier victims."[5] White southern men as archetypes of honor, gentility, and chivalry: this myth dominates the U.S. South for much of the cultural imaginary, yet its veracity need not be tested as much as continually reiterated. As Eugene Genovese notes of cultural practices in the U.S. South, "'Tradition' is . . . an embodiment of 'givens' that must constantly be fought for, recovered in each generation, and adjusted to new conditions,"[6] and such mythic constructions of history as encoded in the cavalier legend of chivalric masculinity need to be tended to in the same manner as other southern traditions. In regard to the puncturing of this cavalier legend, however, a myth deflated is not a myth defeated; the enduring legacy of this myth of white southern masculinity as medieval chivalry reborn continues apace.[7]

For if the Civil War and Reconstruction represent for southern men a paradoxically ennobling experience through their reconstitution into a glorious "Lost Cause," the reformulation of white southern manhood from defeated to victorious serves a similar ideological strategy. The "Lost

Cause" ironically defines a dominant and often virulent incarnation of southern manhood, and Craig Friend and Lorri Glover emphasize the heady confluence of history and male desire amid the disarray of Reconstruction that propagated this archaic yet resilient masculinity: "In the late nineteenth century, as white southerners became nostalgic over the Old South and the 'Lost Cause,' memory of that honor—equal parts reality and fantasy—became central to conceptualizations of southern history and southern men."[8] On a similar note, Stephen Berry marks the confused interplay of war and gender: "The Civil War was, like all wars, essentially ironic. Supposed to enforce, amplify, and clarify gender roles, it instead made them murky, distorted, and even inverted."[9] Engaging in war to confirm their culture and masculinity as superior to the North's, white southern men proved their gendered identity to be a "Lost Cause" as well, and the performance of chivalric masculinity exposes these men's failures to protect their geographically inflected masculinity on the battlefield. Alan Nolan sees in the legend of the "Lost Cause" an attempt "to foster a heroic image of secession and the war so that the Confederates would have salvaged at least their honor from the all-encompassing defeat."[10] For these reasons, the "Lost Cause" permeated life in the U.S. South following the Civil War, even, as Charles Wilson asserts, evolving into virtually a religion, as he documents in his *Baptized in Blood: The Religion of the Lost Cause, 1865–1920.*[11]

If southern history brims with mythic potential in its cavalier legend of the "Lost Cause" and its chivalric men, so too does gender in its myriad constructions, but the overarching aggrandizing of southern culture through myth does not extend to all gendered persons of the region. As social constructions founded upon biological reality, myths of gender establish paradigms of identity for people to emulate, and their responses to these myths influence the directions of their lives in myriad ways. In her critique of Western psychoanalysis, Judith Butler describes gender as a coercive force of ideology: "If gender is a norm, it is not the same as a model that individuals seek to approximate. On the contrary, it is a form of social power that produces the intelligible field of subjects, and an apparatus by which the gender binary is instituted. As a norm that appears independent of the practices that it governs, its ideality is the reinstituted effect of those very practices."[12] For the U.S. South, polarized myths of gender identity are interconnected with a vast array of other binary markers. "The stories of southern bodies have been structured in large part by the interlocking logics of dichotomy—masculine and feminine, white and black, master and slave, planter and 'white trash,' Cavalier and Yankee—that have characterized the dominant public written discourse of the South," declare Susan Donaldson and Anne Goodwyn Jones in considering the ways in which gendered myths inflect discourses of the U.S. South.[13] Prevailing divisions of humans into categories based on gender, race, social class, and geographical location affect—if not effect, or infect—a given individual's position in society, yet these cultural categories are myths as well. Although such myths of gender are accorded great ideological weight, their power to alter lives does not transmute them into anything beyond myth. On the contrary, they remain fantastic constructions while simultaneously revealing the brute force of ideological interpellation. Without using this critical lexicon of Althusserian theory, Robert Penn Warren recalled late in his life that he paradoxically could not recall "how my early brand of uninstructed Southernism soaked into me," and his confused memories on this subject capture the tacit function of ideology to create normatively gendered citizens without the individual's awareness of the immersion.[14] In a similar vein, George Tindall describes how southern culture perpetuates itself through racial myths that exclude vast swaths of its population: "It was as if one soaked up from the air one breathed the belief that the southern people comprised a population that was 99.44 percent pure Anglo-Saxon."[15] Viewing history as a "natural" presentation of the past, one that subsequently produces normality in the present through the touchstone deployment of its self-reflexive "natural" qualities, obscures the contingent and fluctuating foundations at its heart, in regard both to its narratives and to the genders defined within them.

As a subset of mythologized genders, masculinities evolve in the contested yet shared space between history and myth, thereby reflecting the historical circumstances conducive to the ideological propagation of a culture. Men live and die embedded in history, in the passage of time that establishes the beginning and terminus of their lives, and in many ways, time defines the masculinities available during a given historical period. The masculinities conceivable to a fifteenth-century peasant, a seventeenth-century king, a nineteenth-century slave, and a twenty-first-century male homosexual vary widely, and the historical times of these men's lives delimit the contours of their masculinities. In terms of ideological and cultural privilege, dominant forms of masculinity create male power within a given chronological period, and, as Stanley Aronowitz posits, the maintenance of dominant forms of masculinity wields debilitating effects for those not accorded the benefits of such a gender when it is projected as an "essentialized identity defensively invited by men to reassert their privileges."[16] For the U.S. South, the myth of chivalric masculinity dominates the cultural and historical landscape, creating a vision of white southern men through the mutually mythologized histories of the Middle Ages and the U.S. South as lands and times of chivalric honor, with little regard to the historical actions (and, at times, atrocities) of such men.

To bolster its ideological status as normative, white chivalric masculinity of the U.S. South appropriates invisibility as its defining feature: it is silently naturalized as the de facto standard of southern manhood so that its cultural construction as normative is overlooked. Holly Crocker analyzes masculine invisibility and finds it complicit with the ideological maintenance of gender: "Invisibility . . . is directly relevant to gender constructions, particularly the ways that dominant masculinity establishes its quiet claim to power over others, especially women. Aligning itself with an expansive invisibility that subjects others to its machinations and designs, masculinity asserts its comprehensive dominance by passing unnoticed."[17] Similar to masculinity, whiteness and heterosexuality also erase their traces while propping up prevailing ideological power structures. Pointing to the invisible power of racial and sexual normativity, Julian Carter declares: "'[N]ormality' made it possible to discuss race and sexuality without engaging the relations of power in which they were embedded and through which they acquired much of their relevance."[18] White heterosexual southern men have historically and invisibly claimed normativity and chivalry as exclusive to themselves, relegating African Americans, women, homosexuals, and others to a subjected and secondary status.

Queer theory, however, demands that the "natural," the "normal," and the "invisible" undergo the same analyses as that which historically has been deemed unnatural, abnormal, and conspicuously visible in terms of race, social class, gender, and sexuality, in contrast to white masculinity's invisibility. Rather than accepting masculinity as a natural foundation of analysis, queer theory asks for every performance of gendered identity to be taken as tentative and unproven, to be subject to exposure for its contradictions, its paradoxes, and how it often passes unnoticed. White masculinity of the U.S. South, provocatively and defiantly presented as the definitive model of manhood, depends upon the white-black, male-female, and homosexual-heterosexual binaries to project itself as superior, yet the inherent instability of these binaries bears the potential to subvert the manhood it defends. By troubling history and gender as epistemological categories, queerness exposes what some versions of history might hide, and white southern men's appropriation of medieval chivalry compellingly exemplifies the queer anxieties at the heart of such a defensive ploy. It must not be forgotten, as Sally Robinson posits, that invisibility is not free from history but bears its own history, too: "To be unmarked means to be invisible—not in the sense of 'hidden from history' but, rather, as the self-evident standard against which all differences are measured: hidden *by* history."[19]

If this chivalric myth of white southern masculinity were not treated with such dutiful respect in some quarters, its inherent implausibility would shine through and the myth would be subject to ridicule in its very pronouncement. But here the myths of the U.S. South converge with myths of the medieval past, and cultural fantasies unite as a glorified vision of southern masculinity merges with a glorified vision of the Middle Ages. Neither of these visions is grounded in historical reality, for the medieval past is not summoned to perform ideological work for subsequent cultures due to its history as archivally recorded but due to a romanticized, aestheticized, and often literary version of its history more connected to fantasies of romance than to actual living conditions during the roughly one thousand years designated as the Middle Ages. As Umberto Eco trenchantly argues, "the Middle Ages have always been messed up in order to meet the vital requirements of different periods."[20] In regard to southern chivalric masculinity, the tropes of medieval romance define knightly masculinity, and the standard plots of these narratives feature the quest of a single knight seeking valiantly to win his lady's love. Along this narrative trajectory, the knight proves his worthiness by fighting in tournaments and slaying monsters for his beloved or for any forsaken and suffering women encountered during his journey. Medieval romances stress the ideals of courage, courtesy, loyalty, honor, etiquette, and mercy and, in so doing, glorify chivalric masculinity as a gendered panacea to a range of narrative obstacles and cultural traumas.[21] Maurice Keen considers chivalry to be "an ethos in which martial, aristocratic, and Christian elements were fused together,"[22] and its usefulness during the Middle Ages and subsequent temporal periods arises in its succinct yet malleable definition of ideal and virtuous masculinity.

In terms of the historical foundations of this ultimately queer myth of southern chivalric manhood, it should be noted that some scholars discount as historical "fact" the proposition that chivalry emerged in response to the U.S. South's veneration of the Middle Ages. Eugene Genovese concludes that antebellum southern slaveholders "were consciously looking toward a bright future, not toward the past and toward some restoration of a lost world. In consequence, with few exceptions, they regarded the Middle Ages as backward, superstitious, static, and on balance as unattractive."[23] Here we see the dismissal of a historical "fact" through Genovese's reassessment of archival records, yet the same society can embrace simultaneously both progressive and regressive fantasies, and Gregory VanHoosier-Carey's intriguing study of the rise of Anglo-Saxon studies in southern universities after the Civil War traces how this "discipline enabled Southerners to reinterpret the disorienting events of the Civil War and Reconstruction as a comprehensible narrative that both legitimized Southern defeat and promised eventual Southern victory."[24] The U.S. South's conflicting turn to chivalric medievalism as regressive and progressive, depending upon the circumstances of its enactment, reflects the amorphousness of the past when used to construct the present (and thus to create a vision of the future as well).

As the studies of Genovese and VanHoosier-Carey illustrate, medievalism frequently moves in contradictory currents in relation to time and history, and in this regard Michael Alexander outlines it as "the offspring of two impulses: the recovery by antiquarians and historians of material for the study of the Middle Ages; and the imaginative adoption of medieval ideas and forms."[25] Both of these diverging impulses in medievalism are in play in the chivalry of the U.S. South. Scholars will likely continue to disagree over the extent to which medievalism and chivalric masculinities define southern history (as evidenced in Woodward's analysis of mythmakers and iconoclasts), but what is nonetheless apparent is the persistence of this myth and the cultural work it continues to perform. Moreover, the shadow of this medieval myth is long and long-standing, and it does not appear to be fading from the U.S. cultural imaginary. "The South today is as much a fiction, a story we tell and are told, as it is a fixed geographic space below the Mason-Dixon line," Tara McPherson comments,[26] and although the story of the U.S. South changes in each retelling, the trope of southern chivalric masculinity proves intransigent, although not entirely stable, in its popularity, which also highlights the protean resilience of the Middle Ages as a tool for commenting on the present.

In appropriating chivalric values into their fictions, many southern writers select the gendered elements of medieval romances conducive to their narrative and ideological goals while ignoring the tropes that would render these reconceived avatars of southern manhood laughable rather than laudable. Southern culture's turn to medievalism hinges more upon such heroes as Roland in *The Song of Roland*, Thomas Malory's depictions of Arthur and Lancelot in the *Morte D'Arthur*, and the mythologized masculinity of historical figures such as Richard the Lion-Hearted than upon medieval visions derisive of such unimpeachable manhood, including the parodies depicted in Chaucer's "Tale of Sir Thopas" from the *Canterbury Tales* and Cervantes's *Don Quixote*. The kinship between medieval romance and southern literature, despite their shared focus on the chivalric virtue of heroically masculine protagonists, is actually rather superficial, but this dominant trope of masculine honor nonetheless shores up white southern masculinity by bestowing upon it an honored pedigree. Southern masculinities also depend upon idealized re-creations of medieval literature in subsequent eras, most notably those of Sir Walter Scott and his *Waverley* novels, but any such turn to medievalism to define southern masculinity belies the necessity of such a defensive ploy to defend what is already under duress.[27]

To describe white southern masculinity—a culturally dominant identity that often defended its privileges through horrendous acts of violence and oppression—as under duress will undoubtedly offend many readers, particularly those who (or whose ancestors) have suffered mightily under such brutality. It is nonetheless essential to see the queer foundations of identities mounted in defense of their own gendered vulnerability. The need to perform chivalry reveals a chink in the armor of white southern masculinity, in that chivalry projects a narcissistic claim regarding the attractiveness of southern men, but such narcissism, as Sigmund Freud argues, is a defensive strategy in response to cultural anxieties, as well as, I argue, a strategy that bears queer undertones. Freud delineates a link between narcissism and homosexuality in that narcissism "denotes the attitude of a person who treats his own body in the same way in which the body of a sexual object is ordinarily treated—who looks at it, that is to say, strokes it and fondles it till he obtains complete satisfaction through these activities." Narcissism rapturously celebrates the self, but such pleasure depends upon the aesthetic and sexual contemplation of one's physical body as the ideal object of desire. Expanding on this point, Freud also sees the possibility that narcissism assists in the development of a healthy ego, "that it might claim a place in the regular course of human sexual development," in its function as a "complement to the egoism of self-preservation."[28] Desiring narcissistically, and thereby creating a vision of oneself as desired, defends the ego from an endless parade of doubts that would fracture one's self-image as desirable to others. Narcissism may be a tautological desire, yet it is one that performs important defensive work for the maintenance of individual identity, as well as for a culture at large.

The narcissistic project of chivalric masculinity cannot forever uphold the virile claims at its heart, and Julia Kristeva underscores the inherent unlikelihood of narcissism protecting an individual's claims of identity: "The fragility . . . of the narcissistic elaboration, underpinning the ego image as well as ideal cathexes, is such that its cracks immediately reveal the negative of our image films to those that others consider to be 'narcissistic.'"[29] Paradoxically, these fissures within chivalric masculinity are not without their cultural function to uphold subverted masculinities. Kaja Silverman explores how masochistic pleasures arise in the assumption of such failed narcissistic identities, how power is continually perpetuated through these cracks. She terms such a strategy "reflexive masochism," in which a man's investment in cultural conditions apparently subversive of his masculinity buttresses his dominant position: "Because reflexive masochism does not demand the renunciation of activity, it is ideally suited for negotiating the contradictions inherent in masculinity. The male subject can indulge his appetite for pain without at the same time calling into question either his virility, or his paternal lineage."[30] The claim of white southern chivalry is both narcissistic and masochistic: it posits southern men as bounteously attractive, yet this declaration reveals a masochistic dissonance between the beautiful image and the need to project and protect this image ceaselessly and thus, ultimately, fruitlessly. The turn to chivalry and medievalism queerly reveals what the ideological superstructure behind white southern masculinity would hide—its inherent vulnerability.

The theoretical construct of queer chivalry denudes the conflicted play of white male narcissistic posturing in southern literature, in that, in the interplay of history, myth, medievalism, race, and masculinity emerges the potential for a queer analysis, one that examines the fanciful exchanges between history and myth as chronicled in the literary record and exposes both the coercive power of normative masculinity and sexuality and their hollow bravado. Scott Bravmann argues that scholars "need to stretch rather than reinforce the boundaries that define queer history and its academic study, to think outside the historically specific formations that distinguish absolutely between the literal and the figurative, the real and the imaginary—between, in other words, 'fact' and 'fiction.'"[31] History, myth, medievalism, race, and gender combine in the ideological formulation of the U.S. South, a region that frequently metamorphoses history into myth—and also treats its myths as history—and obscures the borders between the two even more throughout the literary record. In this study, the terms *history*, *myth*, and *literature* both represent separate spheres of narrative and culture and are inextricably intertwined with one another in the construction of white southern manhood.

As a concept, *queer chivalry* captures the paradox of southern chivalric masculinity, with this oxymoronic term also pointing to the disorienting effect of myth in the re-creation of gendered histories. Chivalry, of course, should not be queer, since it refers to the decidedly heterosexual endeavors implicit in courtships between valiant knights and beautiful maidens, but performances of chivalry metamorphose into queerness when the suspect nature of heterosexuality becomes evident through these very performances. In this regard *queer* refers to disruptions of normative gender and sexual identities, but it is critical to realize that such subversions of heteronormativity need not entail homosexuality. Carolyn Dinshaw notes that queer theory asks readers to recognize the cultural work that must be undertaken to produce "normality": "Queerness works by contiguity and displacement, knocking signifiers loose, ungrounding bodies, making them strange. . . . [I]t makes people stop and look at what they have been taking as natural, and it provokes an inquiry into the ways that 'natural' has been produced by particular discursive matrices of heteronormativity."[32] Eve Sedgwick likewise defines *queer* as signifying "the open mesh of possibilities, gaps, overlaps, dissonances and resonances, lapses and excesses of meaning when the constituent elements of anyone's gender, anyone's sexuality aren't made (or *can't be* made) to signify monolithically."[33] Homosexuality, in regard to amatory desires shared between members of the same sex, frequently clashes with heteronormativity, but such collisions between sexual desire and a governing ideology of normativity reflect a cultural construction, not a "natural" state of affairs. Little of the literature under consideration in this monograph directly addresses homosexuals or homosexuality, yet these narratives insistently highlight the queer difficulties inherent in maintaining gendered and sexual normativity.

From this perspective, southern chivalric masculinity as historical "fact" and as literary "fiction" reveals the flimsiness of these binary terms, for the relevant facts and fictions circuitously support and undermine each other in a manner that renders masculinities queer. Recent studies of southern queerness ponder history's effects on gendered identities and address the ways in which people negotiate their sexualities within particular geographical and sociocultural landscapes. As John Howard claims in his study of southern homosexuality, "notions and experiences of male-male desire are in perpetual dialectical relationship with the spaces in which they occur, mutually shaping one another."[34] White southern chivalry reflects an ideological desire to see men in a certain gendered fashion, one emerging from a romanticized historical landscape of de facto heteronormativity and divorced from the emasculating force of defeat in the Civil War. Within this overarching paradigm, great differences emerge in how authors deploy these tropes. The authors who serve as the primary focus of this monograph—Mark Twain, Flannery O'Connor, John Kennedy Toole, Robert Penn Warren, Walker Percy, and Ellen Gilchrist—write from remarkably different cultural perspectives despite their shared status as southerners, and their play with southern chivalry reflects varied conceptions of how masculinity functions in the U.S. South to subvert male privilege and heteronormativity as they are simultaneously lionized.

In using queer theory to analyze constructions of southern masculinity, I am not attempting to "out" the authors or the characters examined in this study as homosexual; on the contrary, in this move I join scholars such as Michael Bibler and Gary Richards who locate queerness in southern literature and highlight its conflicted position within southern culture. Bibler explores queer relationships in mid-twentieth-century southern literature, particularly those involving "same-sex intimacy [as] part of a larger nexus of queer relations specific to the plantation mythologies" found in the works of William Faulkner, Tennessee Williams, Lillian Hellman, Katherine Anne Porter, Margaret Walker, William Styron, and Arna Bontemps.[35] Gary Richards investigates the ways in which the "quarantining of homosexuality to the South in the popular national imagination dictated to some degree that the region's writers must represent sexual otherness"; he analyzes the ways in which such authors as Truman Capote, Richard Wright, Lillian Smith, Harper Lee, and Carson McCullers employ "acts of strategic subversion [to] reconfigure these representations with depth and complexity."[36] Richards refuses "to isolate same-sex desire from other components of sexuality or to hold sexuality as extricable from biological sex, gender, race, and class" in his analysis,[37] and this monograph builds upon his and Bibler's work by moving beyond the potential queerness latent in homosocial relationships to explore the ways in which straight men are rendered queer through the fantasy of chivalry. Desires that are gendered masculine—to be a man, to win a woman, to achieve a victory—circulate throughout southern literature, but men cannot sate such desires with teleological certainty: a man can approach a model of masculinity, can near it and approximate its characteristics, but such a vision can never be achieved in its entirety. As Jane Gallop observes of the virtual paradox inherent in defining the self, "Identity must continually be assumed and immediately called into question."[38] This foundational assumption guides the questions at the heart of the subsequent analysis: how are fictions of southern masculinity established in a text, and how are these fictions subsequently reified or subverted, performed successfully or denuded as a fraud in regard to the famed chivalry of white southern men?

The enduring myth of white southern masculinity and chivalry is elegantly and elegiacally expressed in the opening screens of the film version of Margaret Mitchell's *Gone with the Wind*, perhaps the most iconic pronouncement of southern medieval masculinity within the U.S. cultural imaginary:

> There was a land of Cavaliers and Cotton Fields called the Old South . . .
> Here in this pretty world Gallantry took its last bow . . .
> Here was the last ever to be seen of Knights and their Ladies Fair, of Master and of Slave . . .
> Look for it only in books, for it is no more than a dream remembered.
> A Civilization gone with the wind . . .[39]

These lines mythologize antebellum southern culture by haphazardly laying claim to historical models of masculinity, including cavaliers and knights, as well as by articulating an argument against the future through their lament for the eternal loss of gallantry. One is not expected to probe the accuracy of such mythic pronouncements with historical questions, such as How did knighthood and feudalism, waning historical institutions in Europe by the time of the founding of Jamestown in 1608, cross the Atlantic Ocean to inspire generations of white southern men? Even lexical questions can disrupt these myths, if one ponders which type of cavalier modeled masculinity for southern men—the fictional courtly lovers of medieval romances, the historical knights who fought in the Crusades, the supporters of Charles I in his seventeenth-century war with Parliament, or the literary reincarnations of medieval chivalric figures in nineteenth-century novels such as those of Sir Walter Scott?

One need not digress deeply into the literary and historical incarnations of cavaliers to note remarkable distinctions in these men's treatment of women and thus to note as well the inherent confusion of chivalry as a marker of masculine identity in the U.S. South. Medieval knights displayed their chivalric virtue by performing feats of bravery while chastely adhering to ideals of courtly love, an amatory ritual codified by Andreas Capellanus in his twelfth-century text *De amore* (often loosely translated as *The Art of Courtly Love*).[40] In contrast, the cavaliers of Charles I wrote notoriously lascivious verse, such as Sir John Suckling's "Out upon It!" and

Robert Herrick's "To the Virgins, to Make Much of Time." Walter Scott's chivalric fictions reimagine the gendered relations of medieval romance by concentrating more on armed conflict between crusaders and "infidels" and by largely stripping women of their courtly roles as arbiters of masculine conduct. In the text quoted from *Gone with the Wind* and other such melancholic paeans to southern manhood, the politics implicated by historical nostalgia for a largely imaginary past, one cobbled together from models of masculinity no longer particularly relevant to their actual historical foundations in medieval Europe, posits an idealized vision of geographical and temporal masculinity both as timeless and as extinct. Any sense of historical accuracy is rendered irrelevant in the retellings of the cavalier legend and its fantastic scaffolding of white southern masculinity, as southerners have themselves noted. In her 1894 tribute to the southern cavalier, Maud Wilder Goodwin praises this model of manhood while dismissing the necessity for historical accuracy in its roots: "The men who settled the Southern Colonies, Virginia, Maryland, and the Carolinas, were Cavaliers; not necessarily in blood, or even in loyalty to the Stuart cause, but Cavalier in sympathies, in the general view of life, in virtues and vices."[41] The need to label white men as cavaliers trumps the need to know precisely what is meant by this term for Goodwin and many other commentators who endorse this masculine legend.

Chivalric myths of white masculinity offer a powerful model of social self-definition for the U.S. South. Yet at the same time that myths are promulgated as an essential truth of a culture, members of the culture often realize the shallow protection that such ideological fancies afford. For even as southern identity is venerated through historical misappropriations, the inherent anachronism of chivalric masculinity can also be apparent within its own value system. Chivalry guides southern manhood, but it is only one model among many conflicting myths of masculine identity. Returning to *Gone with the Wind,* it is apparent that the same text can lionize and subvert mythic history, such as when Rhett Butler dismisses southern chivalric masculinity because of its preemptory claims: "Scarlett, our Southern way of living is as antiquated as the feudal system of the Middle Ages. The wonder is that it's lasted as long as it has. It had to go and it's going now. And yet you expect me to listen to orators like Dr. Meade who tell me our Cause is just and holy? And get so excited by the roll of drums that I'll grab a musket and rush off to Virginia to shed my blood for Marse Robert? What kind of a fool do you think I am? Kissing the rod that chastised me is not in my line."[42] Rhett considers southern culture an anachronism, an outmoded way of life detached from the social conditions of antebellum America, and he links his rejection of southern culture and its medievalism to its demands upon his gender, specifically the presumed assumption of a heroic and martial masculinity of crusading and chivalry. Furthermore, in his image of men kissing a chastening rod, Rhett defends his masculinity by linking other men's performances of chivalric masculinity to homoerotically phallic acts of subservience.

Quite simply, chivalry generates for Rhett Butler and other men like him a model of masculine identity that constrains them into a rigid gender role with potentially fatal repercussions in war, and this trope carries over into other texts of southern literature derisive of such performances of male chivalric identity. As humorist Florence King trenchantly points out in recalling her childhood visits to neighbors, family, and friends, lethal side effects accompany chivalric masculinity: "There were never any men in the homes we visited. They had all died somewhere between forty and fifty, felled by the rigors of chivalry, leaving fragile, helpless, desperately ill widows to 'cope'—the Southern woman's favorite verb—as best they could."[43] King's satire comically overstates the burdens of chivalry, yet she also highlights the ways in which antiquated myths of masculinity bear unexpected repercussions for the men enacting them. If death is in some ways the final and irrevocable status of all men's masculinities, chivalry hastens its proponents to their graves, as they are prematurely forced to confront the ways in which gendered myths cannot defend their narcissistic claims forever.

In regard to the historical trajectory of southern literature, masculinity and medieval chivalry run hand-in-hand throughout many of its classic texts, and their conjunction has greatly influenced how readers view this literary canon. Paul Jones outlines how mythological and romanticized versions of history inform popular thinking about the "medievalness" of the U.S. South and its literary roots: "[M]ost of the literature of the antebellum South was written by a handful of white, wealthy, landowning, and slave-owning historical romancers—including William Gilmore Simms, John Pendleton Kennedy, William Caruthers, and Nathaniel

Beverley Tucker—who imitated the model of Sir Walter Scott's historical novels in order to paint a portrait of the South that would promote an aristocratic social structure, based on class hierarchy and slavery. Since Mark Twain diagnosed the region as having 'the Sir Walter disease,' antebellum southern literature has been depicted by literary studies as little more than glorified propaganda, poorly written copies of Scott's Waverley novels."[44] Jones's study complicates and questions this simplistic myth, as he provides readings of voices antithetical to this paradigm and delineates the variety of viewpoints, many of which were somewhat radical, expressed in antebellum fiction. Once again, myths—in this case, a simplistic assessment of early southern literature denying its artistic complexity—need not be true in order to wield a powerful influence on a culture.

Mark Twain's famed diagnosis of the U.S. South as suffering from "the Sir Walter disease" humorously yet accurately assesses many texts of southern literature that naively reflect medieval courtly values. The "disease" of an inflated sense of aristocratic and chivalric privilege provided ample fodder for humorists other than Twain, as is also evident in such works as Henry Clay Lewis's *Odd Leaves from the Life of a Louisiana Swamp Doctor* (1850), in which a chapter is titled "The Man of Aristocratic Diseases."[45] Twain's derogatory evaluation of southern literature appears to be an example of history being written by the winners, as his canonical pronouncements on the aesthetic value of this body of writing contributed to a view of it and the U.S. South as antiquated and backward (while leaving his own literature unscathed despite its many southern and medieval themes). Twain's words from *Life on the Mississippi* (1883) merit quoting at length, as they mockingly cement a vision of the U.S. South in terms of its myths of medieval chivalric manhood:

> Then comes Sir Walter Scott with his enchantments, and by his single might checks this wave of progress, and even turns it back; sets the world in love with dreams and phantoms; with decayed and swinish forms of religion; with decayed and degraded systems of government; with the sillinesses and emptinesses, sham grandeurs, sham gauds, and sham chivalries of a brainless and worthless long-vanished society. He did measureless harm; more real and lasting harm, perhaps, than any other individual that ever wrote. Most of the world has now outlived [a] good

> part of these harms, though by no means all of them; but in our South they flourish pretty forcefully still. . . . There, the genuine and wholesome civilization of the nineteenth century is curiously confused and commingled with the Walter Scott Middle-Age sham civilization, and so you have practical, common-sense, progressive ideas, and progressive works, mixed up with the duel, the inflated speech, and the jejune romanticism of an absurd past that is dead, and out of charity ought to be buried. But for the Sir Walter disease, the character of the Southerner . . . would be wholly modern, in place of modern and mediaeval mixed, and the South would be fully a generation further advanced than it is. It was Sir Walter that made every gentleman in the South a Major or a Colonel, or a General or a Judge, before the war; and it was he, also, that made these gentlemen value these bogus decorations.[46]

Twain's vision of the U.S. South, which he characterizes as deluded by regressive fantasies of manners and chivalry, yields none of the supposed charms of the land but only the pathetic attempts of its citizenry to assert an anachronistic view of military masculinity unhinged from any historical foundations and embodied in a legion of spurious majors, colonels, generals, and judges. Queer potential lurks in the background of such imaginary constructions of manhood, as the "bogus decorations" that Twain locates as foundational to southern manhood bespeak the dishonesty necessary to proclaim and protect masculinities created through myth, as well as the hollow narcissism of masculine attractiveness paradoxically predicated upon the failure of these men to win the Civil War.

Twain's disparaging assessment of "the Sir Walter disease" in southern life and literature greatly oversimplifies a complex sociocultural and literary heritage, yet many southerners agree with his claims and virtually diagnose themselves with cases of this "affliction." Describing his late-nineteenth-century childhood, Henry Seidel Canby, a founding editor of the *Saturday Review of Literature*, confesses how the allure of Scott's novels shaped him and his peers: "[W]hat we fell upon, read besottedly, thought about and were moulded by were . . . the novels of Sir Walter Scott." Beyond the ways in which Scott's medieval romances influenced his generation of male readers, Canby also discerns a connection between the memories of his elders and Scott's novels: "The eccentrics, the temperamentals, and the powerful living people I knew were nearly all old in the [eighteen-]nineties, and the stories they told were paralleled in what I read in Scott, even if far less romantic."[47] In his 1941 memoir *Lanterns on the Levee,* William Alexander Percy recalls how his father believed that Scott's novels were essential for a man's proper moral development and determined for his son that "there would be no other novel-reading to poison my mind until I had finished Scott."[48] The parallels between the U.S. South after the Civil War and England after the Norman invasion—in which two conquered peoples (southerners and Saxons) struggled to retain cultural pride while living with their conquerors (northerners and Normans)—bolstered the allure of Scott's novels for many southern male readers such as Canby and William Alexander Percy. Indeed, Scott's *Ivanhoe* can be read as virtually a pre-facto allegory of the defeated U.S. South.[49] Reality filtered through the lens of Scott's medieval fictions in the U.S. South of chivalry reborn: Canby and William Alexander Percy testify that this heady combination marked their perceptions of life and literature.

One does not need to look far to find examples of chivalry and medieval masculinities in southern fiction. They pervade the literary record, but for the purposes of this study, their divergent use in Harriet Beecher Stowe's *Uncle Tom's Cabin* (1852) and Caroline Lee Hentz's *The Planter's Northern Bride* (1854), antebellum novels representing opposing sides of the slavery debate, provides thumbnail sketches of their conflicting deployments. In his climactic battle with Simon Legree, Stowe's hero George Harris transforms into a modern-day reincarnation of the epitome of knightly virtues, St. George: "George turned, and, with one indignant blow, knocked Legree flat upon his face; and, as he stood over him, blazing with wrath and defiance, he would have formed no bad personification of his great namesake triumphing over the dragon" (597).[50] In contrast, St. Clare, the genteel figure of whom such chivalric virtues should be expected as well, laughingly dismisses his inability to embody a chivalric ethos: "I can't turn knight-errant, and undertake to redress every individual case of wrong in such a city as this" (313). Hentz's protagonist Eulalia Hastings recalls descriptions of the U.S. South and its chivalric character, detailing her impressions of its positive and negative features to her suitor Mr. Moreland. She initially holds antislavery views, in contrast to his stance opposing emancipation:

"I love to think of your sunny clime, . . . of your magnolia bowers and flowery plains. I have heard a great deal of your chivalry and liberality, and love to listen to their praises; but I do not love to think of the dark spot in your social system, that is gradually spreading and deepening, and destroying all its beauty and happiness" (54).[51] As a result of her chivalric suitor's heroism, Eulalia realizes her error and, by novel's end, rewards her lover by agreeing with him about the necessity of slavery. Perhaps the most egregious deployment of supposed chivalric values arises in Thomas Dixon's celebration of the Ku Klux Klan, which he imbues with medieval chivalry in his *The Clansman: An Historical Romance of the Ku Klux Klan* (1905).[52] The subtitle of this novel bears a trace of "the Sir Walter disease" in its statement of genre, with Dixon acclaiming the Klan's purportedly noble and medieval character in their document "The Prescript of the Order of the Invisible Empire": "This is an institution of Chivalry, Humanity, Mercy, and Patriotism: embodying in its genius and principles all that is chivalric in conduct, noble in sentiment, generous in manhood, and patriotic in purpose" (320). The vision of chivalric men-at-arms merges with the medievalism of a holy war akin to the Crusades: for Dixon, the Klan triumphs in its incarnation as modern-day crusaders for whiteness.

Numerous examples of the ways in which medieval chivalry and white masculinity influence southern literature could be added to the ones in the previous paragraph, but in the interests of expediency, it would perhaps be best to direct the reader to Harnett Kane's *The Romantic South*, a miscellany stocked with numerous illustrations of southern medievalism as an ideal virtue, such as James Avirett's pronouncement in 1857: "It is a mistake to say that the age of chivalry has passed. . . . It is fashionable to sneer at these imitations of the amusements of the middle ages; but when it is remembered that they are done in the daytime, and bring together from distant places the young and old of both sexes, and excite to courtly emulation, whilst they perfect our young men in the elegant accomplishment of horsemanship, they are far more worthy of commendation than the midnight revels of the ballroom."[53] The contrast between chivalry in the daylight and an unmentionable licentiousness assumed to correspond with "midnight revels" lionizes the former as the most prized virtue of the U.S. South. In this antebellum homage to the Middle Ages and southern gentility, Avirett lauds the chivalric performances that Twain later found so laughable, and his praise points to chivalry's honorable effects on masculinity as its defining feature.

In the gaps among history, myth, and literature arise much subversive potential, in that myth colors history, yet this coloring takes on a queer tint when fantasies of masculinity are revealed as empty performances of gendered and narcissistic bravado. The cavalier myth, when exposed as a white masculine facade to bolster the ideological regimes of the U.S. South, can no longer conceal its queer foundations of masculinities manipulated through fantasies of identity. For southern writers who do not replicate the chivalric myth at face value, the deconstruction of this dominant trope of southern masculinity subverts the fictional and historical foundations of the U.S. South. In his study of literary representations of the cavalier figure, Ritchie Watson notes that many authors employ the ideal figure of the southern gentleman to criticize the values represented by such men: "All of Virginia's writers have recognized at least dimly that there is something inadequate and insufficient in the Cavalier ideal."[54] Watson's insightful readings of the limitations of the cavalier figure in the novels of George Tucker, John Pendleton Kennedy, William Caruthers, and John Esten Cooke point to the necessity of deflating culturally lionized stereotypes of masculinity. This study builds on his by considering chivalric and medieval masculinities as queering forces that unexpectedly undermine performances of culturally valorized manhood.

Following this introductory chapter, *Queer Chivalry* turns to Mark Twain's dismissive treatment of medieval masculinity in *A Connecticut Yankee in King Arthur's Court* (1889), as this text in many ways provides a satirical superstructure for understanding subsequent dismissive accounts of southern masculinity. After Twain, four canonical writers of the mid to late twentieth century—Flannery O'Connor, John Kennedy Toole, Robert Penn Warren, and Walker Percy—are discussed in regard to their varying treatments of southern chivalry and masculinity, which nonetheless unite in subverting chivalry as an ideal value. The book concludes with a brief reading of Ellen Gilchrist's rewriting of chivalry as a woman's virtue. These writers reconsider tropes of medieval masculinity approximately seventy-five to one hundred years after Twain's indictment of them in *Life on the Mississippi* and *A Connecticut Yankee in King Arthur's Court*, as they investigate the ways in which such myths continue to inflect southern literature at a time when U.S. masculinity, in the wake of World War II, appeared imperially triumphant. These authors showcase the limitations of white male chivalry, although they do so from a variety of perspectives: O'Connor writes as a woman denied the privileges of southern masculinity; Toole as a homosexual alienated from prevailing cultural constructions of sexual normativity to the point of suicide; Warren as a former southern apologist in *I'll Take My Stand* (1930) who shifted to more progressive racial views later in life;[55] Percy as a Catholic responding to the cultural shifts inaugurated both by Vatican II and by the feminist and gay rights movements of the 1960s and 1970s; and Gilchrist as a woman condemning the rampant sexism of the U.S. South. Despite the wide variety of their worldviews, these authors agree in their fictions that the clichés of southern chivalry have become ripe for reassessment, and in particular they respond to the historical shifts of U.S. manhood in the years following World War II.

Of course, authors prior to O'Connor, Toole, Warren, Walker, and Gilchrist, and those prior to Twain as well, also play with southern medievalism as a literary trope; medieval themes, images, and ideas, although frequently more muted in tone, can readily be found in the works of such esteemed southern authors as William Faulkner, Truman Capote, Eudora Welty, and Tennessee Williams, among others. Perhaps most notably, James Branch Cabell assaults chivalric values in his *Jurgen: A Comedy of Justice* (1919), and this novel, remarkably popular and controversial in its day, lampoons chivalry as a value in defining masculine virtue.[56] My goal, then, is not to create a linear literary history of a protean trope but to explore its contradictions and queering effect on the construction of southern masculinity within a subset of southern literature contemporaneous to society's reevaluation of gender roles in the period roughly between the 1950s and 1980s. Concomitant to the narrative trajectory outlined in this monograph, a vision of shifting southern masculinities emerges, yet I avoid the implied telos of many historical studies implying progressive evolution: this study seeks not to delimit the queer intersections of chivalry and masculinity but to provide linking snapshots of an overdetermined trope that insistently resonates throughout southern culture.

Chapter 2, "Dialectical History, White Indians, and Queer Anxiety in Mark Twain's *A Connecticut Yankee in King Arthur's Court*," explores how protagonist (or antihero) Hank Morgan's insistently masculine identity fractures through the dialectic tension between his modern self and the medieval past he must negotiate throughout his time-traveling adventures. Hank establishes himself as an embodiment of American industrialism and progress, one who, like Twain himself, would never succumb to "the Sir Walter disease," but sixth-century England seduces him into realizing the limits of modernity. The homosocial bonds prevalent in the Arthurian court threaten Hank's masculinity, as he comes to grips with the ways in which interpersonal relationships are mediated through historical visions of masculinity, ones that are a good deal more appealing—and queering—than he initially suspects. Twain presents his notoriously vexed text as a satire, but he subverts its satirical foundations when narrator Hank Morgan finds himself seduced by the archaic visions of masculinity that he first derides.

Themes of medievalism, masculinity, chivalry, and sexuality unite in Flannery O'Connor's short stories and novellas, and chapter 3, "Medieval Masculinity, Southern Chivalry, and Redemptive Homosexuality in Flannery O'Connor's Fiction," focuses on "Everything That Rises Must Converge," "The Comforts of Home," "The Geranium," "A Late Encounter with the Enemy," "The Enduring Chill," and *The Violent Bear It Away* to discuss the ways in which O'Connor's beleaguered male protagonists face queering potential in their quests for spiritual revelation. The protagonists of these narratives must confront the fictions of their southern manhood. Each man enacts a version of southern chivalric or saintly masculinity, and most of them remain mired in normative conceptions of manhood at the narrative's close; in so doing, they foreclose the possibility of Christian revelation that O'Connor establishes as the telos of her short fiction. Inversely, O'Conner exposes some of her male protagonists to a queering cure for their masculine pretensions, in that she envisions homosociality and homosexuality as painfully reparative therapies for men suffering from an inflated sense of male privilege. O'Connor abases these protagonists so that they can achieve a chivalry of the soul rather than of the body, if such enlightenment is possible for them at all.

Chapter 4, "'It's prolly fulla dirty stories': Queer Masculinity and Masturbatory Allegory in John Kennedy Toole's *A Confederacy of Dunces*," considers how the Middle Ages queers southern literature both textually and metatextually. Toole's novel mercilessly satirizes medievalism, and antihero Ignatius J. Reilly is far too ridiculous and Rabelaisian a figure to be confused with a positive avatar of chivalric masculinity. Medievalism nonetheless inspires his quests throughout the madcap environs of New Orleans, as it also inspires his allegorical interpretations of their significance. Allegory, in many ways, establishes an intensely personal relationship between reader and text, in that readers are called to interpellate themselves within the narrative. Here arises the queering potential of medievalism, in that readers must confront the emptiness of modernity and the lure of the Middle Ages by witnessing Ignatius's unsettling yet hilarious performances of historical masculinities, which are ultimately seductive, albeit in a most quixotic fashion.

The lunacy of *A Confederacy of Dunces* finds its inverse image in Robert Penn Warren's *A Place to Come To* (1977), because both narratives focus on medievalists seeking to imbue their lives with meaning through their re-creation of outmoded values in modern society. Warren's protagonist Jed Tewksbury could not be more dissimilar from Ignatius Reilly, in the former's philosophical musings on the meaning of life and love and in the latter's farcical questing, but in chapter 5, "'I *am* the Lost Cause': Queer History, the Southern Phallus, and the Quest for Medieval Timelessness in Robert Penn Warren's *A Place to Come To*," unexpected similarities emerge in Jed's quest to create a life of meaning by refracting medieval qualities into his search for romance. Jed rejects his southern roots and replaces them with his passion for medieval literature, and in so doing, he exposes the hollow fantasy of masculinity and the deep difficulties of merging chivalry, gender, and southern identity into a unified person. The return trip to his Alabama home after years of self-imposed exile entails realizing a newly refurbished yet haunted sense of medieval masculinity, through which he ultimately resolves the dilemma of a self fractured by its southern foundations.

Walker Percy's interest in chivalry and medievalism provides the focus of chapter 6, "'The Sir Walter Disease' and Queer Quests for Masculinity in Walker Percy's Novels." Of Percy's six novels, *Lancelot* most forthrightly proclaims its interest in medievally inspired chivalric masculinities through its title, but this theme percolates throughout all of Percy's novels to varying degrees. In an intriguing passage of autobiographical reminiscence recorded in the essay "Why Are You a Catholic?" Percy "diagnoses" himself as suffering from "the Sir Walter disease" in his childhood and considers its effect on his spiritual worldview.[57] If one reads his novels through the lens of his distrust for Scott's chivalric fictions, it becomes apparent that Percy sees medieval incarnations of heroic masculinities hindering the path to spiritual growth by inspiring chivalric actions in environments spiritually inhospitable to them. His protagonists—Binx Bolling, Will Barrett, Thomas More, and Lancelot Lamar—all face pressures to their sense of chivalric southern masculinity, and their varying responses to these pressures outline how "the Sir Walter disease" queerly deconstructs pretensions of southern manhood.

Queer Chivalry concludes with a study of Ellen Gilchrist's *The Annunciation* (1983), a novel in which myths of southern male chivalry are reimagined from a feminist perspective. As Gilchrist's narrative asserts the possibility of female chivalry, this turn of the trope puts a lasting queer spin on an intransigently heterosexual posture. *The Annunciation* asks readers to consider how the myth of southern chivalry relegates women to secondary and often subservient positions, and the story of Amanda McCamrey's escape from southern history powerfully revises the meaning of gender. As is apparent from Gilchrist's literature, exploring the U.S. South is itself often a queer process, in that it demands that authors, readers, and citizens see a geographical and literary landscape through the gendered fictions of identity created by southerners to define themselves, as well as by northerners to define themselves in contrast to southerners. In this imaginary interplay of past and present, the past's power is often presumed to be incontrovertible and its problems irresolvable. In 1950 William Faulkner memorably pronounced of southern history, "The past is never dead. It's not even past," and in a similar vein, Robert Penn Warren eulogized in 1946, "[I]f you could accept the past you might hope for the future, for only out of the past can you make the future."[58] These haunting admonitions bespeak the impossibility of freeing a culture or a person from history. Without history, one is lost, cast adrift, and bereft of a sense of place and culture.

But with history, southerners are often queered as well, because history outlines a model of identity that many find restrictive or otherwise uncomfortable. Hence the queerness of white southern masculinity, in that its power stems from its ubiquitous invisibility, which itself depends upon its continual reenactment to mask the deceptions at its perverse and narcissistic core. At the beginning of William Gilmore Simms's *Southward Ho! A Spell of Sunshine* (1885), the narrator's traveling companion ponders the necessity of traveling from North to South and hints at the queerness of such a journey: "What does all this mean? . . . Back to the south? In the name of Capricorn and Cancer, why this most perverse of all determinations?"[59] The perversity accorded to the U.S. South is somewhat erased in Simms's reimagining of Chaucer's *Canterbury Tales*, in which various travelers offer narratives glorifying the region and its chivalric values, yet a shadow of perversity lingers throughout the narrative in that chivalric fictions continually and narcissistically pronounce values that can never fully shore up the statements of masculinity at their heart. Writing in the mid-twentieth century, C. Vann Woodward notes in his critique of American historical texts that the "perversity" of the U.S. South accompanies scholarly accounts of it: "[T]he general histories of the United States have been governed by the tacit assumption that the South is adequately covered by the various phases of national history, and the perverse section is disposed of with cursory reference to progress, poor whites, and the race problem."[60] In the end, the ghostly penumbra of chivalry attached to white southern masculinities cannot withstand the queering interplay of fact and fiction. History only bears the meanings we give it, and now it is time to examine how some of the most vaunted writers of the U.S. South use chivalry and the medieval past to queer the men of their fictions and, in so doing, to question the meaning of southern manhood.

2

DIALECTICAL HISTORY, WHITE INDIANS, AND QUEER ANXIETY IN MARK TWAIN'S *A CONNECTICUT YANKEE IN KING ARTHUR'S COURT*

Mark Twain derided the symptoms of "the Sir Walter disease" in southern culture as the mawkish and sentimental attachment to chivalric identities celebrated in Walter Scott's novels. Hank Morgan, the protagonist of *A Connecticut Yankee in King Arthur's Court* (1889), appears to display no such traces of this affliction in his flagrant Americanism characterized by gritty independence and technological know-how.[1] Most important in this regard is Hank's eponymous identification as a Yankee, an identity that ostensibly inoculates him from the nostalgia for chivalric social codes prevalent in the nineteenth-century U.S. South. Hank instead ridicules the Middle Ages for espousing and practicing chivalric values; his criticism of the past tautologically condemns the Middle Ages for its very medievalism. Despite this overarching color to his character, Hank has proved troublesome for scholars to construe as the representative of a specific ethos: he appears to represent nineteenth-century American industrialism and progress in an anachronism-ridden vision of sixth-century medieval England, yet, by the novel's end, he is seduced by the past and wishes nothing more than to remain in the history that he at first has despised. This conflict in Hank's desire—to introduce innovation in a land and time he both scorns and adores—hampers a clear-cut interpretation of his motives and sensibilities. By creating these antitheses in Hank, Twain places contradiction at the heart of his protagonist's relationship to the past. As Richard Pressman argues, "The key tension [in *A Connecticut Yankee*] . . . is within Morgan's own personality—a personality that reflects and renders not only Twain's own conflicts but those of his social class."[2]

Hank Morgan's conflicted critique of the Middle Ages reflects Twain's ambivalence about the period and its influence on the U.S. South. Certainly, the author's familiarity with medieval history and literature was extensive, and throughout his corpus he draws upon this body of knowledge to structure his narratives and to deepen their themes. To look at one example, *The Innocents Abroad* (1869) contains numerous (and humorous) medieval moments: a tongue-in-cheek account of Abelard and Heloise's love affair (141–47); a consideration of Petrarch's beloved Laura, with a sympathetic nod toward "Mr. Laura" ("But who says a word in behalf of poor Mr. Laura?" [184]); his retelling of a "thrilling medieval romance" (211–16); and a description of Dante's tomb, as well as his somewhat ghoulish satisfaction that the body was not buried therein (245).[3] Twain particularly extols Cervantes' *Don Quixote,* which he refers to as the "*beau ideal* of fine writing": "Don Quixote is one of the most exquisite books that was ever written, & to lose it from the world's literature would be as the wresting of a constellation from the symmetry & perfection of the firmament."[4] Also, it is well documented from Twain's notebooks and journals that he studied medieval history for his writings and that he relied heavily on W. E. H. Lecky's *History of European Morals from Augustus to Charlemagne* (1869) while penning *A Connecticut Yankee.*[5] Lecky's historiographical influence, however, did not compensate for Twain's lack of interest in the historical contours of the Middle Ages and preference for its fictional potential. Twain affirms his antihistoricism in the novel's preface by excusing himself from the obligations of historical accuracy: "It is not pretended that these laws and customs existed in England in the sixth century; no, it is only pretended that inasmuch as they existed in the English and other civilizations of far later times, it is safe to consider that it is no libel upon the sixth century to suppose them to have been in practice in that day also" (xv). Twain's fictions are inspired by the Middle Ages, yet not for the period's history but for his own fantasies of how the past could be used to consider his present culture. These various examples of Twain's medieval interests illuminate how he found much satiric potential in medieval literature, and his admiration for Cervantes aligns their authorial voices as jointly stimulating laughter by juxtaposing medieval narrative conventions with contemporary social concerns.

In complementary contrast to his satiric penchant for medieval literature and history, Twain frequently reiterates his distaste for Walter Scott's novelistic re-creations of the Middle Ages. In a personal letter he condemns *Ivanhoe* as particularly dreadful: “I am reading Ivanhoe. Ivanhoe was a knight in Sir Walter Scott’s time. He is dead, now. . . . All the characters are well sustained, especially that of the Atlantic Ocean. You know all that is necessary to know about this romance, now, Livy darling, & so if you have not read it subsequently you needn’t.”[6] Twain likewise writes to his friend Brander Matthews that he “lie[s] here dying, under the blight of Sir Walter” after enumerating Scott’s many failings as an author.[7] As much as Twain derides Scott, there is reason to believe that the truth of his critical assessment was more complex than such diatribes reflect. At the very least, he paid Scott the honor of owning his books, as detailed in his correspondence: “Our books have come—a rare thing we have been on the track of for ten days—got it at last—the famous ‘Abbotsford Edition’ of Scott’s works—12 huge volumes elaborately illustrated. Pretty scarce book.”[8] Lin Salamo and Harriet Smith suggest that “Clemens evidently purchased two sets of this twelve-volume edition of Sir Walter Scott’s thirty-two ‘Waverley’ novels . . . one for his own library, and one as a gift for someone in the Langdon family.”[9] Would Twain buy a deluxe edition of books or give them as a gift if he truly detested them? Other correspondence hints that he appreciated some of Scott’s fictions more than others:

> I’m still in bed, but the days have lost their dulness [*sic*] since I broke into Sir Walter and lost my temper. I finished Guy Mannering—that curious, curious book, with its mob of squalid shadows jabbering around a single flesh-and-blood being—Dinmont; a book crazily put together out of the very refuse of the romance-artist’s stage properties—finished it and took up Quentin Durward, and finished that.
>
> It was like leaving the dead to mingle with the living: it was like withdrawing from the infant class in the College of Journalism to sit under the lectures in English literature in Columbia University.
>
> I wonder who wrote Quentin Durward?[10]

The answer to Twain’s coyly rhetorical question, and the author of *Guy Mannering* as well as *Quentin Durward*, is Sir Walter Scott. These words were written approximately twenty years after Twain penned *A Connecticut Yankee*, but his purchase of the editions of Waverley novels occurred prior to writing this text, and so it appears that his views of Scott’s fictions, as well as his view of their medieval roots, were more complex than simple rejection or approval.

In regard to *A Connecticut Yankee* and its ambivalent medievalism, scholars have explored the conflicts between Hank Morgan and his construction of the medieval world as an incomprehensible Other. This chapter expands on their work by addressing Hank's conflicted reactions to the predominantly masculine world of chivalric knights and nobility. Male-male relationships offer readers of Hank's adventures another focal point for analyzing his conflicted responses to a sixth-century world that refuses to conform to his desires, as well as for understanding the vexed status of homosocial relationships in Twain's nineteenth-century United States of America. As Linda Morris argues, Twain's play with gender "subverted Victorian notions of fixed gender roles and essentialist constructions";[11] his depictions of sexuality (and the anxieties that sexualities provoke) likewise undermine conceptions of seamless masculine identities both in the medieval past and in the frontier culture of Twain's nineteenth-century America.

Hank views the medieval past as barbarically ignorant, and his bias surfaces in his racist construction of "white Indians," his opprobrious term for the Arthurian knights, whom he describes as savages. In their hybrid identities as both "civilized" whites and "savage" Indians, these knights expose Hank's anxiety over the possibility of hybridism disrupting cultural purity; such an anxiety also underscores the potential for queer tensions to arise from the prevailing homosocial relationships of the chivalric Arthurian world. Hank affirms such close male relationships through his friendship with Clarence, his creation of the Man-Factory, and his eventual respect for Arthur, but he unceremoniously rejects and disparages all such homosocial friendships after marrying Sandy. Hank's anxieties over masculine bonds in medieval England echo the difficulty of distinguishing between conventionally homosocial and queer male friendships in nineteenth-century Great Britain and the United States, in which homosocial practices known as romantic friendships blurred the borders between heterosexuality and homosexuality. Hank's dismissal of his male friendships in favor of marriage with Sandy exposes the ubiquitous queer potential of the chivalric world of knighthood that Hank bluntly rejects yet finds quite appealing (if only after he has lost it forever).

This chapter's following section, titled "Hybrid Identities, White Indians, and Cultural Anxieties," examines how Hank's repeated references to "white Indians" reflect Twain's construction of identities on the borders between normativity and Otherness, of normative whiteness cloaking a hidden savagery underneath. The phrase "white Indians," along with its cultural baggage, also emphasizes Hank's inability to dialectically view himself in relation to the actors of history. The privileges accorded to whiteness and aristocratic status are therefore presented as mobile rather than static, and this paradigm highlights the necessity to continually reassert their ideological valence. Moving to Hank's queer anxieties over homosociality and Arthurian masculinity, the next section, "Hank Morgan's and Mark Twain's Queer Anxieties," addresses the tension between his homosocial and heterosocial relationships. Romantic friendships between men often warranted social approbation in nineteenth-century America, yet the apparent normality of these relationships could nonetheless provide cover for homoerotic affection. The chapter's final section, "Hank's Massacre of Queer Chivalry," explores Hank's participation in the homosocial milieu of Arthurian knighthood and the ways in which this fraternity upsets his construction of himself as normative through his antimedievalism. In sum, the tragic conclusion of *A Connecticut Yankee* results from Hank's sense of privileged, white, heterosexual masculinity and his inability to accord a place in his masculine worldview for men in homosocial groupings who, according to his cultural logic, do not merit the privileges of invisible whiteness. In this instance, the potential queerness of chivalric masculinity necessitates a massacre to quell its gendered tensions.

HYBRID IDENTITIES, WHITE INDIANS, AND CULTURAL ANXIETIES

At the heart of Hank's failure to come to grips with the medieval Other lies his vision of the novel's Arthurian characters as failed representatives of a nineteenth-century capitalistic ethos. The medieval characters inevitably disappoint him because they cannot be other than who they are—figures steeped in and molded by the cultural mores of the sixth century. Through Hank's inability to envision the past as both alien and accessible,

Twain illustrates the need for dialectical crossings between past and present: viewing the Otherness of the Middle Ages as predicated not upon unbridgeable differences but upon comprehensible similarities would enable his protagonist to establish a viable relationship with the people of the past rather than merely to dismiss them as uncivilized. In this light, the brutality of the massacre at the novel's conclusion appears all the more incongruous, especially in consideration of Hank's numerous successes in his educational agenda: his newspaper and his efforts to improve personal hygiene bespeak his benevolent, if arrogant, interest in enhancing English living conditions, as well as the people's willingness to acculturate themselves to these innovations.

As Frederick Jameson argues, the dilemma created by attempts to comprehend history necessitates a dialectical understanding of present and past. Assuming either the past's comprehensibility or its incomprehensibility dooms one to misread that past, to become trapped in a world fabricated by rigid preconceptions or empty ignorance: "If . . . we decide that Chaucer, say, or a steatopygous Venus . . . are more or less directly or intuitively accessible to us with our own cultural *moyens du bord*—then . . . our apparent 'comprehension' of these alien texts must be haunted by the nagging suspicion that we have all the while remained locked in our own present. . . . Yet if . . . we decide to reverse this initial stance, and to affirm . . . the radical Difference of the alien object from ourselves, then . . . we find ourselves separated by the whole density of our own culture from objects or cultures thus initially defined as Other from ourselves."[12] The inherent difficulty of studying the past either as an alien reflection of a lost world or as a recognizable variant of the present necessitates dialectic and dialogue, traversals back and forth that respect similarities as well as differences. Hank refuses both to see the sixth century on its own terms and to admit that its Otherness from his own world mocks his objectives. In his attempts to refashion sixth-century England into a facsimile of capitalistic Western culture in the nineteenth century, Hank shows little interest in understanding the interactions of past and present; indeed, few characters in American literature would benefit more from introspection, analysis, and dialogue than Hank Morgan, who steadfastly refuses any hesitation in his assault on the cultural mores of sixth-century England.

Hank's reform of medieval England builds the plot of *A Connecticut*

Yankee, but one of the novel's deeper themes emerges as he fails to address the tensions between himself and the people of the Middle Ages as Other. Bruce Michelson argues that the "problems with Hank, and the major structural and moral problems in the novel, seem to grow from Twain's anxiety about the nature of the self and from his uncompromising idea of freedom—as a way to find that self while sustaining a novel about both the hope and the terror in being alive."[13] Striving to unify and advance England, Hank models himself as an integrated individual, but he fails to achieve his ambitions because his relationship with the medieval Other taints this egoistic narcissism. Lesley Kordecki likewise notes that "as the book progresses Hank Morgan changes and finds that although he is drawn to it, he (and Mark Twain as well) cannot fully partake of the medieval consciousness."[14] *A Connecticut Yankee* is thus the tale of a fractured consciousness, of Hank's destructive insistence on his psychosexual wholeness despite the fissures increasingly apparent in his public performance of normative masculinity.

Hank's uncompromising mind-set dooms his lofty ambitions to rebuild the past as the present, but his failure rings with irony in light of his repeated realization of the need for mutual understanding. When traveling with Sandy, he recognizes, "I had to put myself in Sandy's place to realize that she was not a lunatic. Yes, and put her in mine, to demonstrate how easy it is to seem a lunatic to a person who has not been taught as you have been taught" (252). Later, when startled by King Arthur's allegiance to the aristocracy in light of the tragedy of the Small-Pox Hut, he criticizes Arthur for the ideological indoctrination that blinds him to the needs of his people: "There it was, again. He could see only one side of it" (381). For Hank, this obtuseness to the suffering of his people marks Arthur as unfit for his regal position. Twain's irony here—as his protagonist criticizes Arthur for failing to accord the Other a due humanity—underscores Hank's own fluctuating sense of narcissistic identity in himself and in relation to others.

Hank further discerns the limitations of nondialectical communication when the Arthurian court cannot comprehend his own difference. This Yankee, who views medieval people through an alienating perspective based on his assumption of cultural superiority, recognizes this degrading dynamic when it is directed toward him, as exemplified in his metaphor of himself as an elephant in an Arthurian zoo: "You know how the keeper and the public regard the elephant in the menagerie. . . . [T]hey speak with pride of the fact that he can do a hundred marvels which are far and away beyond their own powers. . . . But does that make him one of them? No; the raggedest tramp in the pit would smile at the idea. . . . Well, to the king, the nobles, and all the nation, . . . I was just that kind of elephant, and nothing more" (98–100). Hank stresses here the problems evoked when miscommunications sabotage intercultural dialogue. Realizing the need for dialectic with Sandy and resenting the Arthurian court's ideological construction both of peasants and of himself as degraded incarnations of humanity, Hank nevertheless fails to pursue a shared understanding of the past as zealously as he pursues industrial and business innovations, such as the introduction of nineteenth-century financial markets to the sixth century. His more prevalent mode of communication entails the failure of dialectic and the degradation of the Other, and the disturbing carnage of the Battle of the Sand-Belt ensues from his troubled relationship to the history he must live. The contrasts among these situations—whether riding through the countryside with a woman whom he sees as a lunatic, or pitying himself for the court's suspicion of him, or facing an army pitched for battle—are indeed great, but the armed conflict results directly from Hank's refusal to seek dialectical understanding with a variety of the medieval characters he encounters, not merely the ones with whom he chooses to communicate.

Because he understands neither the history he must live nor the citizenry of Arthurian England, Hank's inability to control the past generates cultural anxieties over his own identity. *Anxiety* may appear an incongruous word with which to characterize Hank's relationship to the Arthurian world, since Twain presents him more as a man of ready action than of nervous introspection. His very quickness to act, however, masks the uncertainties that arise from his difficulties in understanding this alien world. Within the Arthurian past, the failure of dialectic is most evident in Hank's anxieties about whiteness, aristocratic privilege, and heterosexuality. Sigmund Freud famously located the roots of anxiety in the sexual repression that results from the conflict between individual pleasures and societal strictures, and he notes that "[a]nxiety is always present somewhere or other behind every symptom; but at one time it takes noisy possession of the whole of consciousness, while at another it conceals itself so completely that we are obliged to speak of unconscious anxiety or . . . of possibilities of anxiety."[15] Slavoj Žižek expands on Freud's ideas, theorizing that "what causes anxiety is the elevation of transgression into the norm, the lack of the prohibition that would sustain desire. This lack throws us into the suffocating proximity of the object-cause of desire."[16] That is to say, experience with the Other, and with the Other's unsettling cultural norms that need not mirror one's own, raises the possibility that transgressions need no longer be deemed transgressions, and thus one must confront taboo desires without the pretense of distance. Such unconscious anxieties, or anxieties not directly expressed, surround Hank's considerations of race and sexuality as related to issues of cultural hybridity. According to Hank's narcissistic cultural logic, whiteness, aristocratic privilege, and heterosexuality should mark a man's high status in the Arthurian world, but these qualities paradoxically threaten men through their inability to identify consistently which members of society should receive their incumbent privileges. Because whiteness and heterosexuality should reign transhistorically in their apparent ubiquity as shared yet invisible values of the Arthurian aristocracy and of Hank's nineteenth-century America, their cultural construction is never questioned. Nonetheless, whiteness, aristocratic rank, and heterosexuality reveal themselves to be malleable, thereby undermining the very privileges they are thought to uphold.

Hank's vision of race and whiteness highlights the ways in which he construes others' identities as fractured and mutable but his own as narcissistically consistent and attractive. When he views the twenty or more prisoners with whom Sir Kay brings him to court after his capture, Hank describes the appropriateness of the fate of "the rascals" because "they have served other people so in their day" (40). This initial description of the captives' situation denotes a Boethian conception of medieval fate: Fortune's Wheel has turned, and these men who inhabited its top position now fall to the bottom. He proceeds to condemn the moral mind-set of these prisoners, to lambaste their indoctrination into the social order in which they were born: "[I]t being their own turn, now they were not expecting any better treatment than this; so their philosophical bearing is not an outcome of mental training, intellectual fortitude, reasoning; it is mere animal training; they are white Indians" (40). In this fractured description of these men as both white, and thus presumably civilized, and Indians, and thus presumably savage, Hank reveals his cultural prejudices; but more than this, he reveals himself to be the arbiter of the knights' racial purity and, therefore, of their identity as a whole. Nancy Oliver observes Hank's attention to other characters' intelligence, commenting that he "perceive[s] intelligence as the key to individualism but [Hank] determine[s] what type of individuals were created."[17] His assessment of the knights' intelligence grants him authority to judge their entire being, and similarly, his derision of certain men as "white Indians" stresses that these men were formerly "civilized" whites who have metamorphosed into "savage" Indians.

The initial description of these Arthurian "white Indians" suggests that Hank perceives whiteness as a marker of personal identity that an individual can lose; in a similar vein, he describes the Round Table as "a sort of polished-up court of Comanches" (178). Here readers see a similar fractured identity, but now Hank's judgment of a given knight's experience and intelligence does not detract from his whiteness; rather, according to Hank's racial logic, these members of the Arthurian court have not yet earned their whiteness. They represent Indians insufficiently civilized to become white, as opposed to whites degraded to the status of Indians. In Hank's view, white identity fractures either when white people lose their whiteness or when they fail to earn it. The essential point in this regard is that Hank's self-constructed and ideologically invisible whiteness is never in jeopardy, no matter the brutality of his actions. The fact that other men may lose their whiteness indicates that racial constructions provoke anxiety: the vast majority of Hank's activities can be seen as his attempts to impose on the people of England not merely his views of civilization, but his views of whiteness, while simultaneously preserving the necessary cultural invisibility to his own white body.

Hank's conception of "white Indians" demonstrates his tendency to construct others in terms of fractured identities, and the epithets "The Boss" and "Sir Boss" correspondingly highlight his own transformations of identity within the aristocratic order of the Arthurian realm. Similar to the "white Indians" who lose the patina of civilization, Hank is stripped of the veneer of nineteenth-century American progressivism through his contradictory appellations when he discloses that his new title "would be THE

BOSS"; he then proceeds to muse on its merits: "There were very few THE's and I was one of them. If you spoke of the duke, or the earl, or the bishop, how could anybody tell which one you meant? But if you spoke of The King or The Queen or The Boss, it was different" (103). "The Boss," a title alluding to Hank's nineteenth-century entrepreneurial and industrial talents, merges with aristocratic titles of royalty when he reveals its alternate form to be "Sir Boss." Like the "white Indians" who lose their whiteness by metamorphosing into savagery, Hank begins as a "pure" representative of nineteenth-century values only to become increasingly seduced by royal prerogatives. Twain uses the titles "The Boss" and "Sir Boss" interchangeably throughout much of the novel, but toward its conclusion, he refrains from referring to Hank as "Sir Boss." In the letters and declarations for the final war and in Clarence's closing words, Hank becomes simply "The Boss." Twain's consistency on this point indicates his protagonist's rejection of the aristocratic privileges he has garnered in light of his final showdown with the Arthurian knights; the metamorphoses of Hank Morgan from "The Boss" to "Sir Boss"/"The Boss" and back to solely "The Boss" reveal that his identity suffers as much flux and turbulence as the "white Indians" of the nobility. The significant difference emerges in the violence engendered by Hank's anxiety over others' identities and his unquestioning acceptance of his own.

In addition to the conflict of identity evident in the title "Sir Boss," Hank Morgan's name plays upon the shifting aspects of his character. He is tied to the world of thievery, capitalism, and industrialism through the eponymous allusions to the seventeenth-century pirate Henry Morgan and the nineteenth-century monopolist J. P. Morgan. Additionally, the name "Morgan" connects him to the novel's other character sharing that name: Morgan le Fay, Arthur's half-sister and traditional villain of Arthurian narratives. Mary Shanley and Peter Stillman outline many points of comparison between Hank Morgan and Morgan le Fay, including their names, their superficial charm, their status as magicians, their rigid political views, their quick propensity to murder (Hank kills Sir Dinadan as heartlessly as Morgan kills her page), and their aesthetic enjoyment of murder.[18] Edmund Reiss sums up the hypocrisy in Hank Morgan's attempt to depict himself as shocked by Morgan's savagery: "[W]hat appalls the Yankee in the character of Morgan le Fay are the same insensitivities

Twain objects to in the Yankee's character."[19] Here Twain highlights the haziness of Hank Morgan's relationship to sixth-century England: it is unclear whether his protagonist will be the father of industrialism to this age or just another magician pursuing selfish goals. Hank's alignment with Morgan le Fay also undermines his performance of masculinity, as in many ways le Fay serves as the feminine foil who unapologetically performs atrocities similar to his own.

"White Indians," "Sir Boss," and even Hank's name—these terms indicate Twain's conceptions of the divergent and conflicted identities of the sixth-century Arthurian knights whom his protagonist encounters, as well as how their internal inconsistencies parallel Hank's personal contradictions. Twain's corresponding depiction of Hank, with the character's failure to recognize that his construction of the medieval as alien to himself discloses more about his personal anxieties of identity than about the medieval people he describes, establishes a basis of latent hypocrisy that comes increasingly to the novel's surface. This dynamic of identity construction, in which Hank critically assesses others' identities and unreflexively promotes his own as normative, also arises in his troubling response to homosocial relationships. The bonds that he shares with several male characters suffer from the vagaries of his personal anxieties and whims, and the resulting tensions make possible the conflicted visions of masculinity and male friendship that so unsettle the text.

HANK MORGAN'S AND MARK TWAIN'S QUEER ANXIETIES

Hank's homosocial relationships pique his cultural anxieties about participating in the Arthurian world, and ironically, these anxieties surface most strikingly through the depictions of his heterosexual romance. Given Hank's initial disparaging reaction to Sandy, it seems more likely that he would prefer the homosocial community of the Arthurian court and his Man-Factory than the heterosocial realm of courtly love and marriage. Although he admires Sandy's beauty and comments that "[s]he was a comely enough creature" (129), he scorns her intellect ("[S]he didn't know as much as a lady's watch" [129]) and repeatedly insults her, labeling her a "perfect ass" and a "wandering wench" (132–33). When Hank thinks

Sandy will leave him after their adventure concludes, he revels in his new freedom: "[T]he relief of it was like pardon to a prisoner." When Sandy then states that she plans to continue traveling with him, he humorously (but with latent seriousness) affirms, "This was recalling the pardon" (240). Hank also degrades Sandy with terms similar to a "white Indian" when he comments on her bathing and eating habits: "And how had it fared with the nobly born, the titled aristocrat, the Demoiselle Alisande la Carteloise? Why, she was as fresh as a squirrel; she had slept like the dead; and as for a bath, probably neither she nor any other noble in the land had ever had one, and so she was not missing it. Measured by modern standards, they were merely modified savages, those people. This noble lady showed no impatience to get to breakfast—and that smacks of the savage too" (153). Hank's distaste for Sandy is provoked because she has not yet earned the civilizing marks of her whiteness; a mere "modified savage," she represents a slightly elevated barbarian whose grooming and dietary customs offend Hank's American sensibilities. Here Hank criticizes Sandy for her uncivilized qualities and, in so doing, reiterates his position as arbiter of cultural standards.

The blatant misogyny of Hank's diatribes against Sandy is surprising, for he needs this woman to narcissistically reflect the attractiveness he claims for himself as England's lead reformer. Through his dehumanizing epithets for Sandy, Hank models a particularly virulent form of masculinity that is constructed upon the denigration of the female Other whom he both despises and, as soon becomes apparent, latently desires. In light of Hank's hostility toward Sandy, their marriage takes many readers by surprise. The only hint that he bears any affection for her appears in his statement that he is "gradually coming to have a mysterious and shuddery reverence for this girl" (258), but this realization comes before she falls to the novel's background when Hank travels and shares numerous adventures with Arthur. In a scene late in the novel, Hank affectionately reminisces over his girlfriend in nineteenth-century Connecticut: "Across my mind flitted the dear image of a certain hello-girl of West Hartford, and I wished she could see me now" (503). Bruce Michelson notes how Sandy is slighted in terms of narrative attention: "Hank's memoir expends more words on his triumph in publishing a newspaper than on his own daughter or his three years of domestic life with Sandy."[20] Nevertheless, Sandy returns to the novel's forefront when readers learn that not only has Hank married her, but they are parents of a sick daughter as well.

The marriage creates an interpretive conundrum, as it represents a social and sexual alliance between these oppositional avatars of nineteenth-century and medieval values, in Hank's self-construction as civilized and his construction of Sandy as savage. In this moment, Hank "goes native" by aligning himself with a woman he describes as uncivilized, in a scene precursory to (but not as extreme as) Kurtz's metamorphosis in Joseph Conrad's *Heart of Darkness* (1902). "Going native," the assimilation of cultural characteristics assigned to the Other during an act of conquest, paradoxically defines the whiteness of the character who undergoes such a transformation. As Shari Huhndorf argues, it is "a means of constructing white identities, naturalizing the conquest, and inscribing various power relations within American culture."[21] Within Hank's worldview, a marriage to a "savage" woman would more likely taint the husband with the wife's savagery than elevate him into a deeper understanding of romantic affection, but his disparaging opinion of Sandy nonetheless showcases the narcissistic necessity that she reflect his desirability as a heterosexual man, despite his propensity for homosocial, rather than heterosocial, relationships.

Sandy and Hank's marriage affirms the heterosocial realm of courtship and procreative romance, yet this celebration of normative sexuality carries with it his condemnation of homosocial bonds. His words testify to the utility, if not desirability, of women in disproving homoerotic valences to homosocial friendships: "Now I didn't know I was drawing a prize, yet that was what I did draw. Within the twelvemonth I became her worshiper; and ours was the dearest and perfectest comradeship that ever was. People talk about beautiful friendships between two persons of the same sex. What is the best of that sort, as compared with the friendship of man and wife, where the best impulses and highest ideals of both are the same? There is no place for comparison between the two friendships; the one is earthly, the other divine" (524). Here readers see a dichotomy similar to that embodied in the figure of the "white Indian": "earthly" homosocial friendships, debased in a manner similar to the construction of American Indians and Arthurian knights as savage, are inferior to "divine" heterosocial romances, elevated in a manner similar to the construction of whites as culturally superior. This condemnation of homosociality accompanying the paean to Hank's wedded bliss in many ways undermines the claim to normative sexuality inherent in marriage. Hank's bonds with Clarence and Arthur structure much of the novel, and few contextual clues indicate that these friendships represent earthly and trivial matters to him. Indeed, Hank's friendship with Clarence appears the strongest of his relationships throughout the novel, yet he now characterizes it as "earthly," as one in which the "best impulses and highest ideals" could not exist. These lines are especially jarring when one realizes that Hank's partner in his lofty ambition to reform England is Clarence, not Sandy.

Twain's understanding of male-male relationships in nineteenth-century America surfaces in Hank's condemnation of medieval same-sex friendships. In denigrating such masculine bonds, Twain implicitly addresses the queer potential latent in homosocial romantic friendships, a paradigm of same-sex attachment valorized in many social settings in nineteenth-century and early-twentieth-century America and Britain. Of course, friendships need not carry any latent hints of queerness, and philosophers such as Ralph Waldo Emerson extolled the virtues of friendship for exalting a man's life to a higher plane: "But the sweet sincerity of joy and peace which I draw from this alliance with my brother's soul is the nut itself whereof all nature and all thought is but the husk and shell. Happy is the house that shelters a friend!"[22] Nothing particularly homoerotic colors Emerson's words from this essay of 1841, and in Twain's America, most male friendships offered simply the chaste pleasures of another man's company. Nonetheless, queer potential lingered in the possibility that apparently asexual attachments might cloak homosexual romantic attractions.

Romantic same-sex friendships blossomed frequently in such sex-segregated institutions of the nineteenth and early twentieth centuries as colleges and boardinghouses. In these cloistered spaces, intense friendships flourished between members of the same sex, and the surviving records of such relationships prove their passion and, at times, their eroticism. Leila Rupp documents the sexual nature of romantic friendships in nineteenth-century America, noting in particular the distinct cultural expectations for men and women: "Although male romantic friends shared the female ones' sense that only same-sex friends could truly understand one another, they differed in the loosening of these bonds after the period of youth, at least if they married. Like women, young men formed ardent and romantic attachments and engaged in touching, kissing, and caressing. But they were expected to move beyond such intense attachment when they became adults and married."[23] Romantic friendships provided homosexual men and women a respite from expectations of heterosexuality while simultaneously retaining them within the hazy borders of socially acceptable behavior. Despite the apparent normativity accorded these deep friendships, such attachments could generate anxiety when suspicions emerged concerning whether a particular homosocial friendship masked homosexuality and thus breached heteronormative mores.

Within the cultural context of nineteenth-century homosocial relationships and romantic friendships, Walt Whitman openly celebrates such fraternal affection in his "Calamus" poems of 1860. Twain's fiction is significantly less erotically tinged than Whitman's poetry, yet many of his works consider the cultural implications of male homosociality, including *Tom Sawyer* (1876), *The Prince and the Pauper* (1881), *Pudd'nhead Wilson* (1894), and his masterpiece *Huckleberry Finn* (1885). These texts and others depict male friendships and homosocial pairings, and Twain's portrayals of male groupings complicate an understanding of his views of homosociality in the nineteenth-century United States. During his travels throughout the American West, he lived in a society largely without women, in which men outnumbered women by a significant proportion in many areas. Reading Twain's ribald verse in light of men's communities in the frontier West, where Twain traveled and worked throughout the 1860s, Chris Packard suggests that "Twain's sub-rosa material reveals how he promoted homosocial if not homoerotic bonds as a way of consolidating privilege and power without violence."[24] The line between the homosocial and the homoerotic is notoriously difficult to identify precisely, and Andrew Hoffman, also documenting Twain's life and relationships during his western travels, compiles "evidence—circumstantial, but incontestable; inconclusive, but suggestive—that Clemens had a series of strong, loving, and romantic relationships with other men." Hoffman's intriguing study captures the gendered hurly-burly of the American West in the mid-1800s, especially in regard to Twain's Bohemian circles in San Francisco that "boasted an especially high tolerance for sexual ambiguity." Hoffman counterbalances readings of homoeroticism in Twain's works as primarily allegorical or otherwise literary in nature, such as those initiated by Leslie Fiedler.[25] Given the somewhat ambiguous nature of the biographical evidence culled by Hoffman, questions about Twain's homosocial (and possibly homosexual) experiences will likely persist, but, despite the cloudiness of these records, it is clear both that Twain spent many years of his life in exclusively male settings and that he would have witnessed how the meanings of masculinity fluctuate within male circles depending on the ways in which men negotiate the border between the homosocial and the homoerotic.

Beyond its appearance in *A Confederate Yankee*, queer homosociality similar to the gendered Bohemianism of the nineteenth-century American West is featured in several of Twain's works, albeit often with a humorous edge. His short story "A Medieval Romance" (1869), itself a parody of Walter Scott's romances, flirts with lesbian themes when Princess Constance accuses Prince Conrad (who is actually a woman disguised as a man) of impregnating her.[26] Likewise, the short story "How Nancy Jackson Married Kate Wilson" (ca. 1902) plays with the homosocial nature of female relationships, again through the plot device of enforced transvestism. John Cooley suggests that this "story may reflect Twain's troubled mind regarding his daughter Susy's lesbian relationship with Louise Brownell, a college classmate."[27] Frank Kaplan, although not explicitly labeling the two young women's bond a "romantic friendship," describes their relationship in similar terms: "Within a short while, she and one of her classmates, an attractive, bright girl from New Jersey, Louise Brownell, were in love, a deeply emotional attachment without any necessary physical expression other than hugs, and not unusual among young Victorian women who were well protected from the casual company of men."[28] Twain's exposure to homosocial relationships in general and to romantic friendships in particular, both before and after the penning of *A Connecticut Yankee*, testifies to the prevalence of such pairings throughout the nineteenth century, and reading Hank's disavowal of homosociality through this lens, it seems likely that the character expresses some of the author's anxiety about same-sex friendships eclipsing heterosocial romances.

Certainly, conceptions of human sexuality were shifting in the latter years of the nineteenth century. Michel Foucault famously locates the "birth" of the homosexual in 1870,[29] and this increasing awareness of homosexuality bleeds into concerns about homosocial relationships. In regard to *A Connecticut Yankee,* Twain does not depict Hank (or any other character, for that matter) as homosexual; rather, Hank's queer anxieties arise over the ways in which the Arthurian world privileges the homosocial over the heterosocial, as in the romantic friendships of nineteenth-century America. The end result of this anxiety, gruesomely enacted in the massacre of the Arthurian knights, exposes the brutal repercussions sparked by cultural fears surrounding masculinity, as Calvin Thomas discerns: "[M]asculine anxieties . . . [and] fears . . . are often (and often quite ludicrously) phantasmatic. . . . reproducing social consequences that are all too hideously real."[30] In fiction, the hideous "reality" of the slaughter of twenty-five thousand knights contradicts readings of Hank as a sympathetic character; interpreting his actions as the result of queer anxieties concerning normative sexuality offers a groundwork of explanation for these actions. As his construction of "white Indians" reveals anxieties about the slipperiness of racial identity, so too his condemnation of homosocial bonds bespeaks anxieties about male-male friendships. Moreover, as Twain's story of his Yankee is written over the Arthurian legend, so too does Hank's marriage to Sandy, the woman he so mockingly dismisses in numerous passages of virulent misogyny, write over and reconfigure Morgan's male friendships. A major symbolic and interpretive model for *A Connecticut Yankee* is the palimpsest, through which Twain underscores the ways in which he reimagines past literary traditions in his novel. In the story's frame, the Twain character receives Hank's Arthurian manuscript, which has been written over Sir Thomas Malory's *Morte D'Arthur;* likewise, Hank's rejection of his homosocial relationships and concomitant marriage to Sandy resignify the meaning of his male friendships and thus question what it means to be a man in any sort of relationship with another man.

HANK'S MASSACRE OF QUEER CHIVALRY

The title "Sir Boss" suggests Hank's engagement in an aristocratic world he disparages, and likewise his bond with Clarence emphasizes his enjoyment of "earthly" homosocial relationships that he similarly mocks. Akin to nineteenth-century romantic friendships, Hank's relationship with Clarence appears asexual and heteronormative from the outside, but suggestive passages whisper of a latent sexual attraction. For Hank, the boy is "pretty enough to frame" (34), as well as being a "butterfly" (61) and a "darling" (120). Clarence refers to himself as Hank's "pet" (540), and their shared physical closeness is evident when Hank describes how "[t]he boy nestled himself upon my shoulder and pretended to go to sleep" (57). The sexualized depiction of Clarence also appears in Daniel Beard's illustrations of the novel, about which Twain declared his "unqualified praise."[31] Beard modeled Clarence on the actress Sarah Bernhardt for the novel's illustrations, and the drawing in which Hank meets Clarence shows the man gazing down at the boy's girlish thighs (38). After a time of separation that ends in the two men's joyful reunion, Hank fondly declares, "It was good to hear my boy's voice again. It was like being home" (304). Nothing definitively homosexual colors this friendship, but it is deeply and affectionately homosocial, and Hank never mocks Clarence in the manner in which he repeatedly insults Sandy.

Throughout the majority of the novel, Clarence remains more in Hank's thoughts than Sandy. When praying for rescue from imminent execution, Hank daydreams about his longed-for reunion with the boy, not with his future bride: "Sandy passed within ten yards of me on a mule—hunting for me, I imagined. But the thing which clean broke my heart was something which happened in front of our old barrack in a square. . . . It was the sight of a newsboy—and I couldn't get at him! Still, I had one comfort; here was proof that Clarence was still alive and banging away. I meant to be with him before long; the thought was full of cheer" (467–68). Here Hank does not consider the comforts of closeness with Sandy; rather, she serves as a failed conduit of escape and thus as a disappointment. But a possible reunion with Clarence comforts Hank in this dire moment before his scheduled execution, and the failure to resume this homosocial friendship, as Hank recalls, is what "clean broke my heart."

Another scene stressing the emotional cathexis shared by the two men depicts Clarence saving Hank from execution with the theatrical display of Arthurian knights on bicycles. Clarence admits this spectacular rescue is little more than a "chance to show off" (491), and the boy's showmanship reflects Hank's hope to stage a rescue with "a more theatrical aspect"

(480). Through their shared penchant for theatricality, their intimacy reaches such a high pitch that Clarence intuitively enacts Hank's vision of the rescue. The homosocial bond between Clarence and Hank here takes precedence over heterosocial coupling, but this affection must be refocused when Hank marries Sandy. Discerning a homoerotic subtext in Hank's relationship with Clarence may appear to be casting too much weight on innocuous descriptions of their friendship, but Hank himself provides the rationale for suspecting such sexual undertones through his denunciation of male bonds when he marries Sandy. The needless dismissal of male friendships casts a queerly anxious light on homosocial relationships in general, and on his own male friendships in particular.

If the child they share is one of the factors that raises marriage with Sandy to an earthly experience of the divine, an irony emerges in that Hank first experiences such blissful and procreative joys with Clarence. No human child blesses their homosocial union, but their friendship produces a newspaper, and when their creation first elicits other men's adulation, Hank's joys reach heights both divine and maternal: "These grouped bent heads, these charmed faces, these speaking eyes—how beautiful to me! For was not this [newspaper] my darling, and was not all this mute wonder and interest and homage a most eloquent tribute and unforced compliment to it? I knew, then, how a mother feels when women, whether strangers or friends, take her new baby, and close themselves about it with one eager impulse, and bend their heads over it in a tranced adoration that makes all the rest of the universe vanish out of their consciousness and be as if it were not, for that time. I knew how she feels, and that there is no other satisfied ambition, whether of king, conqueror or poet, that even reaches half way to that serene far summit or yields half so divine a contentment" (344). Hank's words strangely contradict his own position in this passage: surely poets would be able to share such a "satisfied ambition" with Hank when an audience dotes on their literary creations. Recognizing no affinity to the world beyond him, Hank accords the aggressive inclinations of kings and conquerors to poets, whom he fails to recognize as his fellow wordsmiths; furthermore, by the novel's end, Hank evinces more the hostile qualities of tyrannical kings than the artistic qualities of ruminative poets. Twain suffuses this passage with irony in its attack on poets, and Hank's metaphoric construction of himself as a woman who gives birth develops the irony further. Like the "white Indians" on the border between civilization and savagery, Hank here represents the hybrid identity of a man giving birth as a result of homosocial bonding. Note, too, the "divine . . . contentment" Hank experiences through his relationship with Clarence and the "birth" of the newspaper: Hank later replaces such "divine" homosocial attachments with heterosexual ones, but their presence here underscores both the satisfactions aroused by his male friendships and the oddness of his subsequent reconstruction of this and other such moments as "earthly."

Hank's contentment with Clarence and their newspaper fades in contrast to marital and paternal joys with Sandy and Hello-Central, but because this relationship with Clarence appears so satisfying to the two men, Twain must suggest why Hank denounces "earthly" homosocial bonds and rejects his dear friend. The sole moment when Clarence frustrates Hank occurs prior to Sandy's announcement of Hello-Central's illness, with Clarence humorously suggesting that the monarchy should be replaced with cats. Hank grumpily muses: "[Clarence] never could be in earnest. He didn't know what it was. He had pictured a distinct and perfectly rational and feasible improvement upon constitutional monarchy, but he was too feather-headed to know it, or care anything about it, either. I was going to give him a scolding, but Sandy came flying at that moment" (515). This scene rings false, as if Twain grasped for a reason for Clarence to anger Hank and devised one in Hank's boneheaded and surly response to Clarence's humor. In contrast, Clarence's potentially more disastrous gaffe—when he mistakes the date as Hank plans his eclipse prophecy—calls forth only the Yankee's rueful affection: "I choked out some words through my grief and misery . . . for which the lad's eyes paid me back with such deep and loving gratitude that I had not the heart to tell him his good-hearted foolishness had ruined me and sent me to my death" (73–74). Although this calamitous mistake might reasonably trigger Hank's ire with his young friend, Clarence's silliness about a feline monarchy sparks his annoyance more than the mistake with potentially fatal repercussions.

Before marrying Sandy, Hank builds his Man-Factory, an act that highlights his propensity toward and preference for male homosocial communities.[32] Like his friendship with Clarence, Hank's sponsorship of the Man-Factory also carries latent hints of sexuality, as evidenced in his admiration of the boys' beauty: "Ah, they were a darling fifty-two! As pretty as girls, too" (553). The blood sacrifice required for a recruit's admission underscores Hank's attempt at egalitarian brotherhood: "I got him to lend me a little ink from his veins; and with this and a sliver I wrote on a piece of bark—*Put him in the Man-Factory*" (160; italics in original). The Man-Factory, however, ultimately fails, as do all of Hank's fraternal visions. As Justin Kaplan suggests, "the very names the Yankee gives his institutions—'civilization factories' and, a dehumanizing pun, 'man factories'—suggest not the fervent brotherhood of Whitman's utopian democracy but instead a bleak, industrial collectivism, the nightmare society of a monolithic state ruled by the Boss."[33] Kaplan's suggestion that the Man-Factory fails because it cannot embody a Whitmanesque fraternity returns readers to Hank's failure to maintain and nourish his homosocial relationships. Without maintaining these bonds, they suffer: Hank is so disenfranchised from the Man-Factory by the novel's end that Clarence must inform him how many of their number remain. In the crucial connection between the development of the Man-Factory and his goal to revolutionize England, the "earthly" nature of homosocial bonds weakens Hank's ties to his followers and subverts his political agenda.

Homosocial anxieties and his marriage to Sandy lead Hank to reject his male relationships, and the literary codes of Arthurian literature also necessitate that Hank pursue romance with Sandy. As Betsy Bowden observes, Malory's tales of Sir Gareth and Linet and of La Cote Male Taile and Maledisant "contribute to Morgan's obligation toward his talkative protégée"; Bowden then argues that the chaste love expected in chivalrous tales at times surrenders to a masculine ethos in which "sporadic acts of sexual intercourse function as means to various ends that enhance male status."[34] Simply put, Hank's marriage to Sandy proves his sexual normativity, but it also indicates that Twain felt compelled to give such evidence of his protagonist's heterosexuality amid the homosocial environment of Arthurian knighthood. Certainly, at key moments in the text, Hank responds to the physical attractiveness of the knights, such as in the following declaration: "There was a fine manliness observable in almost every face, and in some a certain loftiness and sweetness that rebuked your belittling criticisms and stilled them. A most noble benignity and purity reposed in the countenance of him they called Sir Galahad, and likewise in the king's also; and there was majesty and greatness in the giant frame and high bearing of Sir Launcelot of the Lake" (44). Hank's litany of insults to the Arthurian world, with all of his arrogant superiority, here slows due to the "fine manliness" of the knights' faces, as if their beauty silences his torrent of vitriol. Interesting, too, is Hank's slippage into second-person narration, detailing "your belittling criticisms" of these men, when it is his words—not the reader's—that denigrate them. Hank further reveals that Sir Gareth holds a special place in his heart: "Garry was my private pet name for him; it suggests that I had a deep affection for him, and that was the case" (111). The protagonist's homoerotic response to the knights' physical attractiveness, however, is not the key issue in these scenes; rather, the significance of these moments is that they must later be resignified to disprove even a remote possibility of queerness. Asexually attracted to chivalrous men, Hank responds to knighthood in a manner that accentuates both the amorphousness of his desires and his difficulty in dividing life into gendered binaries.

In addition to Hank's friendship with Clarence, his creation of the Man-Factory, and his aesthetic appreciation of handsome knights, the homosocial bonds of the Arthurian court also feed his queer anxieties over chivalric knighthood, especially in light of the failures of such friendships within the Arthurian tradition. Upon waking in sixth-century England, Hank enters a world where men fight one another for women, as Sir Kay challenges him to "try a passage of arms for land or lady" (22). In many Arthurian romances, men establish supremacy in comparison to their fellow knights through their relationships with women; a particularly striking example of this paradigm is Arthur and Launcelot's triangulated desire for Guenever that eventually destroys the men's friendship, with disastrous results for the members of the Round Table and all of England. Twain incorporates this plotline of the Arthurian legend at several key points of his narrative, such as when Hank notes that "it was touching to see the queen blush and smile, and look embarrassed and happy, and fling furtive glances at Sir Launcelot that would have got him shot in Arkansas, to a dead certainty" (45). Hank sees trouble brewing when he comments of Guenever, "Many's the time she had asked me, 'Sir Boss, hast seen Sir Launcelot about?' but if ever she went fretting around for the king I didn't happen to be around at the time" (334). When the homosocial bonds between Arthur and Launcelot sever, Hank foresees the impending disaster: "Oh, dear, only one thing could result—I see that. War, and the knights of the realm divided into a king's party and a Sir Launcelot's party" (533). Commenting on the horror of the situation, Hank adds with wrenching pathos, "Oh, you tear out my heartstrings" (533). This scene once again highlights his conflicted relationship to sixth-century England: rather than rejoicing at the subversion of nobility that this combat offers, his goal throughout the novel, Hank laments the bloodshed that the dissolution of homosocial bonds promises.

Hank's mournful response to Arthur and Launcelot's fractured friendship and the chaos it generates ironically prefigures his destruction of the English nobility. Significantly, his targets in his bid to emancipate the lower classes from their enforced subservience are the two most influential, hierarchical, and homosocial structures of the Middle Ages—the Church and the aristocracy. As Hank's title "Sir Boss" reflects his conflicted identification with the nobility, his relationship with the Christian Church similarly highlights his attempts to construct it as Other while exploiting its own practices, such as his use of its missionary system in service of soap advertisements. The more troubling aspect of Hank's attack on the medieval Church, in all of his Protestant fervor, is that, within the fictions of the novel, it appears truly to mediate divine authority: "[T]housands of the lame and sick came and prayed before [the picture of the Virgin's miracle] every year and went away whole and sound. . . . Of course when I was told these things I did not believe them; but when I went there and saw them I had to succumb. I saw the cures effected myself; and they were real cures and not questionable. I saw cripples whom I had seen around Camelot for years on crutches, arrive and pray before that picture, and put down their crutches and walk off without a limp" (337–38). Despite this realization, Hank fails to reevaluate his beliefs. He extols the healing power inherent in religious belief in this scene yet never alters his perception of the Church that fosters such miracles. Yet again Twain depicts his protagonist's distrust of medieval structures of homosociality, despite, in this instance, the miraculous cures granted to believers.

The carnage brought forth by Hank's apocalyptic attack on the chivalric community destroys the homosocial order of knighthood, but Twain also stresses that male friendships suffer as well. The first two victims are good friends, and in a poignant yet disturbing tableau of homosocial affection and death, the electrified body of one man kills his friend: "'Why dreamest thou here, good Sir Mar—' then he laid his hand on the corpse's shoulder—and just uttered a little soft moan and sunk down dead. Killed by a dead man, you see—killed by a dead friend, in fact. There was something awful about it" (562–63). In the gruesome scene that follows, Hank becomes the savage and merciless revolutionary he declared he would never be, as he pronounced earlier that "it being immutable law that all revolution that will succeed, must *begin* in blood, whatever may answer afterward. . . . What this folk needed, then, was a Reign of Terror and a guillotine, and I was the wrong man for them" (242; italics in original). In the intervening pages, Hank transforms into just such a man due to his inability both to communicate dialectically with the sixth-century Other and to understand his relationship to the homosocial order of Arthurian knighthood. The true horror of his transformation is then registered on the dead bodies of male friends, and this putrefying carnage traps the remaining members of his Man-Factory to their own lingering deaths. As Justin Kaplan records, Twain intended his climactic conclusion not to inspire an awed admiration for the military victory but sympathy for its wanton destruction of men: "[Twain] was determined, he said, that the dissolution of the Round Table and the final battle—'the Battle of the Broken Hearts, it might be called'—should lose none of their 'pathos and tears' through his retelling."[35] Dubbing this conflict the "Battle of Broken Hearts," Twain underscores the deep emotional connections apparent in brothers killing brothers. The phrase "broken hearts" typically refers to jilted lovers, and Twain's use of this term tacitly points to the homosocial bonds among men destroyed in response to Hank's queer anxieties over the chivalric world of Arthurian knights.

For a man who condemns homosocial bonds for their "earthly" nature, Hank suffers deeply without them. In nineteenth-century England, he mourns their loss in the same breath with which he laments losing Sandy: "Yes, I seemed to have flown back out of that age into this of ours, and then forward to it again, and was set down, a stranger and forlorn in that strange England, with an abyss of thirteen centuries yawning between me and you! Between me and my home and my friends! Between me and all that is dear to me, all that could make life worth the living! It was awful—

awfuler than you can ever imagine, Sandy" (574). Here Hank seeks both the homosocial and the heterosocial, realizing his need for friends and family. This passage, in detailing Hank's desire for romance with Sandy and friendship with the Arthurian knights, ironically recalls his earlier praise of the heterosocial and dismissal of the homosocial in his words lauding his marriage to Sandy. His realization that enjoying the former need not entail rejecting the latter comes too late to save the twenty-five thousand knights or himself.

"Sir Boss," "white Indians," and the debased depictions of homosocial relationships all attest to Hank's attempts to identify himself as an ideal representation of nineteenth-century masculinity as mediated through capitalism, whiteness, and heterosexuality, even though such purities of male identity are virtually impossible to maintain. In the final analysis, Hank is as much a foreigner and an Other to himself as he is to his sixth-century companions. As Bruce Michelson explains, "And so the 'foreigner,' as that figure takes shape in [Twain's] . . . fiction, was anybody . . . who had constructed or settled into a self made too firmly out of the pathologies and mentalities of one place and group of people."[36] The climax of the Battle of the Sand-Belt highlights this failure one last time, through Hank's failure to see Merlin as anything other than a fraud: by denouncing Merlin as a charlatan, Hank leaves himself vulnerable to his enemy's real magic and the curse of a thirteen-hundred-year sleep. Failing to communicate both with the past as Other and with his very Self, Hank suffers at the novel's conclusion almost as much as the victims of his savage attacks. The "white Indians" that he identifies in others reflect his own barbaric inclinations, and this blindness to the repercussions of his self-construction brings forth the horrors of his massacre of the Arthurian homosocial world. Through his American rejection of medieval ideals, Hank queerly exposes his own hybrid identity as a man desiring homosocial and heterosocial pleasures in the Middle Ages. By succumbing to the chivalric and romanticized view of a time so alien to his own, Hank proves the queer allure of medieval chivalry to seduce and to disorient, and thus medievalism estranges him from a stable vision of his gendered self.

And where does the author fit in regard to his protagonist's adventures? In many ways, Twain's critique of the Middle Ages in *A Connecticut Yankee* is tied to his criticism of the nineteenth-century U.S. South. Certainly, he establishes parallels between the South of his time and England in the sixth century, such as when Hank laments for "the 'poor whites' of our South who were always despised, and frequently insulted by the slave-lords around them . . . [and who] were yet pusillanimously ready to side with slave-lords in all political moves for the upholding and perpetuating of slavery" (387; cf. 449). Here readers witness the tendency of post-medieval authors employing medieval settings in their fictions to address the cultural conditions of their own era, as medievalism offers an ultimately transparent means to critique the present (often, even more than the past). William Dean Howells enthusiastically endorses the novel's time slips: "The elastic scheme of the romance allows it to play freely back and forward between the sixth century and the nineteenth century; and often while it is working the reader up to a blasting contempt of monarchy and aristocracy in King Arthur's time, the dates are magically shifted under him, and he is confronted with exactly the same principles in Queen Victoria's time."[37] Howells hints at Twain's view of the U.S. South as suffering from "the Sir Walter disease" in his analysis, yet his observations also emphasize that, as much as Twain dismissed medievalism, he also found it deeply alluring.

Despite his personal interest in the Middle Ages, Twain condemned southern writers for their enthusiastic embrace of medieval chivalric themes, but this stance ironically reveals the disingenuous foundations of Twain's authorial agenda. Beyond *A Connecticut Yankee in King Arthur's Court*, Twain's medievalism is most apparent in his *Personal Recollections of Joan of Arc* (1896), his last novel, which he declared to be his personal favorite and the best of his fictions: "I like the *Joan of Arc* best of all my books. . . . [I]t is the best; I know it perfectly well."[38] Most critics would disagree with this assessment, as *Huckleberry Finn* receives the lion's share of critical acclaim. Twain's medievalism, in this instance, blinded him to the aesthetic qualities of his own literature: as he accused others of being duped by the appeal of the Middle Ages, he also found medieval values an ultimately seductive—if somewhat disorienting—theme for his fictions, in the impossibility of chivalry communicating more than a befuddled and queer vision of medieval and modern men.

3

MEDIEVAL MASCULINITY, SOUTHERN CHIVALRY, AND REDEMPTIVE HOMOSEXUALITY IN FLANNERY O'CONNOR'S FICTION

Medieval men in modern times: this unlikely blend of medievalism, masculinity, southern chivalry, and sexuality runs throughout much of Flannery O'Connor's fiction. In particular, her short stories "Everything That Rises Must Converge," "The Comforts of Home," "The Geranium," "A Late Encounter with the Enemy," and "The Enduring Chill" and the novella *The Violent Bear It Away* focus on men (or, in the case of *The Violent Bear It Away*, on a boy growing into manhood), and more specifically, on men reacting to the pressures of chivalric history and its bearing on their masculinity and sexuality.[1] Recent studies of O'Connor's fiction examine the repercussions of race and gender in her canon,[2] and this chapter expands on such analyses by taking into account the effects of sexuality as well. Conceptions of race, gender, and sexuality constitute much of an individual's sense of personal identity, but they are not free from ideological inflection; rather, they are forged in and through history. For O'Connor, the two most compelling yet oddly commingling histories for the construction of southern manhood belong to the Middle Ages and the U.S. South due to their converging models of chivalric masculinity. Spiritual Catholicism and martial chivalry collide in these fictions, resulting in men queerly bewildered by the meaninglessness of their masculinity.

For the most part, O'Connor's protagonists, whether male or female, are not readily rewarded with Christian revelation for partaking in sexual relationships and carnal pleasures. Quite unlike Constance Chatterley and Oliver Mellors in D. H. Lawrence's *Lady Chatterley's Lover* (1928), the adulterous lovers who "fucked a flame into being" and thereby imbued their lives with transcendent possibility,[3] O'Connor's characters typically experience sexuality as a red herring on the path to salvation: it promises a transcendent experience yet ultimately diverts attention from the divine. Thus, she parodies and ridicules heterosexual affairs throughout her fiction, as in the hilarious leg-stealing scene of "Good Country People" and in Calhoun and Mary Elizabeth's ridiculous "courtship"—undertaken so they can meet the homicidal lunatic Singleton—in "The Partridge Festival." Little affection is evident in the marriages depicted in "Parker's Back" and "The Life You Save May Be Your Own," and O'Connor portrays nuclear families, the ostensibly blessed result of sexual congress in marriage, as dysfunctional in such stories as "A Good Man Is Hard to Find" and "The River." In her focused attention on the tortuous spiritual path of a lone protagonist who finds damnation or redemption in the final paragraph, O'Connor sees little salvific possibility in sexuality, as it cannot help her protagonists to achieve immanent realizations beyond their solipsistic concerns.

From this perspective, historical models of whiteness, masculinity, and heterosexuality frequently ensnare O'Connor's male protagonists into roles that limit their potential to experience revelation. O'Connor satirically aligns many of her male characters within the paradigm of southern chivalric manhood, and medieval role models of saints and martyrs also guide, while simultaneously curtailing, the range of actions possible to them. In this manner, southern chivalric masculinity is predicated upon a historically myopic view, in which illusions of male gender roles constrain O'Connor's protagonists from realizing the potential of salvation, as is evident in the spiritually pessimistic conclusions of "Everything That Rises Must Converge," "The Comforts of Home," "The Geranium," and "A Late Encounter with the Enemy." In contrast to the immuring qualities of chivalric masculinity and heterosexuality in these narratives, the tension inherent in historically constructed masculinities achieves a grotesquely illuminating revelation in "The Enduring Chill" and *The Violent Bear It Away*, in that Asbury's homosexuality and Marion Francis Tarwater's sodomitic rape are figured as precursors to their spiritual awakenings. Redemptive homosexuality may appear to be an incongruous term given O'Connor's abiding Catholicism, yet her carnivalesque and grotesque topoi consistently undermine the purported values accorded to any number of identities, acts, and peoples. In O'Connor's medievally inspired world of carnivalesque spirituality, the road to salvation traveled by her male protagonists necessitates a decidedly queer journey through medieval and southern models of chivalric and/or saintly masculinity.

O'Connor's play with masculinity reflects its growing amorphousness as a cultural category in the late 1940s, the 1950s, and the early 1960s, the period in which she wrote most of her published fiction until her death in 1964. Following World War II, the achievements of the "Greatest Generation" trumpeted a model of military masculinity then elevated to civil authority in the presidential election (and subsequent reelection) of General Dwight D. Eisenhower. With the expansion of U.S. global influence after World War II, American masculinity appeared to be both dominant and truly united: the successful conclusions of two world wars contributed to a sense of reconciliation between North and South, even if such reconciliation was rather short-lived with the advent of the civil rights movement. During these apparently halcyon days for U.S. masculinity, popular culture celebrated the paradigm of the benevolent patriarch in television shows such as *The Adventures of Ozzie and Harriet* (1952–66), *Father Knows Best* (1954–60), and *Leave It to Beaver* (1957–63).

Although much of governmental and popular culture promulgated the prevailing and stereotypical view of maleness during this period as one of organic and uncritical wholeness, in which white masculinity reigned uncontested in its cultural superiority, questions about the meaning of masculinity and sexuality were beginning to undermine its sacrosanct status as inviolate. With the publication of Alfred Kinsey's *Sexual Behavior in the Human Male* in 1948 and with Christine Jorgensen's sex change surgery in 1952, visions of seamlessly heterosexual masculinity were revealed to be cultural illusions designed to bolster the ideological privileges of white heterosexual masculinity. The breakdown of this ideological illusion culminated in cultural anxieties about the meanings of masculinity, and of femininity as well. In their 1952 exposé of the United States, *U.S.A. Confidential,* Jack Lait and Lee Mortimer uncovered a world in which gender roles, believed to be strictly delineated, now merged, resulting in deleterious effects for the culture at large: "The masculinization of women, which had its counterpart in the feminization of men, is obvious wherever one travels in this nation, in all the forty-eight states and the territories. It is as pitiful a menace as the nation faces."[4] In a 1958 article in *Esquire* entitled

"The Crisis of Masculinity," Arthur Schlesinger summarizes the gendered shifts of the decade and ponders, "What has happened to the American male?" He then laments the "multiplying signs . . . that something has gone badly wrong with the American male's conception of himself." Approximately a decade after the triumphs of World War II, the rising influence of women threatened male prerogatives, and Schlesinger notes various attempts "to blame 'the decline of the American male' on the aggressiveness of the American female."[5]

The apparent paradox of white masculinity undergoing a crisis in the 1950s, in that it would then represent a tormented rather than a socially dominant identity, points to the ways in which a "crisis" of gender can be used to reassert dominant forms of ideologically sanctioned identities: a crisis demands a response, and in this instance, the proper antidote for American men, apparently besieged and under duress due to pressures on their masculinity, would be to bolster their authority (although it was never truly in jeopardy). Thus, to locate a crisis of masculinity in the 1950s is to oversimplify the contours of the Western social order, one that Lynne Segal characterizes as "pathological[ly] silencing" women within this time frame.[6] Within this complex sociocultural period, men dominated, yet a crisis was claimed; women shared little of men's political or economic power yet were somehow seen as subverting masculine authority. As James Gilbert notes of U.S. masculinity in the 1950s, "Worry about masculine identity thus had its origins partially in the desire to maintain clear cultural and social distinctions between men and women and in the belief in the historical certainty and efficacy of such distinctions."[7]

Against this cultural backdrop, O'Connor witnessed during the apex of her writing career how masculinity was ideologically lionized while dependent upon cultural performances that undermined its cultural invisibility and normativity. Within this world of cultural imbalance, O'Connor turned to the Middle Ages for a sense of narrative unity and to highlight the contemporary vagaries of identity that result from shifting cultural mores: "I am often told that the model of balance for the novelist should be Dante, who divided his territory up pretty evenly between hell, purgatory, and paradise. There can be no objection to this, but also there can be no reason to assume that the result of doing it in these times will give us the balanced picture that it gave in Dante's. Dante lived in the thirteenth century, when that balance was achieved in the faith of his age. We live now in an age which doubts both fact and value, which is swept this way and that by momentary convictions" (*MM* 49).[8] Certainly gender roles of the 1950s constituted such a shifting set of values, and O'Connor's treatments of gender and masculinity shore up her personal sense of moral balance while highlighting the transitory nature of gendered identities in relation to Christian salvation. In much of her fiction, race, gender, and sexuality blind her protagonists to important truths of eternal significance, and so they must reluctantly confront the hollow protections afforded by their performances of such archaic roles. O'Connor proclaimed not to see critical distinctions between the sexes—declaring that "[o]n the subject of the feminist business, I just never think . . . of qualities which are specifically feminine or masculine. I suppose I divide people into two classes: the Irksome and the Non-Irksome without regard to sex" (*HB* 176)[9]—yet her fiction evinces her critical engagement with the ways in which gender delimits narrative possibilities, as well as the potential for salvation as mediated through sexuality.

Through her medievalism O'Connor tacitly addresses the ways in which her male contemporaries—notably, "the little group of Agrarians that flourished at Vanderbilt in the [nineteen-]twenties" (*MM* 238)—valorized southern culture for its supposed medieval ancestry. Agrarians such as Frank Lawrence Owsley and Allen Tate nourished the fantasy of chivalric masculinity in their paeans to the medieval character of southern culture. Owsley traced the lineage of the men of the U.S. South to the medieval yeomanry, who "were from rural England with centuries of country and farm lore," as well as to Anglo-Saxon and Scottish cultures.[10] Tate likewise saw southern culture as an offshoot of medieval roots: "All great cultures have been rooted in peasantries, in free peasantries, I believe, such as the English yeomanry before the fourteenth century; they have been the growth of the soil."[11] For O'Connor, then, playing with masculine medievalism allows her to engage in a discussion of southern gender through the lens of grotesque allegory. This is not to imply that O'Connor rejected the agrarians, as she commended *I'll Take My Stand* as a "very interesting document" that reflects "the only time real minds have got together to talk about the South" (*HB* 566). Nevertheless, given its emphasis on chivalry, southern medievalism is primarily a masculine value, and so for O'Connor to tackle southern medievalism in her fictions is also to address southern masculinity as espoused by her male contemporaries.

Similar to Mark Twain in his derision of southern masculinity as a symptom of "the Sir Walter disease," O'Connor satirized some southern writers as "old gentlemen who have impossible historical novels on the way" (*MM* 29), an oblique yet trenchant jab at southern men mired in the romances of the past. O'Connor also shares with Walker Percy a view of the U.S. South as a fallen land: "When Walker Percy won the National Book Award, newsmen asked him why there were so many good Southern writers and he said, 'Because we lost the War.' . . . What he was saying was that we have had our Fall. We have gone into the modern world with an inburnt knowledge of human limitations and with a sense of mystery which could not have developed in our first state of innocence" (*MM* 58–59). Part of the "Fall" of the U.S. South entails the realization that military masculinity could not solve the problems that precipitated and followed the U.S. Civil War; O'Connor's male protagonists must grapple with a fallen legacy of chivalric masculinities and the cultural fantasies that attempt to compensate for defeat. In this queering view of southern manhood, modern men assert a medieval masculinity that they can never successfully perform and, in so doing, prove the inherent fantasy of their puissance.

MEDIEVAL SAINTS, SOUTHERN CHIVALRY, AND HETEROSEXUAL PERILS

John Desmond proposes that a tense relationship between history and individuals permeates O'Connor's fiction, particularly in how history molds people into ideologies: "O'Connor's development of character cannot in fact be separated from the whole order of reality in which her characters exist. . . . [H]er stories constantly raise one question: what does it mean to be a person in history?"[12] One might also ask: what does it mean for O'Connor's characters to be a person in *which* history? Whether local or international, yesterday or centuries past, history cascades upon a consciousness, and the repercussions of the historical past often affect the perceptions of a given person in unfathomable ways. O'Connor's dual deployment of medieval and southern history testifies to the impossibility of delineating precisely a historical root to a modern identity, for history's pulse can seldom be tamped down to one particular sociotemporal field. Such is the case with O'Connor's merging of medieval and southern historical models to address modern masculinity.

O'Connor's medieval themes and images surface throughout much of her corpus, and she explicitly advocates writing and reading literature in accordance with medieval hermeneutic principles: "The medieval commentators on Scripture found three kinds of meaning in the literal level of the sacred text: one they called allegorical, in which one fact pointed to another; one they called tropological, or moral, which had to do with what should be done; and one they called anagogical, which had to do with the Divine life and our participation in it. Although this was a method applied to biblical exegesis, it was also an attitude toward all of creation, and a way of reading nature which included most possibilities, and I think it is this enlarged view of the human scene that the fiction writer has to cultivate if he is ever going to write stories that have any chance of becoming a permanent part of our literature" (*MM* 72–73). In her endorsement of medieval hermeneutics, O'Connor implicitly integrates medievalism within her fiction's worldview. She also indicates that her role as a writer necessitates adhering to aesthetic and artistic values articulated by medieval thinkers, citing St. Thomas's assertion that "the artist is concerned with the good of that which is made" (*MM* 65; cf. 171).

For O'Connor, medieval interpretive and aesthetic values imbue literature with meaning, but within her grotesque fictions, these medieval values are seldom represented straightforwardly. In his *American Gargoyles: Flannery O'Connor and the Medieval Grotesque*, Anthony di Renzo explores the ways in which "apocalyptic playfulness, which has free reign in medieval festivals, permeates the fiction of Flannery O'Connor,"[13] noting how her fictional world overturns the typical rules and expectations of polite society, with the medieval grotesque inspiring these carnivalesque inversions. As Mikhail Bakhtin writes of medieval festivals, "Carnival with all its images, indecencies, and curses affirms the people's immortal, indestructible character. In the world of carnival the awareness of the people's immortality is combined with the realization that established authority and truth are relative."[14] In her carnivalesque depictions of sexuality, O'Connor rejects protagonists who model purity and innocence because of her own incomprehension of their spiritual significance: She notes, "Purity strikes me as the most mysterious of the virtues and the more I think about it the less I know about it" (*HB* 117). She concentrates instead on characters whose purity is very much in doubt, and Hazel Motes of *Wise Blood* (1952) could serve as O'Connor's archetype of the impure man falling into purity. This carnivalesque trope colors the depiction of her male characters who succeed in finding a deeper spiritual realization at their narrative's end, but such a revelation hinges upon medieval hermeneutics leading one to decode correctly the play of grotesque inversions.

O'Connor frequently deploys the chivalrous stereotype of southern men to undermine pretensions of cultural identity, but she also exploits another medievalized construction of southern masculinity—that of the saintly martyr—to consider the meaning of southern masculinity. As the "Lost Cause" ideology led southern men surviving the Civil War to cast themselves as chivalrous models of honor, the slain soldiers were similarly remembered as saintly martyrs to a righteous mission. In the words of Richard Wilmer, the bishop of Alabama, speaking two years after the war's end, the fallen Confederate soldiers were "a noble army of martyrs . . . [who] rejoice[d] that they were counted to suffer shame and death for a cause which they honored and espoused."[15] For O'Connor these two complementary medievalized models of southern masculinity—chivalric gentlemen and martyred saints—establish historical and mythological paradigms to trouble her male characters' journeys to revelation. Such a combination would be slightly ridiculous in medieval literature, as the expected behaviors of male saints in hagiographies and of chivalric knights in romances vary widely. Saints frequently model passivity in their embracing of martyrdom because they must die to triumph spiritually over their oppressors, whereas knights actively engage in quests and tournaments on behalf of their ladies for a much more earthly victory in which human erotic love trumps other considerations. Of course, O'Connor did not write medieval literature: she exploits its tropes to consider the meaning of masculinity in the U.S. South through this hybrid hermeneutic of medieval masculinities, and so the combination of the saintly and the chivalric highlights her particular authorial strategies to address the vagaries of southern manhood.

Medieval saints and martyrs provide exemplary paradigms of masculinity for many of O'Connor's male protagonists, constituting a veritable touchstone by which they may be gauged, and in her allusions to such holy men, she plays with the masculine forbearance that grounds these legendary figures and imbues her far less heroic male characters with an inflated sense of their importance. Saints model masculinity as it should be performed within a Christological context, yet her male protagonists inversely and carnivalesquely incarnate this masculine paradigm of holiness by mistakenly dedicating themselves to their selves rather than to Christ. Within O'Connor's worldview, however, it is important to note that she believes not even saints attain the ideal expressed in Christian thought: "Ideal Christianity doesn't exist, because anything the human being touches, even Christian truth, he deforms slightly in his own image. Even the saints do this" (*HB* 516). O'Connor's "saintly" male protagonists must fail because their models of masculinity, although closely linked to earthly perfection, incarnate a flawed vision of masculine potential due to the impossibility, the inherent paradox, of humanity acting without sin (from her Catholic perspective). Performances of saintly masculinity become further tainted due to the cultural shadow of chivalric and patriarchal modes of masculinity as enacted in the U.S. South, since these cultural and narcissistic fantasies of masculine identity cannot effectively lead men to the ideals of Christian spirituality represented in her fictions, instead seducing them into performances of gender that queer their ostensibly heteronormative foundations.

In many ways, "Everything That Rises Must Converge" (1961) encapsulates O'Connor's treatment of medieval masculinities and their misappropriation in the modern U.S. South. The narrator ironically describes the glum protagonist Julian as a saintly martyr for his mother: "She was almost ready to go, standing before the hall mirror, putting on her hat, while he, his hands behind him, appeared pinned to the door frame, waiting like Saint Sebastian for the arrows to begin piercing him" (405).[16] The queer iconography of St. Sebastian's martyrdom, in which numerous arrows pierce his nearly naked body, has long been celebrated for its homoerotic and masochistic features, as Jason Goldman records: "Sebastian . . . was a featured subject of a host of Renaissance and Baroque artists . . .

whose works inspired an explicitly homosexual cult of Saint Sebastian in the nineteenth century."[17] By alluding to the legend of St. Sebastian, long associated with homoeroticism, O'Connor undermines her protagonist's heteronormative masculinity. Additionally, a trip to the "reducing class at the Y" (405) with his mother carries little of the consequence of Sebastian's gruesome martyrdom, yet Julian's resentment toward his familial obligations encourages him to see himself as a long-suffering saint.

O'Connor again alludes to the passive masculinity of martyred saints who suffer endlessly when describing Julian's inner torment: "He walked along, saturated in depression, as if in the midst of his martyrdom he had lost his faith" (407). His ridiculous sense of self-importance imbues this trivial incident with momentous meaning and also highlights his failure to treat his mother with the filial chivalry expected of southern men. Julian's name alludes to St. Julian the Hospitaler, the early Christian who mistakenly kills his parents and atones for his sin by building an inn for travelers and a hospital for the poor, and the legend of St. Julian finds its narrative parallel at the conclusion of "Everything That Rises Must Converge" when Julian's mother dies and he finds himself distraught without her. His story is that of a failed man, one with little real appreciation for the masochistic suffering embodied by medieval saints and a hyperbolic sense of his familial travails He succeeds only in prolonging his egocentric solipsism rather than overcoming it in service of a larger Christian plan. Unlike St. Julian, who elevates his family's tragedy into a life of service for others, O'Connor's Julian shows few signs of transforming his loss into spiritual action and thus models impotent inaction as his defining trait of queer masculinity.

This ironic sense of martyred and saintly masculinity informs O'Connor's depiction of many of her male protagonists: they see themselves as suffering martyrs who sacrifice themselves, not for Christ, but to a narcissistic vision of masculinity that aggrandizes their egos while leaving them blind to their human handicaps. A writer steeped in medieval and southern literature, O'Connor consistently uses images of the suffering saints of hagiographies and the chivalric heroes of medieval romance to construct, and then to pillory, her male characters. In her satiric treatment of the chivalric codes of southern manhood, O'Connor degrades the paragons of knightly chivalry as represented by such masculine archetypes as King

Arthur, Lancelot, and Galahad, who undertake grand quests for such inspiring objectives as the Holy Grail or rescuing maidens fair. In contrast, her male protagonists' quests are of a quotidian, if not entirely banal, nature: picking up a flower in "The Geranium," or attending a graduation ceremony in "A Late Encounter with the Enemy." Hazel Motes's "quest" in *Wise Blood* is at best an antiquest. O'Connor explains the inverse meaning of his narrative journey: "For [some readers] Hazel Motes' integrity lies in his trying with such vigor to get rid of the ragged figure who moves from tree to tree in the back of his mind. For the author Hazel's integrity lies in his not being able to. Does one's integrity ever lie in what he is not able to do? I think that usually it does."[18] O'Connor's explanation of Hazel's spiritual development focuses on the meaning of free will, yet her consideration of this issue concomitantly rejects the quest as the traditional narrative form of chivalric masculinity. Her male characters incarnate a fallen and dissolute model of both medieval and white southern masculinity: they may see themselves as long-suffering saints, tortured martyrs, and chivalric avatars of yesteryear's values, but they fail to attain the level of revelatory suffering necessary for Christian revelation, let alone canonization.

Returning to the example of Julian in "Everything That Rises Must Converge," his southern masculinity and ironic "sainthood" are further attenuated due to the chivalric manhood of his forebears that subverts his vision of his masculinity. His mother encourages him to see himself within a narcissistic southern heritage of masculine authoritarian prosperity and feminine religiosity: "'Your great-grandfather was a former governor of this state,' she said. 'Your grandfather was a prosperous landowner. Your grandmother was a Godhigh'" (407). White privilege through governance is tacitly acknowledged in Julian's mother's account of their family history, but the devolution of southern masculinity (through its spiritually enervating connection to the gilded allure of financial prosperity) leaves Julian with little money and hence little masculinity. His matrilineal ancestry as a Godhigh links him to his religious heritage as well, but the family's spiritual history ironically foreshadows the revelation he denies himself in the present by mistreating his mother. The death of Julian's mother brings "Everything That Rises Must Converge" to its bleak conclusion, with the loss of the maternal pointing to the spiritual blindness of a child mired in empty models of medieval and white southern masculinity, both those of the saint and of the chivalric gentleman. Too old to be a child, too weak to be a man, Julian cannot define his male identity other than through his queer inability to achieve any credible performance of southern masculinity.

Medieval and southern histories make a man within O'Connor's fictional U.S. South, and this power of history to construct masculinity is compellingly underscored in "The Comforts of Home" (1960). The reader learns that the protagonist Thomas is embedded in history: his mother reports to the nymphomaniac Sarah Ham that "Thomas writes history" and that "[h]e's president of the local Historical Society this year" (389). The long-standing axiom that "history is written by the winners" is travestied in O'Connor's tale of a white southern man incapable of defending himself and his cultural prerogatives. History cannot protect Thomas in the narrative's present when Sarah Ham, who incarnates uncontrollable and wanton female sexuality, disrupts the protected sanctum of his home. Thomas compares himself to Antony of Egypt, a saint who is credited as "the founder of Christian monasticism and [who] was famous all over the civilized world for his holiness, asceticism, and wisdom,"[19] but his affinity for Antony is based on misinterpreting the meaning of saintly masculinity. He ponders his mother's misunderstanding of history, which reveals his own misperceptions of historical masculinities and saintliness: "Had [his mother] been in any degree intellectual, he could have proved to her from early Christian history that no excess of virtue is justified, that a moderation of good produces likewise a moderation in evil, that if Antony of Egypt had stayed at home and attended to his sister, no devils would have plagued him" (385–86). In a manner similar to Julian's ironic identification with Sebastian, such thinking drains the virtue from Antony's saintly masculinity, which he proved by overcoming, not ignoring, the devil's sexual temptations. Furthermore, O'Connor's deployment of Antony as a model for Thomas's masculinity carries a hint of homoerotic potential through the gender inversion depicted in Antony's story, in which the devil impersonates a woman while attempting to seduce the saint: "The wretched Devil even dared to masquerade as a woman by night and to impersonate such in every possible way, merely in order to deceive Antony."[20] Surely one can see Sarah Ham as a devilish figure of temptation, but within O'Connor's carnivalesque worldview of seduction and sin, Thomas's inability to respond meaningfully to her enticements reveals his shallow sense of masculine identity, as well as his saintly misidentification: her sinful nature sparks less narrative concern than Thomas's inability to respond to her temptations through any sort of action, whether saintly or chivalric.

In complementary contrast to Thomas's inverted incarnation of Antony of Egypt's medieval sainthood, his deceased father models an archaic southern masculinity that Thomas both craves and despises: "It was at these times that Thomas truly mourned the death of his father though he had not been able to endure him in life" (387). Such is the double bind of patriarchal history: it establishes a melancholic regret for what is lost, even if the lost entity was unendurable before it dissolved into the past. Jeremy Tambling argues that a "history which emphasizes ascent, or development, or ages of improvement becomes complicit with the catastrophe" of the failure to achieve continual progress.[21] Because history is, by definition, that which exists no longer, people frequently imbue it with the meanings they wish it to denote and thus accord it a hazy, alluring, and seductive power. Thomas falls into this schema of historical consciousness: he can recall little affection for his father, yet he nonetheless turns to the man's image of southern masculinity for inspiration in handling the troubling vision of female sexuality he must confront in Sarah Ham.

The desire to expel Sarah Ham from his home necessitates that Thomas take action, and in so doing, he aligns himself with his father's historically brutish masculinity. The sexual imagery of Thomas's duplicitous act to free himself from her—stuffing a gun in her bag, his phallus in her vagina—humorously contrasts with his steadfast refusal to copulate with her. In spurning sexual intercourse with Sarah Ham, Thomas successfully emulates Antony of Egypt, who withstood the devil's homoerotic temptations that were cloaked under a veneer of heterosexuality; however, through O'Connor's protean irony, Thomas symbolically fails to emulate Antony's saintly chastity because he does not understand the ways in which his masculinity coerces his decisions. When his mother tells Sarah Ham, "Thomas wouldn't put a gun in your bag," because she believes that "Thomas is a gentleman" (403), his mother ascribes her son's prudery to his southern chivalric heritage. A gentleman would not put his "gun" in a woman's "bag," but Thomas's misreading of saintly and chivalric masculinities and his fear of his father's historical shadow lead him to overturn the expected behaviors of both models of masculine identity, and he thus impotently frames Sarah Ham by placing his gun in her purse: "'I found it in her bag!' Thomas shouted. 'The dirty criminal slut stole my gun!'" (403). Failing to view his father's masculinity objectively and misreading the example of Antony of Egypt, Thomas falls victim to Sarah Ham in his plan to frame her, thus exposing his figurative, if not literal, impotence. Antony withstood the devil's enticements through saintly chastity, but Thomas's metaphorical impotence, as well as his flaccid masculinity, forces this decision upon him.

Although the history of patriarchal culture, writ large, is the image of masculine dominance over the feminine through physical force, Sarah Ham triumphs because she stands apart from the traditions of masculine sexuality that trap Thomas: she is not the salvific virgin who inspires men to salvation but the whore who jolts men out of their sexual complacency. Following his father's lead, as well as yielding to the lure of history, Thomas finally claims an unsaintly and unchivalric masculinity by assuming the posture of an amatory embrace with Sarah when the gun discharges and kills his mother: "Over her body, the killer and the slut were about to collapse into each other's arms" (404). A fallen vision of Antony of Egypt, Thomas succumbs to carnal temptations, if only on a symbolic level. With sheriff Farebrother witnessing the shooting, the ending of "The Comforts of Home" does not celebrate the triumph of historical masculinity (since Thomas now faces arrest for his mother's murder); rather, the conclusion underscores that misinterpreting the example of medieval saints and chivalric heroes and heeding the voice of southern history constrains a man's vision of himself, his gender, and the women around him. The parody of heterosexual intercourse enacted in the narrative's conclusion highlights O'Connor's satiric treatment of sexuality, in which sexual desires frequently lead her characters astray, even when they determinedly avoid such entanglements. A man whose primary desire was not to engage in sexual intercourse with a woman, Thomas symbolically enacts that which he rejects, and as he does, O'Connor inversely queers her character by displaying him in a tableau of undesired heteroerotic passion.

Julian's and Thomas's downfalls highlight the damning effects of misunderstanding the respective moral examples of medieval and white southern masculinities in contemporary society. The relative youth of these men contrasts with two of O'Connor's elderly male protagonists, Old Dudley in "The Geranium" and General Sash in "A Late Encounter with the Enemy," who jointly embody the archaic southern conceptions of chivalrous masculinity that dogged Thomas in his attempt to free himself from Sarah Ham. In "The Geranium" (1946), southern chivalric masculinity constrains Old Dudley's actions to the extent that his ability to create nurturing relationships, whether heterosocial or homosocial, is crippled. Before relocating north, he believed himself to be the guardian of southern womanhood: "He protected the old ladies. He was the man in the house and he did the things a man in the house was supposed to do" (5). The patriarchal codes of the U.S. South encourage Old Dudley to reinforce his masculinity through his relationship with women, yet it is a woman—his daughter—who removes him from this role of paternal authority: "She was seeing that her father spent his last years with his own family and not in a decayed boarding house full of old women whose heads jiggled" (6). Separated from a female community where his patriarchal governance would be inviolate, Old Dudley must reconceptualize his role in society after moving to New York City. In O'Connor's fiction, this metropolis serves as the antithesis of southern culture, for its cosmopolitan milieu starkly contrasts with the agrarian simplicities of the U.S. South, as also evidenced in "The Enduring Chill" and "Judgement Day."[22] Without women whom he might chivalrously protect, Old Dudley is alienated from his prior sense of masculine worth through his geographic relocation from a small, monocultural boarding house in a southern town to a large, multicultural apartment building in a northern metropolis.

Southern chivalry renders Old Dudley an antiquated relic in the unfamiliar environment of New York City, and without any women around him except his daughter, his alienation impels him to look to his personal history for memories of meaningful companionship. His past friendship with Rabie, an African American, kindles Old Dudley's nostalgia. In recalling their fishing and hunting trips, he relives their homosocial intimacy to escape his debilitating loneliness. Recovering this type of interracial relationship might alleviate Old Dudley's isolation in New York, but his historically modulated identity of heteronormative chivalric masculinity cripples his ability to establish new relationships. In particular, he is humiliated to appear in a feminized position in contrast to the African American tenant who helps him up the stairs back to his apartment: "It probably looked like he had his arm locked in the nigger's" (13). This African American man's assistance effeminizes Old Dudley, and his tears register this enervated masculinity: "The pain in his throat was all over his face now, leaking out his eyes" (13). Unmoored in his new environs following the loss of southern masculinity, a masculinity that should establish him as a dominant and privileged member of society, Old Dudley continues to mull over the implications of his physical intimacy with this African American: "And the nigger had pulled him up on his feet and kept his arm in his" (14).

The continued focus on Old Dudley's feminization bespeaks the ways in which southern chivalric masculinity establishes an impossible standard for any man, but especially for an aging man, to maintain. Also, through the African American man's gracious—indeed, chivalrous—actions in assisting Old Dudley, he successfully incarnates the masculinity that Old Dudley can no longer perform in a metropolitan landscape supposedly devoid of southern values. The threat to Old Dudley's white southern manhood is encapsulated in a term absent from this narrative yet present in "The Barber" when the eponymous barber barks at Rayber, "You a nigger-lover?" (15).[23] This term, through its colluded aspersions against African Americans and homosexuals, captures the racist and homophobic cast of southern culture in its tacit argument that a white man should never engage in a friendship—let alone a sexual relationship—with an African American man.

Old Dudley's beliefs in southern chivalry and in heteronormative race relations prohibit him from establishing a friendship with the African American tenant, and he ponders his emasculating circumstances and the contrast between the South and the North: "Him, that had come from a good place. A good place. A place where such as that couldn't be" (13). But what is the "that" that could not be in the U.S. South? Several possibilities register as the "that" that "couldn't be" in his southern homeland: his tears of humiliation based on a homosocial connection with a black man; his relationship with this northern African American man turning upside-down the cultural codes of the U.S. South because the man maintains a cultural position equal, if not superior, to his own; or simply the alienation in which he finds himself trapped. Effeminized by his contact with the African American man, Old Dudley links his new sense of femininity to his antiquated identity as a white southerner: "His throat was going to pop on account of a nigger—a damn nigger that patted him on his back and called him 'old-timer'" (13). As much as the physical contact with this African American effeminizes him, the epithet "old-timer" forces Old Dudley to confront his narcissistic fantasy of southern masculinity, in that southern men in the mid-twentieth century incarnated a model of maleness now found to be outdated, if not irrelevant, approximately eighty years after the Civil War and now contemporary with the nascent civil rights movement. O'Connor's play with her characters' names is frequently noted, and that "Old" is inscribed in Dudley's appellation renders his aging masculinity suspect, as does the "dud" in "Dudley," which bespeaks a man with insufficient puissance to ejaculate.

To escape the constraints of southern masculinity, Old Dudley must paradoxically access and accept his feminine potential through a carnivalesque act of inversion. The eponymous geranium serves as the narrative's chief symbol of femininity, and Old Dudley's compulsive fascination for it highlights its potential role in freeing him from the oppressive force of gender. Once the flower falls off its windowsill, however, Old Dudley cannot descend deep enough into the feminine to salvage his life from loneliness. The narrator describes the insuperable barrier that prohibits Old Dudley from reaching the flower—"The steps dropped down like a deep wound in the floor" (14)—and here O'Connor employs the image of the wound, a misogynistic symbol of female genitalia, to expose the impossibility for Old Dudley to explore his femininity.

At the story's conclusion, the geranium suggests multiple symbolic possibilities, including femininity, a friendship with either the African American man or the male neighbor across the alley, the women in the southern boarding house whom he misses, and even Old Dudley himself. No matter the particular meaning assigned to this protean symbol, it primarily denotes loss and Old Dudley's failure to ameliorate his loneliness because he remains ensconced within a heteronormative view of white southern manhood and race relations. In terms of O'Connor's depiction of martyred masculinity, Old Dudley suffers in his loneliness and refuses to act meaningfully to ameliorate it. The passive and masochistic masculinity of saints celebrates the desirability of suffering, yet O'Connor inverts the positive value of saintly suffering by disclosing how passivity freed from redemption loses any revelatory meaning. Likewise, the chivalric identity that Old Dudley can no longer enact destabilizes his view of his southern self while simultaneously showcasing the potential for black men to perform chivalry more successfully than whites. If chivalry is a signifier freed from the white southern male body, as O'Connor here suggests, its ability to shore up white privilege is rendered a cultural fantasy of phallic power, one revealing the queer underbelly of heteronormative ideology that cannot suture over its internal contradictions.

Of all of O'Connor's characters, none represents white chivalric masculinity and its narcissistic sexual excesses more blatantly (and humorously) than General Sash in "A Late Encounter with the Enemy" (1953). This ancient spitfire embodies phallic authority, as is evident in his self-assessment: despite his 104 years, the General "considered that he was still a very handsome man. When he had been able to stand up, he had measured five feet four inches of pure game cock" (135). The play on "cock" as rooster and as penis metaphorically satirizes General Sash's phallic pretensions. For a man, five feet and four inches does not measure up to an impressive stature, and so this phallic claim fails to register a masculinity sufficient for a typical chivalric hero. As becomes clear throughout the story, General Sash, with his unbridled sexuality, evinces little interest in the chivalric codes of masculinity that might make him a more palatable figure. He is, quite simply, a relic of history: "Every year on Confederate Memorial Day, he was bundled up and lent to the Capitol City Museum where he was displayed from one to four in a musty room full of old photographs, old uniforms, old artillery, and historic documents" (139).

Male sexuality is horrific in "A Late Encounter with the Enemy" because it appears to dominate men to the extent that all other social connections become secondary, if not altogether irrelevant, especially in regard to how carnal desires threaten familial bonds. Chivalry should teach men how to channel their sexual drives into respectful behavior toward women and, thus, within southern fictions, to fulfill the role of the benevolent paterfamilias, but unrestrained male sexuality in this story belies the promises of chivalric virtue and its purported protection of women. General Sash's sexuality terrifies his granddaughter, Sally Poker Sash: "One night in her sleep she screamed, 'See him! See him!' and turned her head and found him sitting in his wheel chair behind her with a terrible expression on his face and with all his clothes off except the general's hat and she had waked up and had not dared to go back to sleep again that night" (135). This dream's incestuous threat bespeaks Sally's dread that, should her grandfather's sex drive prove unvanquishable, he will rape her. Although her fear is not realized, Sally's middle name indicates the aggressive force of southern masculinity, as it points to the possibility of rape and forced penetration with the play between the name "Poker" and its homophonic pun of "poke her." The menacing detail of the general's hat connects General Sash to military history, and the possibility emerges that Sally will fall as the latest conquest of his martial and sexual prowess.

The General focuses on imagined amatory conquests in his past, looking back at his experiences during the Atlanta premiere of a Hollywood movie to relive the fantasized acme of his sexual history. Although the film is not named, it is likely that O'Connor had in mind the 1939 opening of *Gone with the Wind*, especially since both *Gone with the Wind* and the unnamed film in her story focus on the Confederacy.[24] General Sash thus appears to be an aged and lascivious incarnation of Ashley Wilkes or Rhett Butler. In recalling the events of the premiere, he claims, "A beautiful gul presented me with [a tuxedo] that afternoon in a hotel room" (136). Sally corrects her grandfather—"You weren't alone with any young lady in a hotel room" (136)—but General Sash nonetheless claims his sexual potency, even if such an encounter never occurred: "'Was, I'd a known what to do,' the old General would say with a sharp look and the visitors would scream with laughter" (136). Here O'Connor limns the imaginary construction of southern male sexuality. It matters little whether General Sash slept with the young woman, or even whether she delivered him a tuxedo; rather, his performance of virile masculinity, so ingrained in his mind over the years despite its questionable veracity, becomes the truth for him simply due to its constant and narcissistic reiteration. But his truth is most likely false, and thus O'Connor's medieval vision of the carnivalesque comes into play in her creation of Sash's manhood. In this regard, Sash's enjoyment of the carnival spirit of parades and festivities points to his preference for pageantry over substance: "Any procession that came to meet him, he thought irritably, ought to have floats with beautiful guls on them like the floats before the preemy. It must be something connected with history like they were always having" (141–42). Identity is measured through carnivalesque celebrations of history, not its reality, and thus Sash's sexuality increasingly isolates him through a masculinity so excessive that it becomes parodic.

At Sally's graduation, an event suggesting her potential to move beyond the traditions of southern life that trapped her grandfather, General Sash demands that she help him to accentuate his phallic puissance with his sword, the iconic symbol of his masculinity: "'Put the soward acrost my lap, damm you,' the old man said, 'where it'll shine'" (140). These instructions drip with irony, as the old soldier depends on his granddaughter helping him to display his masculine power. The theme of "A Late Encounter with the Enemy" emerges in the importance of history to guide one's life in the present, as voiced by the commencement speaker: "'If we forget our past,' the speaker was saying, 'we won't remember our future and it will be as well for we won't have one'" (142). O'Connor deploys an understated humor here, ridiculing the tangled nonsense often spouted at commencement exercises, in that remembering the future is, by definition, impossible. At the same time, General Sash can recall only sexual affairs with beautiful girls whom he never actually met, rather than his wife and children whom he lost to the passing of time: "He had forgotten the name and face of his wife and the names and faces of his children or even if he had a wife and children" (142). "Remembering" illusory sexual escapades while forgetting his family, General Sash rewrites history to suit his vision of sexual potency, but this performance of masculinity ensnares him within its isolating pressures.

In the end, General Sash is queerly undone by his unrestrained heterosexuality, which sabotages the chivalry he pretends to represent. Immediately before dying, he clutches his phallic sword, injuring himself in the process: "He made such a desperate effort to . . . find out what comes after the past that his hand clenched the sword until the blade touched bone" (143). If Thomas in "The Comforts of Home" is ensnared by a patriarchal past he cannot escape and his dread of female sexuality, General Sash is inversely trapped by a fantastically constructed past that never existed, and he thus loses the family that might provide some sense of emotional cathexis during his dying moments. In this acerbic satire of southern chivalry, O'Connor unsettles pretensions of white chivalric manhood through

General Sash's excessive performances, as her protagonist misreads the meaning of history by mistaking Hollywood premieres and carnivals for his life story.

Julian, Thomas, Old Dudley, and General Sash illustrate the limitations engendered by historical masculinities modulated through the cloudy intermingling of medievalism, saints, chivalry, and white southern heritage. They also share an inability to see women as women, instead viewing them as nuisances, sexual predators, helpless dependents, and sexual objects. Because women cannot simply be women and must instead reflect to the masculine protagonist his ideal view of himself, no matter how ridiculous, exaggerated, or even attenuated such a vision may be, southern chivalry paradoxically erases the women this purported virtue is intended to honor and protect. Beyond the shared foundations of their masculinities, Julian, Thomas, Old Dudley, and General Sash also face dire circumstances at their narratives' conclusions, which indicates that southern masculinity, in these instances, blocks their paths to salvation, or even to social communion. The invisibility of white male privilege blinds them, especially Old Dudley and General Sash, to the selfishness defining their relationships with men and women, and the bleak endings of their narratives indicate an empty future for them all, one devoid of human or spiritual connection, as evidenced by dead mothers, a broken flower pot, and a hand cut to the bone. In contrast, O'Connor's male characters who experience homosexuality—whether as an identity (Asbury in "The Enduring Chill") or as a violent sexual act (Marion Francis Tarwater in *The Violent Bear It Away*)—find revelation and escape the solipsism that queers so many of her other male protagonists from the valorized masculinity they attempt to perform. Within O'Connor's apocalyptic and carnivalesque perspective on salvation, redemption may be found through homosexuality, which entails a topsy-turvy view of southern male sexuality and its narcissistic claims.

CHRISTIAN REVELATION AND REDEMPTIVE HOMOSEXUALITY

O'Connor's carnivalesque spin to her fiction plays out in numerous themes, and much of this topsy-turviness unsettles traditional binaries of gender, race, class, and sexuality. Katherine Prown notes that gender and race, as seen through a lens of white masculinity, affected O'Connor's conception of the U.S. South and its people: "Just as the Southern Tradition centered on the experience of educated white men, so too did the larger 'republic of letters' rest on the opposition between white and black, male and female."[25] In addition to the ideological boundaries between genders and races that have divided the U.S. South, white masculinity is also marked as triumphant in its assumed heterosexuality, despite the ubiquitous possibility of homosexuality. Beyond her treatment of race and gender, O'Connor also portrays boundaries between heterosexuality and homosexuality, and her characters react strongly to the pressures of heteronormativity, even when they simply capitulate to cultural expectations of "normative" sexual desire. Capitulation to heteronormativity does not fully explain the unsettling force of homosexuality within her work, which reflects a carnivalesque view of human sexuality that locates redemptive possibility within ostensibly opprobrious sexual acts and identities. When O'Connor couples homosexuality with Christian revelation, marginalized sexual acts and actors take on a redemptive cast within her fictions.

Such an argument may appear counterintuitive, given some scholars' arguments that O'Connor felt uncomfortable describing sexuality in her literature. Reading O'Connor in light of her contemporaries, Ted Spivey suggests that "O'Connor's sweeping denunciations of Tennessee Williams, Truman Capote, and Carson McCullers obviously owe much to her revulsion at the frankly sexual in literature."[26] This argument ignores O'Connor's depiction of the "frankly sexual" in her own literature, which teems with erotic characters and themes, such as prostitutes in *Wise Blood* and "The Artificial Nigger," the issue of teen sexuality as mediated through hermaphroditism ("A Temple of the Holy Ghost"), and sexual dissatisfaction in marriage ("Parker's Back"). Likewise, *Wise Blood* showcases Hazel Motes's sexual affairs, including his evenings with prostitute Leora Watts and his planned seduction of Sabbath Lily. Surprisingly, J. O. Tate concludes that "in reading *Wise Blood*, we find no hint of the erotic, no allure, hardly even lust. . . . Hazel Motes' sex life on the page has little or nothing sexual about it";[27] he explains his position further, pointing out the mechanical nature of Hazel's sexual experiences. Still, to deny sex acts their identity as sex acts strips O'Connor's fiction of the sexuality that serves as a central means for some of her protagonists to paradoxically access greater levels of self-awareness and Christian revelation. O'Connor theorized pornography as "essentially sentimental, for it leaves out the connection of sex with its hard purpose" (*MM* 148), and that she mused over pornography's thematic evasions of morality demonstrates that she considered the social repercussions of sexuality and its portrayal in narrative.

Sex and spiritual revelation may appear to share little in common, yet O'Connor connects some of her characters' failures to experience redemption to their prudishness about sexuality, especially when they comically consider sex in regard to their relationship to Christ. In "The Displaced Person," Mrs. McIntyre ponders the intersection of Christianity and sexuality and views them as impolite topics: "Mrs. McIntyre's face assumed a set puritanical expression and she reddened. Christ in the conversation embarrassed her the way sex had her mother" (226). The irony of these lines, in that a puritanical facial expression captures her discomfort with both sexuality and religion, mocks Mrs. McIntyre and her inability to experience transcendentally the mysteries both of religion and of intercourse. In "Greenleaf," Mrs. May similarly links Christianity to sexual prudery: "Mrs. May winced. She thought the word, Jesus, should be kept inside the church building like other words inside the bedroom. She was a good Christian woman with a large respect for religion, though she did not, of course, believe any of it was true" (316). These two women are similarly discomfited by religion and sexuality because both necessitate the baring of a person: the baring of the soul in religion, and the baring of the body during sex. For O'Connor, the connection between religion and sexuality arises in their shared insistence on intimate—even naked—kinship with forces beyond one's self that strip away veneers of egotistical solitude.

In her depiction of sexuality, O'Connor builds redemptive possibility in sex acts considered within Catholic thought to be the most flagrant disruptions to God's plans. The sex acts meriting medieval theologian Thomas Aquinas's most forceful disapproval include those representing "the vice against nature, which attaches to every venereal act from which generation cannot follow," and these sins include masturbation, bestiality, and sodomy.[28] These transgressions are transformed with redemptive possibilities in O'Connor's fiction: masturbation in "The Turkey," bestiality in

"Greenleaf," homosexuality in "The Enduring Chill," and sodomy in *The Violent Bear It Away.* In "The Turkey," O'Connor includes several hints that the young protagonist Ruller enjoys masturbatory pastimes, such as when "His father asked Ruller the next day what he had been doing lately and Ruller said, 'playing by himself,' and walked off sort of like he had a limp" (44). "Playing by himself" euphemistically denotes masturbation, and Ruller's accompanying limp suggests his overenthusiastic indulgence in these solitary pleasures. In "Greenleaf," the bull iconographically consummates its relationship with Mrs. May: "[T]he bull had buried his head in her lap, like a wild tormented lover, before her expression changed. One of his horns sank until it pierced her heart and the other curved around her side and held her in an unbreakable grip" (333). "Greenleaf" ambiguously concludes as Mr. Greenleaf witnesses his wife "whispering some last discovery into the animal's ear" (334), which suggests that she has achieved some sense of revelation prior to her death. Putting reviled sex acts in her texts and imbuing them with transcendent possibility is part of O'Connor's carnivalesque view of humanity's fallen nature, and from this inverted view of sexuality, it is then not surprising that she finds latent spiritual possibility, no matter how violently realized, in Asbury's homosexuality in "The Enduring Chill" and Tarwater's anal rape in *The Violent Bear It Away.*

Beyond the borders of the decent in heteronormative southern culture, sodomy often registers as that which is unnamable and thus that which is unknowable. So marginalized within southern culture that it often fails to appear, sodomy nonetheless refuses to disappear and inhabits the marginal hinterlands of society in O'Connor's fiction. And ironically, the U.S. South is frequently linked with sodomy within the cultural imaginary of the United States, as in such works as James Dickey's *Deliverance* (1970). Both when the U.S. South needs to define normative white masculinity and when the rest of the United States needs to construct the South as its internal Other, accusations of sodomy register the panic inherent in claiming normative masculinity. In a scene that testifies to the tacit power of charges of sodomy to regulate male behavior in O'Connor's fiction, Johnson insinuates that Sheppard made homosexual advances toward him in "The Lame Shall Enter First" (1962):

> "He made suggestions to me!". . .
>
> "Suggestions?" the reporter said eagerly, "what kind of suggestion?"
>
> "Immor'l suggestions!" Johnson said. "What kind of suggestions do you think?" (480)

The spectral hint of pederasty lurks in these lines: what kind of "immor'l suggestions" does a widowed man make to a teen-aged boy? Johnson then tells the reporter that Sheppard is "a dirty atheist" who "said there wasn't no hell" (480), and his words quell the rising homoerotic tension in the scene. This moment illustrates the virtual invisibility of sodomy within southern culture while also pointing to its ubiquitous specter. Johnson's allegations suggest pedophilia, but this possibility is then reformulated into the more palatable—the more mentionable—transgression of heresy.

In O'Connor's "The Enduring Chill" (1958), the protagonist Asbury appears to be homosexual and embodies numerous gay stereotypes. With his "part-time job in the bookstore" (358), he labors as a quasi-intellectual, and he also displays a bohemian sensibility: "[T]he trouble was that in addition to being smart, he had an artistic temperament" (361). Asbury's return to his small southern town cements his status as an outsider, and the narrator indicates that his mother senses his artistic inclinations alienate him from the wider community: "She supposed the truth was that she simply didn't understand how it felt to be sensitive or how peculiar you were when you were an artist" (362). Additionally, Asbury stands physically smaller than his sister Mary George ("He and she had the same features except that hers were bigger" [359]), and he speaks with a "high voice" (358). The stereotypical vision of a homosexual man's family involves a distant father and a domineering mother, and this paradigm holds true for Asbury, whose father is dead and whose mother smothers him. He rebukes her for stifling his creativity: "I have no imagination. I have no talent. I can't create. I have nothing but the desire for these things. Why didn't you kill that too? Woman, why did you pinion me?" (364). Asbury's lament focuses on his artistic and intellectual failures, yet his words—"I can't create"—also point to his failure to produce children.

Given these many queer hints to Asbury's character, even his name takes on homosexual connotations. Like Oscar Wilde's "Bunbury" in *The*

Importance of Being Earnest (1895), in whose name Christopher Craft locates "a tongue-in-cheek allusion to Wilde's illegal 'sodomitical' practices,"[29] O'Connor's use of the name "Asbury" connotes anal penetration, a connection made explicit when Dr. Block surmises that Asbury "must have been on the bum up there [in New York City]" (366). The phrase "on the bum" can be found in the American folk song "Hallelujah, I'm a Bum," which celebrates the lifestyles of vagrants, vagabonds, and tramps,[30] but since "bum" also denotes "buttocks," the phrase assumes a decidedly homoerotic coloring in the narrative. The queer play in the name "Asbury" does not exhaust its connotative range, which is also connected to the founder of American Methodism, Bishop Francis Asbury, who is commemorated in the name of Asbury College and Theological Seminary of Wilmore, Kentucky. The sodomitic and theological allusions in the name "Asbury" merge when Mrs. Fox encourages O'Connor's protagonist to form a relationship with "Mr. Bush, the retired Methodist minister" (371), to which Asbury responds, "If you think I need spiritual aid to die . . . you're quite mistaken. And certainly not from that ass Bush. My God!" (371). The phrase "ass bush" conflates two orifices—the anus and the vagina—through slang terminology and indicates that Asbury's redemption is located in neither homosexual nor heterosexual consummation. Finally, when Father Finn questions Asbury—"Do you have trouble with purity?" (375)—O'Connor sketches Asbury's shameful reaction as he pales before the priest. These many aspects of Asbury's character paint him as a homosexual isolated from his family and the gendered mores of the U.S. South.

Asbury counters his alienation from both his family and white southern culture through his desire to form a homosocial alliance with Morgan and Randall, the African American men employed by his mother. Here Asbury demonstrates his desire to repudiate cultural codes of the U.S. South: returning to the language of "The Barber," he embraces the possibility of being labeled a "nigger-lover." As John Duvall notes of O'Connor's treatment of race, "[t]he figurative blurring of racial binaries in O'Connor's fiction is often closely related to the possibility of salvation, but it is a salvation predicated on whites' traumatic awakening to a shocking discovery that they are colored, even if that epiphany encompasses an almost simultaneous repression."[31] For Asbury, friendship with these black men would flout social standards of white southern masculinity while simultaneously ending his social ostracism; thus, he shares cigarettes with Morgan and Randall in his mother's dairy, and this moment of interracial male bonding is predicated upon the communal enjoyment of phallic symbols. As the men smoke, they enact the basic oral posture of fellatio, and by so doing, they contaminate the milk in the dairy with their impure exhalations. Milk typically symbolizes femininity, nurturing, and childrearing, but Asbury's smoky and phallic union with two African American men perverts the purity of the wholesome white milk. When he feels that his death is certain, Asbury seeks to relive this moment of homosocial union with Morgan and Randall, but they simply pocket his cigarettes rather than smoke them with him. Following the removal of these phallic symbols, an act that metaphorically castrates Asbury, Dr. Block diagnoses his illness as undulant fever, with which he became infected after drinking unpasteurized milk. The torturous and feverish chill caused by the tainted milk's purging femininity ironically heals Asbury's corrupted masculinity.

Despite Asbury's failure to achieve homosocial union to escape his solipsistic loneliness, the ending of "The Enduring Chill" is hopeful as this man on the verge of dying prepares to live again: "The old life in him was exhausted. He awaited the coming of the new" (382). Moreover, Asbury's physical recovery from illness is connected to spiritual rebirth as well, and the reader witnesses his redemption: "[T]he Holy Ghost, emblazoned in ice instead of fire, continued, implacable, to descend" (382). In this conclusion, remarkable in its unexpected optimism, Asbury experiences the narrative equivalent of a reformation ministry designed to free homosexuals from their supposedly sinful behavior. His old life is over, and a new one can be commenced. "The Enduring Chill" does not endorse homosexuality any more than bestiality is "endorsed" in "Greenleaf" or heterosexuality is "endorsed" in *Wise Blood;* rather, sexuality is surpassed rather than embraced in these narratives' conclusions. By giving this homosexual character a revelatory experience, O'Connor, in carnivalesque fashion, upends the expected blanket homophobia of the U.S. South and finds transformative, rather than damning, potential therein.

In *The Violent Bear It Away* (1960), Marion Francis Tarwater journeys into saintly manhood through the redemptive potential inherent in homosexuality. His uncle Rayber enunciates his secular goal of helping Tarwater to grow into southern manhood: "It's not too late for me to make a man of you!" (177). Rayber, however, fails to understand that the proper model of masculinity is to be found in the medieval saints and mystics whom he shuns, as is evident in his derogatory opinion of his family's religiosity: "The affliction was in the family. It lay hidden in the line of blood that touched them, flowing from some ancient source, some desert prophet or polesitter, until, its power unabated, it appeared in the old man and him and, he surmised, in the boy" (192). Tarwater's saintliness shines through even in his infancy, which is apparent when Rayber's wife recoils from him: "Its face was like the face she had seen in some medieval paintings where the martyr's limbs are being sawed off and his expression says he is being deprived of nothing essential" (230). Saintly masculinity guides this family as its patriarchal birthright, but the tension between sacred and secular masculinities threatens to undermine Tarwater's achievement of spiritual revelation.

Robert Donahoo declares that Tarwater's spiritual maturation is linked to an increased acceptance of femininity: "[I]n the case of young Tarwater in *The Violent*, development—what O'Connor in her analyses of the novel sees as religious epiphany or 'salvation'—is linked to a movement not just toward acceptance of the feminine but toward emulation and submission to it."[32] The novella's gendered dynamics, however, should not eclipse the ways in which gender and sexuality conjointly effect a change in Tarwater's consciousness. O'Connor foreshadows the carnivalesque significance of her protagonist's anal rape when Rayber blasphemously baptizes the infant's buttocks:

> Old Tarwater had laid the baby back in the crib but the nephew took him out again, a peculiar smile, the old man said, stiffening on his face. "If one baptism is good, two will be better," he said and he had turned Tarwater over and poured what was left in the bottle over his bottom and said the words of baptism again. Old Tarwater had stood there, aghast at this blasphemy. "Now Jesus has a claim on both ends," the nephew said.
>
> The old man had roared, "Blasphemy never changed a plan of the Lord's!" (167)

If Rayber's blasphemy symbolically marks Tarwater's anus with sin, it is then the Lord's plan to resignify the boy's buttocks and soul through the purging degradation of rape. This passage in the novella is not incidental but part of a train of symbolism linking Tarwater to anal and sodomitic images, such as when his father declares, "One bath more or less won't hurt the bugger" (201). A synonym for sodomite, "bugger" foreshadows the centrality of Tarwater's anus and rape to his redemption.[33]

The driver who picks Tarwater up while hitchhiking rapes him, and numerous queer clues foreshadow this violent act. The driver's car, shirt, and handkerchief are all lavender in color (258, 261), and this shade has long symbolized homosexuality. The *Oxford English Dictionary* documents that lavender connoted homosexuals and homosexuality as early as the 1920s, and the first reference listed is Cole Porter's song "I'm a Gigolo," which contains the lyrics, "I'm a famous gigolo, / And of lavender, my nature's got just a dash in it."[34] As a homosexual himself, Porter knew the codes and symbols of queer life, and his song elucidates the ways in which displays of color encode sexuality. In the buildup to Tarwater's rape, O'Connor highlights the driver's lascivious nature by describing him as giving "the boy a long personal look" (258) and by suggesting "that the stranger was watching him with what might be a leer" (260). After drugging Tarwater, the man "was breathing rapidly and sweating" as he "picked him up and carried him into the woods" (261). Tarwater wakes up to discover that "[h]is hands were loosely tied with a lavender handkerchief which his friend had thought of as an exchange for the hat. His clothes were neatly piled by his side. Only his shoes were on him" (261). Stripped naked, raped, and abandoned, Tarwater then accepts his new Christian identity and undertakes his missionary work.

This shadowy and sodomitic sex act in *The Violent Bear It Away* does not celebrate queer sex as a meaningful union between two consenting adults, yet it underscores the revolutionary and revelatory potential of nonnormative sexuality. This unique moment in O'Connor's fiction, in which sodomy catalyzes redemption, captures her ambivalent depiction of masculinity and sexuality in relation to religion and salvation. It is a moment of grotesque and carnivalesque sexuality, yet Tarwater now sees the "burning bush" of divinity (267). O'Connor most obviously alludes to Moses's vision in Exodus in this line, but the sexual imagery of a burning bush highlights the comic excesses of the scene as well, in that a young man's first vision after his anal rape is a symbolic vision of a fiery vagina.

O'Connor celebrates neither homosexuality nor heterosexuality in these scenes, but instead the purging achievement of spiritual blindness: "His scorched eyes no longer looked hollow or as if they were meant only to guide him forward. They looked as if, touched with a coal like the lips of the prophet, they would never be used for ordinary sights again" (262). Genitals, real or symbolic, are rendered irrelevant, as are eyes that see yet know not, and all must be surpassed as Tarwater achieves a queerly emasculated salvation transcendent of typical codes of southern masculinity.

For many of O'Connor's men, history in its medieval, chivalric, and southern incarnations shapes their identities, and the power of history must be shattered if they are to escape the cultural limitations of their current lives. Surprisingly, of the characters examined in this chapter, the homosexual Asbury and the sodomized Marion Francis Tarwater succeed in moving beyond their histories and their solipsistic sense of their lives. The Holy Spirit descends on Asbury, and Tarwater begins his missionary work, in contrast to Julian's mourning for his mother's death, Thomas's imminent arrest for his mother's murder, Old Dudley's unconquerable loneliness, and General Sash's death surrounded by a "black procession" (143). This is not to suggest that O'Connor took a progressive view of homosexuality: just as she frequently deploys violence to catalyze spiritual enlightenment, she also uses homosexuality and sodomy to destabilize readers' expectations and to instill a lurid symbol of nascent enlightenment within her fictions. In her gothic and grotesque imaginary, the journey to salvation takes place where one might least expect it: on a queer path historically traveled by suffering medieval saints and white southern gentlemen trapped by gendered codes of chivalry. This path, depicted with teleological yet carnivalesque logic, leads to a sodomized anus and the salvific pleasures of a burning bush.

4

"IT'S PROLLY FULLA DIRTY STORIES"

Queer Masculinity and Masturbatory Allegory in John Kennedy Toole's A Confederacy of Dunces

As the antiheroic protagonist of John Kennedy Toole's comic masterpiece *A Confederacy of Dunces,* Ignatius J. Reilly embodies a queer masculinity modulated between the solipsistic physical pleasure of masturbation and the esoteric mental study of medievalism.[1] Antichivalric in the extreme (and provocatively antisouthern), Ignatius's masculinity plays a pivotal role in the character's unlikely triumph at the narrative's end. Throughout his madcap adventures, the seductive force of allegory stimulates Ignatius, despite his stringent asexuality, into erotic action as he casts himself as the protagonist of medievally inspired allegorical crusades against modernity. These masturbatory and medieval allegories structure the reader's understanding of Ignatius's crusades in the decadent milieu of twentieth-century New Orleans, as they also illuminate the ways in which queerness permeates allegorical meaning in the disjunction between text and metatext. As Ignatius's medievalism estranges him from the social world around him, it also models for the reader the sheer pleasure in absurdly ahistorical masculinities divorced from the cultural touchstone of white southern chivalry.

Through Ignatius's queer masculinity, sexual desires within *A Confederacy of Dunces* disrupt normative constructions of identity and allegorical meaning. Lee Edelman argues that "the queer dispossesses the social order of the ground on which it rests. . . . [Q]ueerness exposes the obliquity of our relations to what we experience in and as social reality."[2] Without doubt, Ignatius challenges contemporary southern values, and these challenges are linked to his unique sexual desires and masturbatory fantasies. Through Ignatius's parodic reinstitution of medieval values in southern culture, Toole considers the cultural meanings of southern masculinity, with his protagonist subverting the dominant social order. A homosexual living and writing during the 1960s in the U.S. South, Toole deploys Ignatius to reflect his own sense of the amorphous nature of white male identity. In a letter to Robert Gottlieb, a senior editor at Simon & Schuster, Toole recalls how his life merged with Ignatius's: "I was beginning to talk and act like Ignatius. No doubt this is why there's so much of him and why his verbosity becomes tiring. It's really not his verbosity but mine. And the book, begun one Sunday afternoon, became a way of life. With Ignatius as an agent, my New Orleans experiences began to fit in, one after the other, and then I was simply observing and not inventing."[3] Reading Ignatius as a mirror of Toole greatly oversimplifies the ways in which some authors invest their characters with elements of their own personality, yet their respective sexualities—Toole's homosexuality and Ignatius's indeterminate sexuality—together represent how nonnormative masculinities were viewed as aberrant in the 1950s and 1960s.

Their shared enthusiasm for the Middle Ages and the Renaissance also links the author to his protagonist: as an academically trained scholar of medieval and Renaissance literature, Toole turned his knowledge of early writers and philosophical traditions upside down in his satirical reimagining of medieval themes in his novels. His literary education included an M.A. from Columbia University's Department of English and Comparative Literature for a thesis on the humor of John Lyly (ca. 1553–1606), who is known for his comic plays and his *Euphues: The Anatomy of Wit* (1578); Lyly's style sparked the term *euphuism* to refer to elaborately artificial and postured language, and their shared penchant for verbosity also connects author to protagonist.[4] In regard to Toole's medievalism, Wesley Britton posits that Toole conceived of *A Confederacy of Dunces* as a modern rewriting of William Langland's *Piers Plowman.*[5] Also, whereas Toole follows Mark Twain's lead in lampooning southern chivalry and medieval masculinity, Ignatius inversely defends medieval values by repeatedly insulting Twain: "You may remember that Mark Twain preferred to lie supinely in bed while composing those rather dated and boring efforts which contemporary scholars try to prove meaningful. Veneration of Mark Twain is one of the roots of our current intellectual stalemate" (55). In a metacritical moment of irony, Ignatius refuses to be confused with one of Twain's creations—"Does she think that I'm one of these perverse Mark Twain characters?" (91)—and he pithily lambastes Twain as "that dreary fraud" (141). Toole unites his critique of southern chivalry to Twain's through his protagonist's distaste for Twain's antimedievalism and thereby circuitously pays homage to his literary forebear for his critique of southern chivalric values.

The fact that Toole was a homosexual does not entail that he lived openly as such. The concept of *pseudohomosexuality* enlightens the ways in which suspect sexualities operated in the United States during the 1950s and 1960s. Pseudohomosexuality refers to the fears of otherwise straight men that they might be gay, as well as to society's perception of some men as insufficiently normative and thus potentially homosexual.[6] In a 1959 essay, no less an avatar of American masculinity than Norman Mailer diagnoses his pseudohomosexuality, wondering whether his homophobia masks latent queer desires: "There is probably no sensitive heterosexual alive who is not preoccupied at one time or another with his latent homosexuality, and while I had no conscious homosexual desires, I had wondered more than once if really there were not something suspicious in my intense dislike of homosexuals."[7] Despite the virile masculinity of his public persona, Mailer concedes the potential for virtually any man to embody heterosexuality while shrouding his latent homosexuality.

Pseudohomosexuality as a category of cultural panic emerged as a result of seismic shifts in understandings of male sexuality in the late 1940s and 1950s. As Barbara Ehrenreich points out, marriage documented a man's heterosexuality during this period, and so unmarried men might be seen as insufficiently normative: "The average age of marriage for men in the late fifties was twenty-three, and . . . if a man held out much longer, say even to twenty-seven, 'you had to wonder.' . . . By the 1950s and '60s psychiatry had developed a massive weight of theory establishing that marriage—and, within that, the breadwinner role—was the only normal state for the adult male."[8] Against this backdrop of rigorous conformity to normative masculinities, the cultural anxiety surrounding pseudohomosexuality in the 1950s offered some small protections to homosexuals, in that this suspect sexual category could be both liberating and imprisoning: pseudohomosexuality provided a thin layer of protection against social reprobation because it screened men from the truly damning label of homosexual. Since pseudohomosexuality was not quite synonymous with homosexuality, a man could be perceived as noticeably different in his sexuality while not meriting the opprobrious designation of homosexual.

Truman Capote and Tennessee Williams epitomize how gay men could live fairly openly as homosexuals despite the conservative environs of the U.S. South, through the social persona of pseudohomosexuality (even if this term itself was not used). In many ways, this cultural phenomenon appears counterintuitive, and Capote denied experiencing shame about his sexual identity or the need to hide it: "I always had a homosexual preference, and I never had any guilt about it. As time goes on, you finally settle down on one side or another, homosexual or heterosexual. And I was homosexual." Many of Capote's friends and family did not share his comfort with his sexuality, and biographer Gerald Clarke documents that some of his closest companions ignored his sexuality altogether: "Not many people talked openly about homosexuality at that time, and though they knew he was different, of course, few of his friends, even sophisticated ones like Tom Flanagan, who had read Oscar Wilde and knew about such things, guessed his sexual inclination."[9] In the case of Tennessee Williams, James Keller observes how homophobic societies exploit gays for their own gain while denying the venerated homosexual's very sexuality: "Queers are symbolically central and socially peripheral. As is the case with Tennessee Williams, the culture is willing to co-opt his fame for its own purposes, to take credit for his work . . . , assuming that somehow his creative impulses are separate from his sexual predispositions."[10] As much as Truman Capote and Tennessee Williams were two of the most famous gay men of their generation, society at large and southern society in particular often refused to see their sexuality.

In this manner, pseudohomosexuality offers a means of conceptualizing how nonnormative sexualities could be purposefully misdiagnosed, in which the refusal to label homosexuality as such served the ideological purpose of rendering the nonnormative invisible. In her chapter entitled "'He's a Little Funny, but He's Nice'; or, The Gay Confederation," from *Southern Ladies and Gentlemen* (1975), Florence King captures how southern culture recognizes but insists on misreading male homosexuality: such a man is a little "funny," and this epithet obfuscates homosexuality by redirecting attention from sexuality to the assumed niceness of virtually any homosexual. King satirically dissects the southern experience for gay men and refers to them as "homosexuals or crypto homosexuals"; this latter term testifies to the ways in which southern culture euphemizes homosexuality even while directly addressing it.[11] Within this mix of human sexuality and its ensuing cultural anxieties, Toole exploits the hazy parameters of pseudohomosexuality to delineate his flamboyant protagonist's odd sexual desires. Surely he had practice in this regard, as biographical evidence records the pseudohomosexual facades that he erected—or were erected for him—in interactions with friends and family. Dalt Wonk suggests that Toole's mother "tended to think that women were after her son, but that he was not interested, 'not that kind of man,'" and pseudohomosexuality, even if not labeled as such, allowed Toole's mother to consider her son's sexuality in terms acceptable to her worldview. Likewise, Wonk records an unnamed friend's murky description of Toole's sexuality: "As one acquaintance put it, 'he had no observable sexual dimension in his life.'"[12]

Still, the cold comfort of pseudohomosexuality should not cause one to overlook the painful homophobia of the period. Even if New Orleans in some ways offered a queer oasis amid the blatant homophobia of the U.S. South, persecution of homosexuals proceeded apace throughout the period, such as in the 1966 case of two women, Mary Young and Dawn DeBlanc, who were charged with "unnatural carnal copulation" in the Criminal Court of Orleans Parish before Judge Frank J. Shea. The women were convicted, and on January 16, 1967, their convictions were upheld after appeal.[13] John Howard documents numerous additional cases of the persecution of gays in the U.S. South, and he also points to the connection between homosexuality and suicide as reported by one of his sources, Damien Martin, who remembers from 1952 in Biloxi, Mississippi, "some of the worst antigay purges the air force has ever known" that resulted in numerous suicides.[14] John Kennedy Toole killed himself on March 26, 1969.

Toole invites his audience to experience the pseudohomosexually gendered fictions of *A Confederacy of Dunces* allegorically, but its allegorical qualities also compel the reader to confront the ever-present possibility of medieval hermeneutics queering the contours of readerly identities. The allegorical qualities of *A Confederacy of Dunces*, as well as their connections to medievalism, provide the subject of this chapter's next section, and the following section examines the text's multiple allegorical registers and how they open a space of queer potential for Ignatius to undermine conceptions of white southern masculinity. The chapter concludes by considering the ways in which allegorical medievalism inspires Ignatius's masturbatory pleasures and sexual desires. Despite his overbearing unattractiveness as a fictional character, Ignatius, through his queerly medieval masculinity, creates manifold literary pleasures, if readers only heed his seductive appeals.

IGNATIUS'S MEDIEVAL ALLEGORY

Toole suffuses numerous characters and incidents in *A Confederacy of Dunces* with allegorical significance, and in many ways allegory provides a generic superstructure to the novel; this genre, however, should not occlude its play with a range of complementary narrative forms. Given the novel's investment in multiple generic traditions, interpretative plurality must structure any explication of its textual strategies. Keith Miller argues that the novel proceeds in a linear manner in the grand comic fashion of such early novelists as Henry Fielding and Charles Dickens, whereas William Nelson reads it as a comic grotesque. David McNeil labels *A Confederacy of Dunces* a reverse satire, "because [Ignatius] epitomizes the very perversions against which he rages," while Elizabeth Bell discerns the novel's picaresque qualities. Robert Regan argues that the tale burlesques Walker Percy's *The Moviegoer.* It is a "Christian comedy particularly fitting for a [nineteen-]sixties setting," according to Pat Gardner, and Hugh Ruppersburg believes it belongs to southern literary traditions due to its "philosophical and cultural attitudes" and its "setting, local color, and characters," although he cautions against viewing the novel as a "conscious response to Southern literary tradition."[15] Reading the novel as a roman à clef inappropriately stretches its allegorical qualities to fit the contours of history, yet Toole appears to have modeled Ignatius both on himself and on Bobby Byrne, "the eccentric New Orleanian" who taught English with him and who specialized in medieval literature.[16] Likewise, readers have discerned additional autobiographical and historical elements in the novel.[17] In regard to his protagonist's pseudohomosexuality, Toole colors Ignatius with his own experiences as a southern homosexual, which highlights his character's alienation from the culture around him. Within this multiplicity of generic forms, allegory provides the necessary backbone to the structure: the play of genres gives the novel much of its lively polyphony, while allegory helps the reader to distill a message from the madness.

A Confederacy of Dunces presents a medievally inspired allegory with twentieth-century twists. Embedded with varying levels of symbolism and meaning, allegory relies on the gap between text and metatext, as Gordon Teskey describes: "The very word *allegory* evokes a schism in consciousness—between a life and a mystery, between the real and the ideal, between a literal tale and its moral—which is repaired, or at least concealed, by imagining a hierarchy on which we ascend toward truth." In his study of the genre, Angus Fletcher argues that "considered as a rhetorical device, allegory has the . . . capacity to provide narrative and dramatic equivalents of visual, geometric diagrams."[18] Such a conception of allegory is readily applicable to *A Confederacy of Dunces* because the reader's first vision of Ignatius offers not merely a description of his clothing but an explanation of its symbolic significance: "The plaid flannel shirt made a jacket unnecessary while the muffler guarded exposed Reilly skin between earflap and collar. The outfit was acceptable by any theological and geometrical standards, however abstruse, and suggested a rich inner life" (1–2). Such allegorical moments in *A Confederacy of Dunces* lull readers into a false sense of interpretive security: how challenging can it be to decode the symbolism of the text, if each piece of the allegorical patchwork comes with a key informing readers of its significance?

Within this allegory, Ignatius represents medievalism fighting against the fallen modern world. He devotes himself to the Middle Ages, and his medieval interests resonate throughout his adventures. He reveres Boethius's *The Consolation of Philosophy,* a sixth-century philosophical treatise written while its author faced execution that addresses Lady Fortune and the vagaries she inflicts upon humanity. Ignatius elevates medievalism into a spiritual touchstone for life in a postmodern world: "As a medievalist Ignatius believed in the *rota Fortunae,* or wheel of fortune, a central concept in *De Consolatione Philosophiae,* the philosophical work which had laid the foundation for medieval thought" (35).[19] Few members of the New Orleans community heed his cry for the return to medieval values, but Ignatius aspires to reclaim the glories of the past in his fight against modernity.

For Ignatius, the loss of medieval ideals precipitated the rise of vulgarity, and he documents this belief in his Big Chief tablet: "With the breakdown of the Medieval system, the gods of Chaos, Lunacy, and Bad Taste gained ascendancy" (33). He believes that spreading medieval values will return order, sanity, and decorum to New Orleans by erasing the foundations of modernity. A defender of medieval sensibilities and an offender of modern ones, Ignatius allegorically represents Boethian medievalism in a world cut adrift from its historical and philosophical moorings, and the failure of this lofty ideal peppers the novel with humor: despite taking Boethius's stoic masculinity as his model, Ignatius repeatedly fails to emulate the medieval manhood that should guide him during his daily endeavors.

In addition to this passionate medievalism, Toole links Ignatius to specific classical and medieval men. His address on Constantinople Street connects him to Constantine (88), the fourth-century Roman emperor who halted persecution of Christians. An allegorical representation of one of Christianity's early defenders, Ignatius is imbued with an air of comic religious righteousness, although no characters recognize the royal masculinity embedded in this allusion and see only Ignatius's empty pretensions. Additionally, the name "Ignatius" recalls Ignatius of Loyola, the founder of the Jesuits. Beyond their joint appellation, the comic protagonist and this sixteenth-century priest share a love for learning, as evidenced by their proselytizing—Ignatius Reilly for medievalism, Ignatius of Loyola for Catholicism. (Ignatius of Loyola also recalls the novel's local setting in New Orleans, home of such Jesuit educational institutions as Loyola University and Jesuit High School.) Medievalism provides more than merely an academic interest for Ignatius, for he proselytizes others to his Boethian worldview: "To pacify his mother and to improve conditions at home, he had given her *The Consolation of Philosophy*, an English translation of the work that Boethius had written while unjustly imprisoned and had told her to give it to Patrolman Mancuso. . . . 'The book teaches us to accept that which we cannot change. It describes the plight of a just man in an unjust society. It is the very basis for medieval thought'" (188). In a manner similar to Ignatius of Loyola's evangelical dissemination of Catholic doctrine through the establishment of educational institutions, Ignatius Reilly shares his learning with the world to convert others to Boethian medievalism. Toole's riotous comic touches often puncture any nascent seriousness, and another feature allegorically linking the two Ignatiuses is their digestive difficulties. Mary Purcell documents Ignatius of Loyola's "gastric trouble" during the closing years of his life,[20] and Ignatius Reilly complains frequently of difficulties with his digestive "valve": "'*Everyone* has a valve!' Ignatius screamed. 'Mine is simply more developed. I am trying to open a passage which you have succeeded in blocking'" (57). Through these connections both elevated and ridiculous, Ignatius carries the allegorical weight of a saint and holy man, despite his expressed antagonism toward the Catholic Church after the reforms of Vatican II: "I do not support the current Pope. He does not at all fit my concept of a good, authoritarian Pope. Actually, I am opposed to the relativism of modern Catholicism quite violently" (61). Walker Percy labels Ignatius "a perverse Thomas Aquinas," which encapsulates how another religious figure is identified with Ignatius and thus ridiculed.[21]

A reincarnation of a dyspeptic evangelist living on a holy emperor's street with an executed philosopher as his role model, Ignatius assumes yet another allegorical register as a medieval crusader when he fights to uphold his spiritual values. He begins his revolt against Levy Pants with the "Crusade for Moorish Dignity" (161, 169), and he observes the ways in which crusading defines his sense of self during his daily forays into the French Quarter: "I was beginning to feel rather like a Crusader" (269). With his lexicon of questing and grailing, Ignatius also casts himself as an Arthurian knight when he bemoans his "quest for work" and, proclaiming its futility, laments that he "might as well have had the Grail set as [his] goal" (182). In his journal he merges medieval themes of crusading and questing when he describes vending hotdogs in the French Quarter as an opportunity for him to wage "a crusade for taste and decency, for theology and geometry"; he signs this journal entry as "Lance" (272), thus evoking Lancelot and the knights of the Arthurian tradition. A crusading and questing incarnation of medievalism, Ignatius embodies the battle between a lost medieval past and a fallen postmodern present. With Arthurian masculinities also inflecting his self-definition, Ignatius appropriates a powerful paradigm of medieval manhood to define himself but, in so doing, does not adhere to this model as much as he subverts it.

Because Ignatius is an allegorical figure embodying numerous connections to masculinities of the classical and medieval past, his travails likewise must be interpreted through the lens of allegory. Ignatius observes during one of his trips to the French Quarter, "The balconies of the old building hung over my head like dark branches in an allegorical forest of evil" (269), both underscoring the allegorical nature of his journey and likening it to the opening scene of Dante's *Inferno*. The allegorical trope of a journey through dark woods humorously devolves into a cliché in *A Confederacy of Dunces* through its overuse and obvious symbolism when Myrna writes a letter to Ignatius detailing the artistic vision of her friend Samuel, who "is planning a dramatic allegory set in a dark woods (Ignorance and Custom)" (208). By immediately explicating this trite allegorical scene, Myrna highlights the potential of the genre to devolve into tendentiousness. Medieval morality plays, which are structured allegorically, also organize Ignatius's worldview: "Like two figures in the medieval Morality play, Pragmatism and Morality spar in the boxing ring of my brain" (317). Medieval tragedies represent a literary tradition typically distinct from allegory, but Ignatius blurs their borders by casting himself as the tragic protagonist of the rebellion at Levy Pants: "*De Casibus Virorum Illustrium!* Of the Fall of Great Men! My downfall occurred. Literally" (143). Despite the generic chasm between tragedy and allegory, Ignatius interprets his "tragic" experience for its allegorical meaning, seeking connections between his mishaps and those of medieval narratives.[22]

In addition to allegory and tragedy, Ignatius believes that another medieval genre, the exemplum, should structure modern life. An exemplum typically consists of a short story illustrating a moral lesson; it is not necessarily an allegorical genre, but as Larry Scanlon explains in his interpretation of Chaucer's *Nun's Priest's Tale*, "the shifting, contradictory space between the allegorical and the ironic" can disrupt a narrative's creation of exemplary meaning.[23] In this fashion, the tension between allegory and exemplum arises in Ignatius's ironic application of allegorical significance to the decidedly nonexemplary text of a television sock-hop. In his condemnation of television dance shows for teenagers, he rants: "Do I believe the total perversion that I am witnessing? . . . The ironic thing about that program . . . is that it is supposed to be an *exemplum* to the youth of our nation" (48–49). For Ignatius the common theme of these medieval genres is that they should edify a fallen world into a new awareness of its sinful condition, and thus even nonallegorical genres take on an allegorical cast in his eyes.

The bulk of the narrative invites the reader to witness Ignatius's two "crusades"—the first leading African American workers at Levy's Pants into rebellion, the second leading a homosexual infiltration of world governments—and concomitantly to seek allegorical meaning within these madcap adventures. The allegorical lesson of *A Confederacy of Dunces* arises in its indictment of modern society for combining church and commerce. Religion and finance commingle throughout the novel, and such moments indicate that money threatens the sanctity of religious experience. For example, Mrs. Reilly tells Ignatius that she bought a "nice little pair of beads filled with Lourdes water" for a friend (91); Mrs. Levy describes a jeweler's "exclusive agreement with a bunch of nuns who peddle the rosaries in about forty Catholic schools all over the city. The money's rolling in" (177); Ignatius is hired by the ironically named hotdog franchise "Paradise Vendors" (179); and Mr. Robichaux excuses his tardiness because he was helping his grandchildren who were "raffling some rosaries for the sisters" (231). The reader witnesses commerce on the consecrated ground of a cemetery with the "poor old colored lady [who] sells them pralines" at "a wonderful, lucrative location at the cemetery" (253–54). Religious kitsch populates the landscape as well, as evident when Mrs. Reilly compliments Santa Battaglia on her "little Our Lady of the Television" (308).

Ignatius proclaims the novels' thematic core when he condemns the consumerism of the present for its rejection of the medieval past: "The luminous years of Abélard, Thomas à Beckett, and Everyman dimmed into dross; Fortuna's wheel had turned on humanity. . . . What had once been dedicated to the soul was now dedicated to the sale" (33). This excessive consumerism also threatens to destroy children. When railing against the television dance programs that he delights in watching, Ignatius thunders, "I would very much like to know what the Founding Fathers would say if they could see these children being debauched to further the cause of Clearasil" (49). In comparison to the medieval past, Ignatius notes that he lives in an "age of deodorants and other perversions" (55). Richard Patteson and Thomas Sauret tersely comment that, in the world of *A Confederacy of Dunces*, "materialism has indeed become the new religion."[24] These moments, which focus on money's cheapening of religion and corrupting of children, set the stage for the wider allegorical framework of Ignatius's commercial adventures at Levy Pants.

Toole paints the allegorical qualities of Ignatius's commercial endeavors with broad strokes, labeling Levy Pants as "that particular inferno" (119), another clear reference to Dante's Hell and the allegorical structure of the *Divine Comedy.*[25] In a moment of brief success before imminent disaster, the crusading Ignatius describes his experiences at Levy Pants positively and allegorically: "[M]y Levy circle-within-a-circle is zooming upward to new successes and heights" (150), which suggests both an ironic inversion of the downward spiral of Dante's *Inferno* and a hopeful reference to Lady Fortune's perpetually spinning wheel. Within this allegorical world and responding to the call of "Levy Pants, the commercial muse" (145), Ignatius introduces religion to the workplace by building a cross with "little gold leaf letters that spelled GOD AND COMMERCE" (134). Ignatius triumphs in merging religion and commerce: "Yes! [The cross] is completed and gives our office a needed spiritual dimension" (140). Miss Trixie, the elderly and virtually blind clerical worker whom Ignatius refers to as "our Earth Mother of the world of commerce" (88), "Mother Commerce" (132), and "La Dama del Comercio" (140), represents the stultifying effects of capitalism, but she responds to the cross with appropriate religious reverence: "Miss Trixie . . . had fallen to her knees again before the cross" (134). In light of Toole's protean irony, the depth of Miss Trixie's religious conversion is suspect, as she is more concerned with receiving her long promised Easter ham than achieving religious enlightenment ("'I want that Easter ham!' Miss Trixie snarled. 'Where's my Thanksgiving turkey?'" [133]). The fact that she remains ignorant of this allegorical lesson does not lessen its impact for the reader or for Mr. Levy, the character for whom it is primarily intended.

The grand teeming narrative of *A Confederacy of Dunces* contains many detours along the way, but Mr. Levy finally learns a moral lesson about himself and his company: "A neglected Levy Pants was like a neglected child: it could turn out to be a delinquent, something that created all sorts of problems that a little nurture, a little care and feeding could prevent. The more you stayed away from Levy Pants, the more it plagued you" (419). As Mrs. Levy points out to Mr. Levy, Miss Trixie is "a symbol of everything you haven't done" (278), and the narrative's denouement depicts Mr. Levy attending to his duties to his employee and enabling her to retire. That one must nurture one's business, workers, and family is a simple lesson, but its core simplicity in no manner lessens its impact. In effect, Mr. Levy needs to be reborn into a life of meaningful activity as opposed to his ensconced existence at home, which Toole describes as "a seventy-five-degree womb connected to the year-round air-conditioning unit by an umbilicus of vents and pipes." This home, which is "as sensually comfortable as the human womb supposedly is" (111), highlights Mr. Levy's stunted emotional development. As William Clark argues, "behind the raucous humor and joyously affirmative ending of *A Confederacy of Dunces* lurks the haunting and ubiquitous figure of the suffering child and the complementary portrayal of parent/child relationships as all but uniformly crippling."[26] An allegorical indictment of the breakdown of the family unit, the rise of meaningless commerce, and the moral failings of religion, *A Confederacy of Dunces* achieves a level of surprising poignancy amid its Rabelaisian backdrop of excess and lunacy.

MULTIPLE ALLEGORIES AND IGNATIUS'S PSEUDOHOMOSEXUAL MASCULINITY

As much as this moral lesson structures *A Confederacy of Dunces*, it cannot contain the allegorical excesses unleashed as Toole's medieval protagonist quests throughout a fallen world. Allegory promises its resolution as the reader pieces together the literal and symbolic levels of a text, and *A Confederacy of Dunces* frequently directs readers to interpret a given character or symbol in accordance with the text's instructions. Despite these expectations, allegory also disrupts readerly interpretations, because it is based as much on the disjunction between text and message as it is on their initial congruency. Medieval allegories purport to lead to Truth, but postmodernism teaches that allegories lead to conflicting truths, which potentially pervert the allegory in question.

All allegories bear the possibility of misreadings, but some texts, through their allegorical excesses, call for multiple and contradictory readings more than others. For example, a great deal of allegorical distance separates the medieval morality play *Everyman* from the seductive fictions of *Roman de la Rose*, and the allegorical play of the latter text elicits pleasurable interpretive frustration by offering up too many allegorical registers for one interpretation to control. As Jon Whitman argues, "If allegory intriguingly suggests its own promise, it also revealingly displays its own problems. In these two conflicting demands—the divergence between the apparent and actual meanings, and yet the correspondence between them—it is possible to see both the birth and the death of allegorical writing."[27] Much like language itself, allegory flourishes and falters in the gap between the signifier and the signified. Carolynn Van Dyke likewise declares, "Allegory bases itself frankly on the disruption of signifier and signified and therefore renounces the illusions of semantic unity and directness promoted by such modes as symbolism," and Frederick Jameson agrees: "Allegory is . . . the opening up of the text to multiple meanings, to successive writing and overwritings which are generated as so many levels and as so many supplementary interpretations."[28] Toole plays with multiple levels of allegory throughout *A Confederacy of Dunces*, both creating and subverting his allegorical structures to undermine hermeneutic stability.

The characters of *A Confederacy of Dunces* appear cognizant of the ways in which allegorical fault lines operate, such as when Mrs. Levy employs allegory as a weapon in her marital battles with her husband. She habitually threatens him that she will manipulate their daughters' opinion of him, and she senses the allegorical potential in depicting him as a bigot: "With [Mr. Levy] cast as a Klansman firing a young crusader, Mrs. Levy could really write a flaming broadside" (175). Thinking in terms of allegorical tableaux, Mrs. Levy structures both the allegory and her audience's understanding of it to advance her causes. Similarly, in regard to his plan for a homosexual takeover of world governments, Ignatius plans to create new interpretive possibilities by restructuring symbols and their meaning: "Degeneracy, rather than signaling the downfall of a society, as it once did, will now signal peace for a troubled world. We must have new solutions to new problems" (317). Manipulating symbolism and allegory allows Ignatius to invert old "truths," and, as he resignifies sodomites into humanity's saviors, this allegorical sleight of hand demands a new engagement with allegory and the world it represents.

Contradictory symbolism obscures the novel's allegorical message, with such contradictions surfacing in Ignatius himself, who dually occupies the position of ludicrous antihero and moral protagonist. Toole invites the reader to laugh at Ignatius for his medievally inspired antics that spark the comically picaresque plot, yet he also imbues Ignatius's medievalism with a scholastic foundation that gives him a hint of credibility. Although never employed as an academic, Ignatius was sufficiently successful as a graduate student to earn an interview with the chairman of the Medieval Culture Department of an unidentified school in Baton Rouge, presumably Louisiana State University (13). Ignatius's medievalism thus constructs him as an outlandish yet simultaneously somewhat respectable figure; he may be a lunatic, but as his mother points out, his postbaccalaureate degree should merit him cultural approbation: "You can get you a good job. Wait till they see a boy with a master's degree" (62). Of course, Ignatius's medievalism is seriously flawed in his interpretations of some medieval texts, such as when he compares himself to William Langland's protagonist Piers Plowman in regard to their relationship to labor and describes his horror over "Piers' new fate. And a vicious fate it was to be: now he was faced with the perversion of having to GO TO WORK" (34). Piers Plowman does not view labor as such a perversion of the social contract, and Langland revised his allegory to renounce the narrative's deployment to spur support for the Peasants' Revolt of 1381.[29] Despite the humor of Ignatius's superficial understanding of medieval literature, his devotion to *The Consolation of Philosophy* highlights the ways in which medievalism inspires and elevates him, rendering him both ridiculous and remarkable for his academic study. Likewise, when Mrs. Reilly pressures Ignatius to seek psychological help, he fears that the treatment will metamorphose him "into a moron who liked television and new cars and frozen food" (358) as punishment for rejecting the values of the establishment and "scorning all that they hold dear within their little latex hearts" (269). In this instance, Ignatius's desire not to be transformed into a blinded consumerist lacking any hint of intellectual depth appears not merely rational but wise. True, Ignatius watches television and cooks frozen pizzas, and so this diatribe also exemplifies his hypocrisy. Ignatius's failure to adhere to his ideals, however, does not discredit the ideals themselves. Similar to his superficial medievalism, his rejection of popular culture highlights both his intelligence and his failure to realize his lofty vision of what life should be.

As Ignatius dually represents lunacy and wisdom, medievalism is likewise constructed alternatively as a life-giving force that sustains him through his daily quests and as an opiate for the masses. Representing life and engagement for Ignatius, the symbolism of medievalism for many other characters suggests its soporific and palliative effects. Mrs. Reilly, Mancuso, and Santa Battaglia frequently drink an alcoholic beverage called "Early Times": "His mother and Patrolman Mancuso were sitting at the table around an almost full fifth of Early Times" (121; cf. 224, 234, 237). Both Ignatius and a range of other characters "imbibe" the Middle Ages, but whereas the past sedates most characters, it excites Ignatius to action.

Given this inherent flux of allegory, Ignatius represents both the fallen world order and its salvation, and the moral lesson that Mr. Levy learns prepares the reader for the text's allegorical depiction of Ignatius as a most unexpected Christ-figure. Although Ignatius's unappealing characteristics should dissever any connection to Jesus and his passive model of suffering masculinity, Mr. Levy realizes "[t]hat Reilly kook had really been worth saving after all. He had saved himself, Miss Trixie, and Mr. Levy, too, in his own kook way" (442). A comic, grotesque, and kooky Christ figure, Ignatius suffers his own stigmata when Miss Trixie "step[s] onto one of Ignatius's outstretched hands" (100). When Ignatius realizes that his favorite soft drink now assumes a bitter flavor ("The Dr. Nuts tasted like gall" [444]), he reenacts Jesus' mortification as the soldiers compelled him to drink gall (Matthew 27.34). Ignatius's hyperbolic view of his suffering is ridiculous in its excesses, and he allegorically paints himself as a suffering Christ-figure while castigating his mother for selling her hat: "[Y]ou have, after all, just sold a memento of my childhood for thirty pieces of silver, so to speak" (29; cf. Matthew 26.15). Moreover, he accidentally saves others by the force of his medieval beliefs: his redemption of Mr. Levy, whose name is suggestive of rising in its French cognate *levé*, parallels Jesus' raising of Lazarus, especially since Miss Trixie believes Mr. Levy, who remains very much alive, to be deceased: "I thought you said he was dead" (103). Burma Jones senses a ghostly quality to Ignatius, noting that "[t]here was something ghostly about that green-cap freak" (63) and referring to him as a "green-cap phantom" (64). Santa Battaglia also calls him a "ghost" (226), which hints at Ignatius's otherworldly and spiritual qualities. If medievalism were a religion with Ignatius as its prophet, the text argues, it might just comically save us all.

Reading Ignatius as a Christ-figure both creates allegorical depth in *A Confederacy of Dunces* and makes the allegory ridiculous. A belching, masturbating, and pseudohomosexual Christ-figure detracts from Jesus' dignity as a symbol of peace and salvation, and Ignatius also represents any number of less appealing allegorical entities, including Cain and anti-Semitism. He forges a letter to the unsuspecting Mr. I. Abelman, abuses him roundly, and then signs Mr. Levy's name to the document; the suggestive name "Abelman" calls to mind Cain's slaughter of his innocent brother (105). In response to one of Ignatius's letters detailing his adventures at Levy Pants, Myrna writes back to him and accuses him of bigotry: "Well, at last I heard from you, Ignatius. And a sick, sick letter it was. I won't go into the 'Levy Pants' letterhead on that stationery. It is probably your idea of an anti-Semitic prank" (251). Myrna's suspicions about Ignatius's anti-Semitism are not explored in the remainder of the text, and since Ignatius does indeed work at Levy Pants, her accusations in this instance are unfounded. Nonetheless, Ignatius's "saving" of Mr. Levy, whose name is indicative of a Jewish heritage, allegorically hints at the conversion of the Jews, which both casts Jews as in need of Christian salvation and gives the novel a quasi-apocalyptic register. Additional anti-Semitism arises in Mr. Levy's amoral commercial endeavors, which cast him under the shadow of a long history of Shylocks. With Myrna rescuing Ignatius in dea-ex-machina fashion at the novel's end, Toole depicts a Jew saving his protagonist from his imminent downfall, and this inversion upends traditional structures of Christian conversion narratives.[30] Through this panoply of oversignification, Ignatius's vexed pseudohomosexual masculinity and confused allegorical positioning undermine the text's hermeneutic stability.

Ignatius's role as an accidental Christ figure who simultaneously represents medievalism, Cain, pseudohomosexuality, and anti-Semitism, along with Toole's conflation of the religious tradition of Christ's perfection with Ignatius's excessive imperfections, blurs the allegorical import promised in the novel's condemnation of religious consumerism. One cannot bring these conflicting visions into shared focus, but the pleasure of *A Confederacy of Dunces* lies in its brazen and unapologetic mixture of the sacred and the profane. The reader's pleasure is predicated upon an allegiance to the queerest of characters and his concomitant perversion of allegorical form. This novel, with its exuberant and overdetermined deployment of allegory, estranges readers from the vacant narrative vantage point pivotal to the form's medieval incarnations. Medieval allegories, particularly in the form of dream visions, frequently depict a nameless, faceless "I" for a protagonist, tacitly asking the reader to inhabit the narrator's position and thus to "live" the narrative. This narrative tactic is baldly apparent in many morality plays, whose eponymous protagonists (e.g., Everyman, Mankind) do not merely represent a character but invite spectators to consider themselves as facing similar salvific situations. In this manner medieval allegories actively attempt to seduce their readers into experiencing their fictional worlds. In his depiction of the *Inferno*'s second circle, Dante condemns the seductive power of literature to tempt lovers into sin by retelling the tale of Francesca and Paolo's adulterous reading practices: the lovers succumbed to sexual temptation while reading the romance of Lancelot. The *Divine Comedy* also seduces its readers, but Dante's purpose is to lead them into a newly realized relationship with Christianity through their metatextual journey paralleling his experiences as narrator. Through this interpretive process, readers are expected to grow as Christians into a deeper awareness of sin and salvation. By muddying the borders between text and metatext, Toole creates an allegorical puzzle for the mind that is intended to bear imaginative and somatic effects upon the body, with allegory demanding self-interpellation into the text's ideology. Given the interest in medieval genres that *A Confederacy of Dunces* evinces, one might therefore expect in Ignatius a narrator along the lines of Dante in the *Divine Comedy* or the Dreamer in the fourteenth-century masterpiece *Pearl*—a partially vacant identity in which the text's audience can cast themselves within the narrative's plot. Readers of *A Confederacy of Dunces* are given no such empty space through which to project themselves: if the reader is intended to read this novel as a medieval allegory and to experience firsthand its fantastic narrative, such a readerly experience is based upon one's fidelity to a grotesquely unappealing, sexually ambiguous, yet erotically driven protagonist.

For along with his medievalism, Ignatius's pseudohomosexual masculinity serves as yet another of his defining characteristics, which is registered through the reactions of a range of characters. Concerned about her son's rigid asexuality, Mrs. Reilly encourages him to indulge in licentious heterosexual pleasures, tacitly asking him to access the privileges of white southern manhood: "'They got strippers in here at night, huh?' Mrs. Reilly nudged her son" (11). Mancuso declares that Ignatius "looked like a big prevert [*sic*]" (18), and Mr. Gonzalez comments on Ignatius's apparent hermaphroditism when he applies for employment at Levy Pants, wondering aloud for which job he is applying: "We're running two [jobs] in the paper, one for a woman and one for a man" (80). Miss Trixie continually mistakes Ignatius for "Gloria" (98), and Myrna accuses Ignatius of homosexuality when she writes obliquely in a letter that "Freud linked paranoia with homosexual tendencies," to which Ignatius responds by shouting "Filth!" (94). Lana tells Ignatius that he "look[s] like a queer with that earring" (345), George calls him a "big fruit" (190), and Dorian Greene employs a variety of clever epithets for him focusing on his apparent femininity, including "Charles Laughton in drag as the Queen of the Gypsies" (289), "Mary Marvel" (289), "Bette Davis with indigestion" (290), "Hungarian Joan of Arc" (290), "Maid of Orleans" (297), "Magyar Maiden" (364), and "Girl with the Golden Earring" (364). The references to Joan of Arc astutely combine Ignatius's hermaphroditic appearance with his medieval sensibilities, and the overarching picture of Ignatius confuses his biological sex such that his gendered identity borders on the hermaphroditic. Whereas Ignatius upholds himself as a paragon of virtue, he also casts himself as an object of depraved desires in the French Quarter, declaring that he feels like "an especially toothsome steak in a meat market" (270) and warning his mother of her suitor Claude Robichaux's latent homosexuality: "That man shall never enter this house while I am here. After he had grown tired of you, he would probably turn his warped attentions on *me*" (428; italics in original). With a masculinity queerly wobbling among heterosexuality, asexuality, homosexuality, and hermaphroditism, and which can be summed up as pseudohomosexual, Ignatius encompasses virtually all sexual possibilities, rendering him a polymorphously open yet decidedly unattractive narrative space through which to consider the meaning of white southern manhood.

IGNATIUS'S MASTURBATORY ALLEGORY

Although readers of *A Confederacy of Dunces* are unlikely to experience the text vicariously by identifying with its pseudohomosexual protagonist, Ignatius nonetheless models for them the sexual and masturbatory thrill of embodying allegories. Allegory bears the potential to eroticize those who live its fantastic plots, as Madhavi Menon argues: "[I]deas of veiling and circularity . . . are central to the trope of allegory in which the tropological impulse makes it impossible to arrive at a certainty that does not immediately question itself. Moreover, this deconstruction of certainty is inevitably tied . . . to the construction of sexuality."[31] Sex is frequently implicated in medieval allegories, from Bernard of Clairvaux's twelfth-century interpretations of the Song of Songs to the antisodomitic allegories of Alan of Lille's *De Planctu Naturae*. When Ignatius lives his allegory as the leader of the Crusade for Moorish Dignity, allegorical fantasy is implicated in bodily arousal: "Ignatius was at last vertically atop the long table, holding the bundled bed sheet over his pelvis to hide from his audience the fact that during the process of being lifted, he had become somewhat stimulated" (160). Living the allegory of the Crusade for Moorish Dignity leads Ignatius to unexpected human contact, which strips away his facade of stringent asexuality. Allegory demands engagement with, if not participation in, the fantastic narrative, and this embodied allegory confronts Ignatius with a sexual desire attested to by his erect penis.

In this manner, allegory lures Ignatius into contact with other humans, and additional allegorical and masturbatory fantasies spark his nascent sexuality. As medievalism humorously defines Ignatius in his crusade against modernism and meaningless commerce, masturbation likewise defines and parodies his academic accomplishment. Onanistic self-gratification serves as no mere idle pastime for Ignatius; this avocation infuses his life with meaning, such as when he prays to Fortuna prior to masturbating and labels his experience a "religious ecstasy" (36). The narrator details his zealous and intellectual pursuit of masturbatory pleasure: "At one time he had almost developed it into an art form, practicing the hobby with the skill and fervor of an artist and philosopher, a scholar and gentleman" (36). Masturbation parallels art and academic study in this wildly humorous passage: rather than solitary pleasure-seeking, it is elevated to a position equivalent to the creative and cerebral fields in which Ignatius aspires but never achieves. When Ignatius prepares to leave New Orleans at the novel's end, incessant masturbation catalyzes him to take this decisive action: "Ignatius spent the day in his room napping fitfully and attacking his rubber glove during his frequent, anxious moments of consciousness" (443).

Ignatius's success as a masturbator ironically calls to mind his failures as an academic medievalist. If the goal of his academic medievalism is the publication of his magisterial study, "the lengthy indictment against our century" (from which he rests "to make an occasional cheese dip" [7]), it is apparent that his predilection for masturbation is more widely disseminated. Ignatius boasts of his academic project that "would show literate men the disaster course that history had been taking for the past four centuries" (34); he ponders titles of works-in-progress for both academic and general audiences: "For the journals of opinion there were 'Boethius Observed' and 'In Defense of Hroswitha: To Those Who Say She Did Not Exist.' For the family magazines he had written 'The Death of Rex' and 'Children, the Hope of the World'" (116).[32] Ignatius "published" his two-page monograph "Blood on Their Hands: The Crime of It All, A study of some selected abuses in sixteenth century Europe" by mailing it to Tulane University's library. Even he, however, is dubious in regard to its fate: "I mailed this singular monograph to the library as a gift; however, I am not really certain that it was ever accepted. It may well have been thrown out because it was only written in pencil on tablet paper" (34). As Ignatius's masturbatory releases parallel his academic interests, so too are his academic interests allegorically revealed as masturbatory in themselves, as they are directed inwardly to himself and bear little chance of leading him to intellectual communion with other scholars.

Although Ignatius fails to publish his academic accomplishments as a medievalist, he succeeds in publishing his masturbatory productions to a small audience of family, neighbors, and fellow crusaders. One of the first physical descriptions of Mrs. Reilly notes that her fingers are "chafed from many years of scrubbing her son's mammoth, yellowed drawers" (4), and the reader later sees "Mrs. Reilly hanging a spotted and yellowed sheet on a line" (45). On public view for any neighbors to see, Ignatius's bodily publications on formerly white underclothes and bed linens find a wider audience than his scholarly writings.[33] If the size of one's audience gauges artistic and scholarly success in any manner whatsoever, Ignatius's triumphs as a masturbator trump his ambitions as a medievalist, and these dirty sheets play a greater role in *A Confederacy of Dunces* than a mere bawdy detail recording Ignatius's masturbatory fantasies, as they intertwine with his Crusade for Moorish Dignity and its allegorical meaning. He creates his banner for the crusade on the yellowed sheets: "Among the yellow stains the word FORWARD was printed in high block letters in red crayon. Below this *Crusade for Moorish Dignity* was written in an intricate blue script" (161). The African Americans whom Ignatius "recruits" for his army view the banner with disgust, and one woman ponders, "I wonder who been sleepin on that old thing"; the narrator reports suggestively, "Several other prospective rioters expressed the same curiosity in more explicitly physical terminology" (161). Another woman declares distastefully, "I ain putting my hand on that" (162). Defending his banner, Ignatius implies the dual significations of the sheet as a banner against racial injustice and for masturbatory pleasure: "'Sheet? What sheet!' Ignatius replied. 'I am holding before you the proudest of banners, an identification of our purpose, a visualization of all that we seek'" (162). With its dual signification of a workers' rebellion through its words and of masturbatory pleasure through its stains, the banner emblematizes the seductive force of allegory in jolting Ignatius into social action (as evidenced by the revolt itself) and sexual desire (as evidenced by his erect penis and stained bed linens). Parodically assuming the spiritually masculine authority of Martin Luther King Jr. and other leaders of the civil rights movement, Ignatius succeeds in calling others to action only then to fail in his quest, revealing the empty bravado of white masculinity to advance the cause of civil rights for African Americans.

In a similar vein, Ignatius's plan for homosexuals to infiltrate world governments promises sexual pleasure more than social reform. In a hilarious double entendre, Ignatius offers the homosexual partygoers an either/or choice: "'The challenge,' Ignatius commanded at full volume, 'Is placed before you. Will you turn your singular talents to saving the world, or will you simply turn your backs on your fellow man?'" (376). The latter half of this choice, offered to a roomful of homosexual men, suggests anal intercourse. Given the ways in which so many characters question Ignatius's masculinity and sexual orientation, the double entendre likely represents a Freudian slip as well. Again merging sexuality with an allegorical crusade, Ignatius infuses the possibility of sexual pleasure into his quests for social justice and the return to medieval values. Sexual pleasure is inextricably intertwined with both of Ignatius's allegorical adventures, suggesting that embodying allegory creates avenues to erotic fulfillment for him to explore, despite his rejection of sexual contact with other humans.

Living the allegory of his crusades allows Ignatius to broach his sexuality, and readers learn that his masturbatory adolescence laid the allegorical foundation for his pseudohomosexual present. Ignatius's masturbatory visions contain a striking symbolic figure in Rex, his childhood pet. In a bawdy union of bestial and divine desire, Ignatius masturbates over the image of his long-lost dog: "Ignatius manipulated and concentrated. At last a vision appeared, the familiar figure of the large and devoted collie that had been his pet when he was in high school. 'Woof!' Ignatius almost heard Rex say once again. 'Woof! Woof! Arf!' Rex looked so lifelike. One ear dropped. He panted. The apparition jumped over a fence and chased a stick that somehow landed in the middle of Ignatius's quilt. As the tan and white fur grew closer, Ignatius' eyes dilated, crossed, and closed, and he lay wanly back among his four pillows, hoping that he had some Kleenex in his room" (36–37). Although long deceased, Rex incarnates God in canine form: the name "Rex" means "king" in Latin, and this word also suggests the Christian "King of Kings." Because collies are sheep dogs, they are suggestive of pastoral depictions of Jesus as a shepherd. The delightful obscenity of this scene, in which a daydream of a dog chasing a stick metamorphoses into its pursuit of Ignatius's erect penis, merges masturbatory fantasy with allegorical and sexual union with God, and thus Ignatius's masturbatory dreams of sexual congress with his long-dead dog are allegorically linked to his desire to experience the divine. This profane mingling of the divine and sexuality, moreover, does not represent an isolated incident but serves as part of a larger narrative pattern, such as when Ignatius dreams of Myrna bearing a sign emblazoned "Jesus will come to the fore, skins or not" (284) or the obviously phallic symbolism of the Paradise hotdogs that Ignatius vends, which he labels as "TWELVE INCHES (12)

OF PARADISE," to the shock of innocent passersby: "A woman read the Big Chief statement and screamed, summoning her companions to draw aside from the ghastly apparition that had appeared at their art show" (285).

As Rex symbolizes God, the dog also symbolizes the death of God in midcentury southern culture and Ignatius's subsequent rejection of religion. Rex died many years ago, but his grave is still marked in the Reillys' yard, and Officer Mancuso notices it while visiting Mrs. Reilly: "Stopping by the grave, he read REX in faded letters on the cross" (43). Mrs. Reilly discloses that Rex's death provoked Ignatius to leave the Catholic Church ("He calls the priest in our parish a heretic. They had a big fight when Ignatius' dog died" [237]), and the Reillys' neighbor Miss Annie details how the dog's demise led to the breakdown of Ignatius's family and his rejection of religious belief: "That Idnatius was okay until that big dog of his died. . . . So Idnatius goes over to the priest and ax him to come say something over the dog. Idnatius was planning on some kinda funeral. You know? The priest says no, of course, and I think that's when Idnatius left the Church" (422–23).[34] Losing Rex, losing God, leaving the Church: through this triad of loss and self-imposed deprivation, Ignatius foundered from his moorings and was left emotionally stunted. According to Miss Annie's ramblings, Rex's death precipitated Ignatius's stringent asexuality, as she also recounts Myrna's failed seduction of her neighbor, in which he defended himself from her advances by prudishly exclaiming, "Put down that skirt," "Get off my bed," and "How dare you? I'm a virgin" (423).

Because masturbation mirrors Ignatius's academic pursuits and stimulates his longing for union with God, his sexual desires are fundamentally intertwined with allegory. That is to say, masturbatory delights coincident with academic medievalism merge in his desire to experience medievalism sexually and to experience sexuality medievally. The subplot involving Lana Lee's pornography ring, in which she poses naked with Ignatius's copy of *The Consolation of Philosophy*, stimulates him outside of his masturbatory self-pleasure to contemplate sexual congress with a woman: "A nude woman was sitting on the edge of a desk next to a globe of the world. The suggested onanism with the piece of chalk intrigued Ignatius. Her face was hidden behind a large book. . . . Ignatius scrutinized the title on the cover of the book: Anicius Manlius Severinus Boethius, *The Consolation of Philosophy*. 'Do I believe what I am seeing?? What brilliance. What taste. Good grief'" (338–39). Jolting him out of his asexuality, the pornographic photograph of Lana as a medievalist renders Ignatius capable of contemplating sexual congress with a human being. Lana is not appreciated for her qualities as a woman; rather, she serves as the antagonist who must be dispatched at the novel's end. Ignatius feels nothing but antipathy for her, as he denigrates her as a "Nazi commandant" throughout the novel (27; cf. 73, 344, 348, 385, and 388). In effect, Ignatius desires to sleep with Lana not as an embodied woman but as allegorically embodied medievalism: "He would describe every lush moment with this scholarly woman. With her background Boethian worldview, she would take a very stoic and fatalistic view of whatever sexual gaucheries and blunders he committed" (343). Emancipating himself from the pressures of performing sexually, Ignatius redefines the meaning of white southern manhood into a predominantly asexual gender characterized by its queer relationship to women, in which women are rendered irrelevant to his intransigently narcissistic vision of himself. Once again in southern literature, a female character is constructed solely for a male character to view as a sexual object, yet Toole subverts this trope by delineating the woman's attractiveness as due solely to her assumed medievalism. She is not even a woman for Ignatius; she is a book come to life with a suitable orifice for pleasure.

As an allegorical incarnation of medievalism, Lana stokes Ignatius's libidinal urges, but his desires are also predicated on the fact that he lacks any sexual experience beyond masturbating over a dead dog and fears humiliation due to his sexual naïveté. When Lana ponders what pose to adopt for her photo, she pays special attention to her juvenile audience and "envision[s] several arrangements that would combine grace and obscenity. There was no need to be too raw. After all, she was appealing to kids" (198). Ignatius's powerful response to Lana's pornography for teenagers testifies to his stunted sexual development after Rex's death, as well as to the ways in which his literary efforts symbolically register as masturbatory. In his cultural study of masturbation, Thomas Laqueur observes, "The connections between literary practices and masturbation are deep and extensive. Masturbation's evils . . . find parallels in the silent but far-reaching revolution of consciousness that private reading both reflects and helped create."[35] In such a manner, the intense connection between literary study and masturbatory pleasure illuminates Ignatius's desires to find a sexual partner who incarnates medievalism and Boethian allegory.

Lana first pornographically perverts the symbolism of Lady Fortune for Ignatius, which he finds enticing because he cannot see the face of the woman behind the pose; when her corrupt persona bleeds back upon Lady Fortune, and when Ignatius discovers that she is the nude model posing with *The Consolation of Philosophy*, any desire for the allegorical figure vanishes against the harsh reality of her humanity. The narcissistic reflection that Ignatius sought through contemplating sexual union with a woman was misplaced, for the woman, when stripped of the book in her hand, could no longer function as an appropriate mirror for Ignatius. The repercussions of Ignatius's failed attraction to Lana reverberate throughout the novel, as he becomes increasingly misogynistic and dismissive of women. Ignatius previously referred to Lady Fortune with respectful terms even while bemoaning the vagaries he must endure: he lamented, "Oh, Fortuna, blind, heedless goddess, I am strapped to your wheel" (35), and resignedly accepted the fact that "Apparently Fortuna has decided upon another downward spin" (171). With affection, he called her a "capricious sprite" (267) and "dear old Fortuna" (268); however, when reality corrodes Ignatius's idealistic and allegorical construction of Lana, Lady Fortune is increasingly depicted as a woman of uncertain morals, and Ignatius labels her both a "vicious slut" (383) and a "degenerate wanton" (399). The resymbolism of Lady Fortune and *The Consolation of Philosophy* is complete when Mrs. Reilly attacks Ignatius with the book: "Mrs. Reilly reached down next to her chair and picked from the floor the large volume of *The Consolation of Philosophy*. She aimed one of its corners at Ignatius' stomach" (398). *The Consolation of Philosophy* and Lady Fortune, formerly Ignatius's defenses against the modern world, now antagonize him into a forced rebirth. Living the allegory of medievalism stimulates Ignatius sexually, as he masturbates almost continuously during the close of the novel, and it finally compels him to act in ways unanticipated and unimagined.

Although Ignatius's sexualized attachment to *The Consolation of Philosophy* is ridiculous, Toole foreshadows this perverse attachment in a conversation between Mrs. Reilly and Santa Battaglia regarding the literary qualities of Boethius's treatise:

> "Well, maybe [Mancuso will] feel a little better after he reads that thing that Ignatius gave me to give him. Ignatius says it's inspirational literature."
>
> "Yeah? I wouldn't trust no 'inspirational literature' I got from that Ignatius. It's prolly fulla dirty stories." (304)

Santa Battaglia's reply is ludicrous, as any reader of Boethius would know, yet ironically, she is correct as well. By so fantastically infusing Boethianism and medievalism with masturbatory sexuality, Ignatius creates a pornographic version of a decidedly nonpornographic text. This gross misreading of *The Consolation of Philosophy* violates the text's meaning in incalculable ways, yet Ignatius's hermeneutic difficulties in deciphering his life as medieval allegory nevertheless spur the possibilities of pleasure both for himself and the reader.

As Mr. Levy needs saving on one level of the allegory of *A Confederacy of Dunces*, so too does Ignatius need to be reborn in the novel's denouement. His home life with Mrs. Reilly infantilizes him, and in this regard Myrna advises him that he must "cut the umbilical cord that binds you to that stagnant city, that mother of yours, and that bed" (95). As his shared home with his mother locates Ignatius within the maternal womb, New Orleans (despite Ignatius's fears of the French Quarter) also serves as a protective zone, which he admits in describing his sole trip away from the city: "Leaving New Orleans also frightened me considerably. Outside of the city limits the heart of darkness, the true wasteland begins" (12). Through its references to Joseph Conrad's *Heart of Darkness* and T. S. Eliot's *The Wasteland*, this passage captures Toole's penchant for embedding allusions into his allegory: as *The Wasteland* is itself based on medieval and Arthurian literatures, Toole's allusions build yet another level of allegorical depth to his text, and Ignatius's escape from New Orleans potentially takes on the symbolic trappings of a journey into darkness and despair.

But all is not lost for this pseudohomosexual quester, and at the novel's close, Myrna rescues Ignatius from the dramatic events unfolding in New Orleans. As the chivalric hero appearing out of nowhere to rescue her beloved, Myrna inverts the gendered codes of medieval romance and also tacitly rewrites Ignatius's dismissal of women throughout the novel: he has howled against women and their demands on him, and yet now he can be saved only by a woman's intervention. When Ignatius drives away from New Orleans while cramped in Myrna's car, the reader sees him in a fetal position suggestive of his arrested development ("I seriously doubt whether I can survive more than a day or two in this fetal position" [460]), but he is now prepared for his rebirth in a new city: "Now that Fortuna had saved him from one cycle, where would she spin him now? The new cycle would be so different from anything he had ever known" (461). Ignatius's valve finally opens, and the rigidly asexual protagonist makes a small gesture toward human contact: "Taking [Myrna's] pigtail in one of his paws, he pressed it warmly to his wet moustache" (462). This poignant gesture, surprising for a man who earlier reminded his mother that he rejects physical contact with other humans—"You know how I feel about touching other people" (12)—indicates that Ignatius is growing into sexual maturity. The queerness of Ignatius's medieval allegory, with its demolition of the distance between gendered text and gendered reader, prepares him for his rebirth into adult sexuality. One may see Myrna as merely a plot device, as a dea ex machina who rescues Ignatius from imminent peril, but if Ignatius is ever to see a woman as a woman and not as an obstacle, it must be Myrna who will educate him.

Although Elizabeth Bell takes a bleak view of Ignatius's escape, declaring that he "has left the secure closed world of medieval allegory for an outer world of torment and chaos,"[36] the potential chaos outside of medieval allegory can hardly be more disorderly than the chaos inside of the allegory that has been unleashed throughout the novel. Toole drops numerous hints that leaving New Orleans is key to Ignatius's redemption, such as when Myrna writes him that he has "a brain that could really grow and flower here in N.Y." (212–13) or when she advises him, "Get out of that womb-house" and "[o]pen your heart" in order to "open your valve" (252). Ignatius earlier recorded in his journal his propensity to undertake such a journey: "If I am ever really well, I may make the trip" (149). The queerness of allegory, its disruption of normative interpretations and desires, catalyzes Ignatius to erotic action, whether it is the allegory of his two crusades, of a lost Rex-cum-God, or of an ersatz scholar in a pornographic pose. If Rex's death stunted Ignatius's emotional development, sexual and masturbatory contact with Rex at last breathes life into his medieval quest for rebirth. Ignatius does not metamorphose into a triumphant chivalric hero at the novel's close, since Myrna's rescue of him effeminizes him into the role of the rescued damsel-in-distress in a medieval romance; he nonetheless now approaches sexual maturity after a stunted development, as evident in his reaching for Myrna, which provides an ending inconceivable at the beginning of this pseudohomosexual's adventures.

Within *A Confederacy of Dunces*, masturbation becomes a hermeneutic for reading and experiencing allegory; it is the exuberant embrace of personal enjoyment that leads one to reality through fantasy and, albeit paradoxically, creates social communion by queering the contours of white southern masculinity. Rather than accepting the conservative ideology of New Orleans and the U.S. South, Ignatius upsets the foundation of his life through his masturbatory and medieval adventures in allegory and spurs himself to new possibilities of gender and sexuality through queerness. The most unappealing of characters—an extravagantly selfish man who cruelly berates his mother and revels in narcissism to the point of many readers' repulsion—Ignatius J. Reilly simultaneously models the sheer queer pleasure of medieval masculinity to upset the parameters of the modern world. And as queerness leads Ignatius to his sexual rebirth, his adventures also serve as a model of the queer pleasures of the Middle Ages. The farcical power of *A Confederacy of Dunces* masks its allegorical import, and the idea of taking Ignatius as a role model for readers to emulate borders on the ridiculous. Yet the novel broaches this idea when Myrna explains to Ignatius how members of her "group therapy group" see themselves through him: "The group has been really pulling for you all along. Some are even identifying with you. If you go, they might go, too" (357). One cannot take too seriously this offhand remark about identifying with Ignatius, but as he queerly updates medieval masculinity in the midcentury U.S. South, he succeeds in freeing himself from the tired models of chivalric masculinity that rendered him an anachronism in the modern world. Aside from the fabliaux, medieval literature (especially *The Consolation of Philosophy*) is not "fulla dirty stories," but should not every act of reading be pursued with the same sort of pseudohomosexual abandon practiced by Ignatius, especially if it liberates one from clichéd gender roles that are prohibitive of achieving one's queer potential?

5

"I *AM* THE LOST CAUSE"

Queer History, the Southern Phallus, and the Quest for Medieval Timelessness in Robert Penn Warren's A Place to Come To

History—its weight and its gravity—underpins Robert Penn Warren's *A Place to Come To* (1977), as the protagonist Jed Tewksbury confronts the shallow fantasies of southern masculinity. Early in the novel, Jed ponders how the past determines the meaning of one's life and concludes that "we are all stuck with trying to find the meaning of our lives, and the only thing we have to work on, or with, is our past. This can be a question of life and death" (15).[1] The quest for life's meaning begins in a person's roots in history; to find the self, one must sift through the past. Warren proclaims this theme frequently in his fiction. In an interview with Bill Moyers, he succinctly posits the impossibility of a life without history: "I don't know how you can have a future without a sense of the past."[2] Such a historically inflected consciousness dogs Jed throughout his journeys, with his past continually undermining his sense of historical agency and gendered identity.

Similar to his protagonist in this regard, Warren was also haunted by history, and he sees in southern literature the abiding need to confront the region's troubled past. In his analysis of Mark Twain's relationship to southern culture, Warren argues that his literary forebear in many ways rejected the U.S. South but was unable to escape it: "Later [Samuel Clemens] was to regard Sir Walter Scott as the source of the Southern disease whose contagion he had thus fled and was, in *A Connecticut Yankee in King Arthur's Court*, to equate chivalry with the barbarous irrationality that the rational Yankee tries to redeem. But though the young Sam did repudiate the historical past, he did not, or could not, repudiate the personal past and for his *doppelgänger* Mark Twain, the story of that past became his chief stock-in-trade."[3] Warren's words apply equally well to his own life and literature: the conflicted history of the U.S. South troubles yet inspires his fictions, leaving a queer vision of conflicted masculinity unmoored from its ostensible cultural privilege.

A Place to Come To, Warren's final novel, depicts fictionally themes of deep importance to the author throughout his career and in many ways summarizes the evolution of his views on the U.S. South. When Jed Tewksbury proclaims, "I *am* the Lost Cause" (313), Warren unites his protagonist's sense of beleaguered chivalric masculinity with the debilitating effects of southern history. A segregationist who later shifted his views and advocated for the civil rights movement in the 1960s, Warren asked men of the U.S. South to reevaluate their masculinity and their values,[4] and he derided the ways in which white southern men dressed up their masculinity with trappings of knightly chivalry to camouflage violently racist acts: "Even now, any common lyncher becomes a defender of the Southern tradition, and any rabble-rouser the gallant leader of a thin gray line of heroes."[5] The devolution of the chivalric ideal from masculine honor to racist violence troubled Warren, and he asked white southerners to study history in its complexity rather than to deceive themselves with bigotries and stereotypes derived from a mythologized past: "Discovering his past, the Southerner might find himself, and the courage to be himself; he might free himself from a stereotype which does violence to some of his own most deeply cherished values and to the complexity of his history. He might realize that the obscene caricatures of humanity who have made Philadelphia, Mississippi, newsworthy are scarcely the finest flower of Southern chivalry."[6] Warren's reference to Philadelphia, Mississippi, alludes to the 1964 murder of three civil rights workers—James Chaney, Andrew Goodman, and Michael Schwerner—and these words also point to the ways in which southerners grappled with the twin legacies of masculine chivalry and horrific violence to reassess the meaning of southern history. For example, during the tumultuous years of the 1960s, many students of southern colleges, dubbing themselves the Southern Student Organizing Committee (SSOC), rejected the traditional values of their culture by titling their manifesto "We'll Take Our Stand," a rhetorical move spurning Nashville's intellectual heritage as articulated by Warren and the agrarians of the 1930s with their foundational document *I'll Take My Stand.* Christina Greene sees in the SSOC's appropriation of the agrarians' title an "explicit and self-conscious appeal to a tradition of indigenous white southern radical dissent" along with an attempt to "transform the racism and white supremacy that marred the vision of the Nashville enclave."[7] In this manner the SSOC rejected the past that Warren represented, mirroring his own misgivings about this past.

In addition to *A Place to Come To*, the question of redeeming white southern masculinity from the past emerges in Warren's consideration of congressional efforts to restore U.S. citizenship to Jefferson Davis, as recorded in his historiographic excursus *Jefferson Davis Gets His Citizenship Back* (1980). On January 25, 1976, U.S. Senator Mark Hatfield of Oregon brought forth an act to restore Davis's citizenship, which President Jimmy Carter signed on October 17, 1978. In recounting these events, Warren describes how conceptions of masculine heroism and mythological memory merged in them: "And the Senator [Mark Hatfield] continued with a quotation from Davis, saying, 'In his memoirs, Davis declared it his purpose to "keep memory of our Southern heroes green, for they belong not to us alone: they belong to the whole country: they belong to America."' Hatfield added, 'I seek to keep his memory green, and to restore to him the rights due an outstanding American.'"[8] Keeping heroes green: this is the goal of commemorative declarations such as those introduced by Hatfield, but keeping heroes green may also entail whitewashing the acts for which they are remembered.

To Warren's mind, Davis would have rejected the pardon as an affront to his sense of honor. Accepting a pardon can be construed as tacitly admitting wrongdoing, and Warren suggests that Davis's sense of chivalric honor was deeper than most southern men's superficial understanding of its codes: "So [Davis] holds eternal franchise in that shadowy, ages-ago-established, rarely remembered nation of men and women who in their brief lives learned the true definition of honor, far beyond the triviality of the code duello once defended by the young Davis."[9] Both in his consideration of Jefferson Davis's citizenship and in *A Place to Come To*, Warren grapples with the meaning of southern honor as queerly mediated through history, as well as its disorienting effects. The melancholic cast of *Jefferson Davis Gets His Citizenship Back* underscores the difficulties in considering southern history and its effect on white southern manhood, and within U.S. history, the reclamation of Jefferson Davis's citizenship sparks deep questions about how the past of Davis's "Lost Cause" inflects the present.

Similarly, in *A Place to Come To*, Warren's protagonist seeks to understand his relationship to his southern roots so that he may achieve some sort of heroic identity, no matter how small the scale of such heroism might be. In describing American history, Warren refers to the Civil War as the nation's "Homeric period," in which its soldiers and generals "loom[ed] up only a little less than gods, but even so, we recognize the lineaments and passions of men, and by that recognition of common kinship share in their grandeur."[10] History ennobles yet stunts the men whose actions it records, and Warren's Jed Tewksbury must determine how history inflects his manhood, how fictions of gender are queerly reconceived through the passing of time and how yesteryear's gods devolve into today's dwarfs.

Given the questioning of masculinity within Warren's novel, queerness seeps into the plotline through considerations of the meaning of history. Within the legacy of the "Lost Cause," white southern masculinity defines ideological normativity, yet Warren highlights the disorienting potential of myth to distort masculinity into a grotesque caricature of chivalry while men nonetheless claim its privileges and their supposed honor. David Eng posits that queer theory asks readers to recognize the cultural work that must be undertaken to produce "normality," in that queer theory "challenge[s] the normalizing mechanisms of state power to name its sexual subjects: male or female, married or single, heterosexual or homosexual, natural or perverse"; he also notes its "commitment to interrogating the social processes that not only produced and recognized but also normalized and sustained identity."[11] Queer theory's utility, in this instance, arises in its potential to expose the duplicitous ideological character of chivalry, which shields horrifyingly violent acts under its mantle of narcissistic privilege. The contortions inflicted upon the concept of chivalry, misreadings so ridiculous in their application of virtue to viciousness, should puncture the chivalric myth of white southern manhood, yet this myth intransigently withstood the stain of countless innocents' blood. For Warren, then, a trip through history to investigate masculinity creates the potential for a queer manhood to emerge, one that reflects the ideological contradictions inherent in being a "chivalric" man in the U.S. South. If one is to narcissistically revel in this culturally lionized position, one must also confront the masochistic emptiness at its core. For pain—insistently melancholic and virtually palpable—defines manhood in *A Place to Come*

To, invoking southern masculinity's sad legacy and leaving chivalric men in emotional tatters.

A tension between the gendered histories of the U.S. South and the Middle Ages resonates throughout *A Place to Come To,* and on the surface, the romanticized and aestheticized vision of European medievalism assuages the crises of incarnated southern masculinity. The Middle Ages as a panacea against solipsistic existentialism, however, cannot wholly undo the vagaries inherent in twentieth-century American masculinity. Jed must reconfigure the meanings of both medievalism and southern history if he is to generate a coherent sense of personal identity. Most notable in this regard is the pleasure Jed finds in Dante and his searching pilgrim as opposed to other medieval literary forms more closely aligned with chivalric manhood. In his personal letters to friends, Warren repeatedly alludes to his affection for Dante, recording that he was "studying Dante for about five hours a day" and concluding wryly that the poet "lives up to his reputation"; he describes himself as "still plugging away at Dante, with great pleasure."[12] These lines foreshadow Warren's depiction of Jed, who bases his scholarly career on interpreting the great Italian poet, and thus it appears that both the human author and his fictional creation liberate themselves through a literary medievalism focusing on spiritual journeys rather than chivalric quests.

While it may appear somewhat incongruous to employ queer theory to analyze Warren's heterosexual protagonist in *A Place to Come To,* the apparent disjunction between text and hermeneutic allows a deeper vision into Warren's sexual politics. In her feminist analysis of Warren's literature, Lucy Ferriss argues for the necessity of "the positive hermeneutics of gynocritics not only to recover texts by women, but to explore areas where whatever we choose to call female consciousness . . . has affected the world created by a text—whether that world be the invention of a male or female writer."[13] In a similar manner, queer theory exposes the cracks in ideals of masculinity and individual identity, especially in regard to identities mediated through sexuality. Jed travels through the separate histories of the U.S. South and the Middle Ages to discover his masculine identity, yet the difficulty of this narrative task underscores the queer foundations of normative southern manhood, especially when its chivalric core so readily cracks under its narcissistic pressures.

THE SOUTHERN PHALLUS AND MEDIEVAL MASCULINITY

To put it bluntly, the U.S. South represents white masculine narcissism, cultural stupidity, and social hypocrisy throughout much of *A Place to Come To,* and Jed's antisouthern sensibility develops as a result of his distaste for his father, Buck, the rejected avatar of southern culture. Zeroing in on his father, Jed pays attention more to the man's penis than to the man himself, and few texts confront the symbolic weight of the father's phallus as forthrightly as *A Place to Come To.* The phallus signifies male power and patriarchy, and from this perspective, it thus denotes the exclusion of women from the symbolic order. Judith Butler criticizes the prominence of the phallus in much psychoanalytic analysis: "The phallus, which Freud invokes in *The Interpretation of Dreams,* is considered the privileged signifier by Lacan, that which originates or generates significations, but is not itself the signifying effect of a prior signifying chain. To offer a definition of the phallus . . . is to posture as if one *has* the phallus and, hence, to presume and enact what remains to be explained."[14] To examine the significance of the phallus in *A Place to Come To* is not to reinstate its symbolic power; rather, such analyses underscore the ways in which the text treats the phallus as a privileged signifier, albeit one that must be resisted. Without doubt, the phallus performs its cultural work as the novel's most insistent symbol, and Jed must confront its meaning if he is to succeed in his narrative quest for a fulfilling home life.

The power of the phallus appears early in the novel, in that Jed is haunted by his patriarchal legacy. He continually recalls the phallic circumstances of his father's death: "I was the only boy . . . of Dugton, Claxford County, Alabama, whose father had ever got killed in the middle of the night standing up in the front of his wagon to piss on the hindquarters of one of a span of mules and, being drunk, pitch[ed] forward on his head, still hanging on to his dong" (1). Here Warren inverts one of the standard tropes of southern literature—a dead mule—by illustrating a man dying next to a team of mules still living; Jerry Mills, with tongue firmly in cheek, suggests that the "litmus-like test for the quality of southernness in literature" should be the simple question: "*Is there a dead mule in it?*"[15] In Buck's death, Warren reverses this hackneyed icon of southern literature, positing a dead man and live mules.

Within the novel's opening scenes, Buck's penis represents the weight of southern patriarchy, as well as its hypocrisies and lies, and his death—tragic in its finality yet comic in its circumstances—demonstrates how little a penis can do to resist the gendered tides of time and history, which confront even the most powerful of men with humanity's inevitable mortality. Grasping his penis as an embodiment of phallic power accentuates Buck's defiant statement of manhood, but since a penis must be flaccid to urinate, this grasping of manhood reveals only the limp expulsion of urine and death rather than the tumescent ejaculation of semen and life. A voice at Buck's funeral chimes in prophetically, "It was about all Buck Tewksbury had left to hang on to, I reckin" (4), and even Buck realized the basic uselessness of phallic strength: "Got the biggest dong in Claxford County—and what the hell good does it do me!" (11). A penis symbolizes phallic strength, but it is not strength itself. In the beginning of *A Place to Come To,* Warren subverts pretensions of southern masculinity through this symbol, and thus the pretensions of the U.S. South as a culture predicated upon chivalric traditions as well.

As a persistent metaphor of phallic culture, the penis stands as the dominant, but not sole, indicator of patriarchal manhood. Within southern culture and literature, Confederate swords frequently complement the phallic authority represented by white men's penises. In particular, they represent the history of masculinity in the Civil War and its aftermath, in that men fought a losing battle with weapons laden with phallic and familial symbolism, which were then handed down to their descendants in an act of cultural pride that simultaneously memorialized the failures of the U.S. South and its "Lost Cause." This trope can be presented with deep gravity, such as when Scarlett clashes with Yankees planning to steal a family sword now owned by Wade in *Gone with the Wind,*[16] or with sharp irony, such as when Colonel Sash cuts his hand to the bone in Flannery O'Connor's "A Late Encounter with the Enemy." Much like Buck's penis, Confederate swords bespeak only the masochistic hypocrisies of southern masculine identity in *A Place to Come To.* After Buck dies, Jed's mother Elvira tosses away his father's sword:

> She was not large but, as I have said very strong, and so the thing went sailing a good distance before it struck water, splashed, and sank.

> I had not believed what I was seeing until the splash. Then I cried out: "But my great grand-dad—he fought Yankees with it!"
>
> "If he was like your dad," she said, "he never fought nothing but a bottle." (9)

This sword captures the legendary and mythic cast of southern masculinity, in which manhood is proclaimed, circularly and tautologically, simply by the act of proclaiming manhood. The sword need never have seen combat with northern soldiers for it to be used to signify southern values of bravery, chivalry, and honor. Elvira further explains that the sword is worthless: "[H]e was drunk and he bought that durn thing at an auction for fifty cents which was forty-nine cents more'n it was ever worth new" (9). The sword's cash value, which should be priceless given its presumptive history, is as false as its historical value; it is also false in its tacit pronouncement of southern chivalric masculinity, with its phallic symbolism glossing over the fact that the "Lost Cause" was indeed lost.

If the phallic symbolism of a father's penis and a Confederate sword in *A Place to Come To* appears a bit obvious, white southern masculinity nonetheless bears complex and far-reaching repercussions to the U.S. South and Jed's sense of self. As much as Jed rejects his father's phallic memory, he must continually confront the meaning of his father, the man who was equipped with the "biggest dong in Claxford County" (289) yet who died before establishing any meaningful relationship with his child. Upon the birth of his own son, Jed wonders, "[H]ad there been a time when Young Buck crept at night into a darkened room and stood to look down at a black-haired male infant, in an improvised cradle, sucking, no doubt, at its thumb or a sugar-tit?" The exquisite agony of these lines—latently querying whether his father loved him—leaves Jed so agonized that he concludes abruptly, "I could barely abide the question" (289). Thus, even if one were to criticize Warren for the simplicity of his patriarchal symbolism, he achieves vivid emotional effects when Jed ponders his relationship with his father. Within the eponymous thematics of *A Place to Come To*, Buck's penis and the Confederate sword establish Dugton, Alabama, as the place Jed comes *from* in his quest for a home, home life, and a sense of self. As Diane Bonds observes, "nothing is real to one who is not real to himself, and Jed's placelessness throughout the novel is merely a sign of his self-alienation, his inability to feel or to act, except intermittently, from what Warren calls 'the deepest personal inward self.'"[17]

Jed's mother, Elvira, instructs him to reject both his father as a role model and the U.S. South as a home, and here again Jed must surpass southern masculinity in his quest for a new identity. After Jed returns home drunk one evening, Elvira breaks his nose—a symbolic castration—for his misbehavior, and he sees his father in himself: "She kept on looking at me, but what I was seeing was the body of Old Buck, face vomit-smeared and plowed into the stone hearth, with eyes closed and a rusty cavalry saber yet slackly clutched in one hand" (38). Jed's vision of himself as his father, complete with rusty sword in hand to reveal the empty promise of phallic power, impels him further in his goal to create a new model of masculinity for himself in a distant (that is, northern) location and an earlier (that is, medieval) time. Through his father's failed masculinity and his mother's castrating authority, he is rendered bereft of any prevalent sense of gendered identity and thus queered from the heteronormative fantasies of southern life, with only the impotent symbolisms of a rusty sword and a broken nose to define his faltering masculinity.

After moving north for graduate school at the University of Chicago, Jed transforms the trauma of Buck's phallic fatality into a rejection of his southern identity by reenacting, for the amusement of his peers, "the hilarious episode of his father's death, complete with hand on hypothetical dong and the lethal plunge" (17). Here Jed represents Warren's conception of the southern exile, the protagonist alienated from his home culture yet unable to find a replacement for his roots. As Randy Hendricks proclaims, Warren's novels in this regard "dramatize universal separation through a local, Southern milieu."[18] It is ironic that Jed distances himself from his southern heritage by enacting his family history in a gendered minstrel show, in which he performs with a comic phallus to deride his paternal roots (rather than with blackface to deride African Americans). In a conversation with Ralph Ellison and Eugene Walter, Warren acknowledges the difficulty of freeing minstrel shows of their symbolic weight:

> Ellison: [Some people] consult with themselves to determine if they can laugh at certain situations in which Negroes are involved.
>
> Walter: Like minstrel shows. A whole world of purely American hu-

mor got lost in that shuffle along with some good songs. Some American art forms have been lost for the same reason.

Warren: It's just goddamned hard, you have to admit, though, to sort out things that are symbolically charged. Sometimes the symbolic charge is so heavy you have a hard time getting at the real value really there. You always can, I guess, if the context is right. But hell, a lot of people can't read a context.[19]

Warren here addresses the racial politics of minstrelsy, and his cognizance of the ways in which virtually any act carries a symbolic charge emphasizes that Jed's performances, too, cannot free themselves of a deeper symbolic meaning than anticipated. By assuming the position of phallic minstrel, Jed comically dramatizes white southern manhood to free himself from its shadow, but the performance can only reiterate his queering patriarchal history, albeit humorously, for a primarily northern audience. As Gary Engle observes of minstrel humor, "Minstrelsy inspired the laughter of cruelty as well as the laughter of affirmation";[20] from this perspective, Jed directs cruel laughter toward the U.S. South as a land of inflated masculinity while channeling affirmative laughter to himself as a minstrel performer denigrating outmoded southern values. Jed retells the story of his father's death not only to northern audiences but to southern ones as well (158–59), and in inviting southerners to laugh at their own regional identity, he highlights the ways in which minstrelsy satirizes audiences who simultaneously enjoy the performance.

Haunted by southern history and masculinity to the extent that he performs that which he rejects, Jed finds in the Middle Ages and its academic study an escape from his father's phallic shadow. Because the Middle Ages offers models of masculinity contrapuntal to his father's brutishness, as well as a redeeming vision of love and romance, Jed is able to assert a masculinity opposed to his father's by studying languages, literatures, and histories culturally distinct from those of the U.S. South. When learning Latin in Alabama, he notes the conflicting masculinities incarnated by ancient Roman and modern southern farmers. Even an occupation as fundamental as *agricola* coincides with historically contingent masculinities—"There was a picture of [a farmer] there, but not like any farmer I had ever seen—wearing sandals and a sort of skirt no farmer in Claxford County would have been caught dead in" (20)—and this realization that gender differs in the past guides Jed in his development from southern boy to medieval man. Learning Latin is itself part of the "magic" of medievalism (21), and Miss McClatty, Jed's teacher, inspires him with her recollections of studying: "Long back, I loved it, Latin, I mean. It sort of . . . It sort of took you out of yourself" (22). Miss McClatty models for Jed the freedoms inherent in finding a new sense of self through the distant past, of finding oneself in another culture by losing oneself in the present.

Although studying literature may appear an effete response to his father's insistently phallic manhood, Jed claims his masculinity as a graduate student through a robust and intellectually demanding medievalism. This is in contrast to his future wife Agnes, whose studies focus on eighteenth-century literature: "[Agnes] . . . was obviously concerned with English literature of the late eighteenth century—a language and a period that I, who now fancied myself as a medievalist in comparative literature, regarded as strictly for women and children" (72). He soon styles himself as a medieval hero of chivalric and knightly masculinity, a sophisticated and worthy figure in contrast to his father's banal oafishness, such as when he recounts the reaction of Rozelle, his longtime romantic interest, to his wartime activities: "[H]ere I had been off fighting with the Partisans . . . which she asserted was wildly romantic, and had got decorated into the bargain, a real hero" (112). Beyond the immediate confines of the Middle Ages, Jed also paints himself as an epic hero while creating a masculinity suitably oppositional to his father's: he compares his relocation to Nashville with Aeneas's journey from Carthage to Italy (103), and he outlines his life in terms of epic matters, such as when he reminisces about his early years as representing the "matter of Dugton" (227) or outlines in Lawford Carrington's death "the climax of the 'matter of Nashville'" (277). Because he does not merit the same legendary cast as such semimythological figures as King Arthur, these mock references to the epic cycles of Rome, France, and Britain bespeak Jed's ironic sense of his masculinity; the heroic figures of these legends nonetheless bolster Jed's masculinity such that it is culturally superior to that of his provincial father. Jed's medieval and epic masculinity may be fraught with self-effacing ambiguity, but in his search for a place to come to, he proves that he is not trapped by the place he has come from.

While establishing his medieval masculinity, Jed seeks a lover to help him create a romance predicated upon the amatory values of yesteryear. In this regard, Rose Hardcastle incarnates numerous medieval allusions and allegories.[21] Primarily, her first name connects her to one of the preeminent medieval allegories, *Roman de la Rose,* Guillaume de Lorris and Jean de Meun's thirteenth-century allegory of a lover's quest to pluck his beloved rose in a garden. Likewise, the surname "Hardcastle" casts her as the imperiled maiden of medieval romance trapped in a castle and in desperate need of rescue. Jed refers to Rose as the "Queen of Dugton High" (243), a figure of royalty attended to by numerous friends who relish their secondary status as "some official lady-in-waiting" (24). Also, he remembers their prom date in terms of the medieval romance trope of the fair beloved taking notice of a lowly squire: "[O]n that afternoon a thousand years back, . . . that afternoon when Rozelle Hardcastle, the true and blushful Princess Lointaine, had asked me to go to the Senior Prom with her" (252). The "Princess Lointaine" is a stock figure of medieval romance; she represents the presumably unattainable woman of higher social rank for whom a knight must prove his honor. To this day, much of the allure of medieval romance emerges in its themes of courtly love and chivalry, and Jed's nascent sense of masculinity interlaces with such a medievally inflected worldview.

The union of medieval romance with Rozelle Hardcastle supplies Jed with the quest necessary to free himself from the U.S. South and its insistent history. She herself is timeless, which is suggested when Jed extemporizes that she is "Rozelle, untouched by time" (106). Likewise, he observes that timelessness is not merely one of Rose's attributes but one of her gifts, which she can share with others: "[A]lways in the moment when Rozelle entered a man's embrace to dance, the effect she gave was, invariably, of nestling, as though this was the place and time God had, for all eternity, intended, and her life had been moving toward" (108). Jed's rhapsody over Rose—"I had managed to lock myself with a dream named Rozelle Hardcastle Carrington" (187)—captures the questing nature of medieval romance, in the masochistic fantasy that female beauty and love can elevate a man's masculinity. Despite the many problems associated with Jed and Rose's relationship, including adultery, deception, and excessive carnality, the medieval cast of this romance posits it as a source of inspiration, timelessness, and freedom.

Jed shares the timeless joys of medievalism not merely with Rose, but also with Mrs. Jones-Talbot, his student and eventual paramour. In the crass world of Nashville, medievalism offers a blissful escape into both aesthetic and romantic delights, and Mrs. Jones-Talbot craves an intellectual outlet to escape the stifling world around her, as Jed recalls: "Originally, Mrs. Jones-Talbot had explained the Dante session to me by saying that she just couldn't subsist on a diet of horse talk and Nashville gossip, that she needed something to get the scum off her mind" (124). Mrs. Jones-Talbot's motives are not solely aesthetic, and she confesses that Dante connects her to her amatory past with her former lover Sergio Gaspari, recounting to Jed her romantic memories of shared literary pleasures: "[W]hile we were snowed in, he'd read Dante aloud to me. In late afternoons. In the evening. He had a strong, beautifully expressive voice. The *Commedia*—he could get both the musicality and that brazen clangor" (125). Here medievalism collides with historical romance, and merely the memory of Dante's literature imbues her stultified life with renewed passion and sensibility.

Mrs. Jones-Talbot's medievally inspired romance parallels Jed's own amatory longings with Rose, and it also establishes his eventual dissatisfaction with his romantic pursuits: "I was jealous of something they had had—Sergio Whatever-His-Name-Was and the young woman Mrs. Jones-Talbot had once been" (201). This scene and similar moments are key to determining the limitations of Jed's medievalism in vivifying his life and escaping the pall of his father's southern masculinity: as much as Mrs. Jones-Talbot's medievalism links her to an eroticizing and enlivening reconstruction of the past, Jed's medievalism cannot elevate him into the position of chivalric hero as he discovers that the Middle Ages, like the U.S. South, bears the potential to queer masculinity as much as to construct it. The course that he teaches at his university is entitled "Love in the Middle Ages: Sacred and Profane" (114), and thus Warren includes a critique of medieval amatory values within the same pages as his paean to it. Love, whether medieval or modern, can be either sacred or profane, either fortifying or enervating, and this tension between spiritual and carnal forms of romantic love reveals medievalism's darker side as a force in Jed's life.

The crux of *A Place to Come To* emerges in the frisson inherent in Jed's medievally inspired love that is sacred yet mired in profanity and the ways in which it queers his sense of masculinity. In confronting Rose about the denigration of their timeless romance into coarse sexuality, Jed steers their relationship back into the sacred realm: "You use the word *love*. And I use it. I'm not too damned sure I know what the word means, but I'm damned sure it doesn't mean me hanging around in this shanty waiting for you to take a half-hour off for a quickie. I'm not cut out to be your stud in a pen" (225). The delicious irony of these lines, as Jed rejects performing as Rose's "stud in a pen" soon after witnessing an equine stud service and sleeping with Mrs. Jones-Talbot, reveals both his hunger for a deeper love and the ways in which medievalism inspires him to look for more than the passion he shares with Rose.

Medievalism and timelessness fluctuate in their symbolic import throughout *A Place to Come To,* which renders interpretive security suspect. In the rapturous vision of timelessness espoused by Jed's mentor Dr. Stahlmann, Warren invites readers to revel in the pleasures of the past, yet it is unclear whether the advocate of this viewpoint should be respected: "'I dreamed,' the gently cadenced voice was saying, 'of a world not of the nations. Of a timeless and placeless, sunlit lawn, like that of Dante's vision, where the poets and philosophers and sages sit, and where we who are none of those things may come to make obeisance and listen'" (58). Dr. Stahlmann again expounds upon the value of timelessness when explaining his desire to free himself from history by transforming into an African American:

> He walked me to the door. Almost there, he stopped. "You know," he said, "there's one kind of American I wish my naturalization papers could make me."
>
> "What?"
>
> "*Ein Neger*—black."
>
> "Jesus Christ," I said.
>
> "You see," he said, "your black man—the black man here—has no history but his blackness. No name but the name stuck on him and not his own. He is the only free man." (64)

The inherent racism of Stahlmann's lines should not be overlooked, as they ludicrously posit the possibility of timelessness through enslavement and the forcible loss of one's connection to home.[22] Nonetheless, such a view of timelessness defines Dr. Stahlmann, and Dante's vision serves as a model for a utopian life, touched by grace and open to all. Jed turns to Dante when his wife Agnes is dying, finding solace in writing his scholarly monograph *Dante and the Metaphysics of Death* (88), and this study offers him a deeper perspective on the interrelationship of life and death: "[I]n my studies in theory I undertook to analyze the idea that for Dante death defines the meaning of life, that, indeed, the core drama of the *Divina Commedia* depends upon this idea" (89).

But to see Stahlmann's medieval vision and Jed's academic success as indicators of an illuminating medievalism would ignore that Stahlmann's paeans precede his suicide and that Jed's medievalism feeds almost vampirically on Agnes's—the lamb's—death. Medievalism inspires the characters of *A Place to Come To*, but it is also thematically linked to solipsism and despair. Dr. Stahlmann's house, dubbed the "Castle of Otranto" (49), blends the concluding Dantean vision of eternal peace with the Gothic medievalism evident in much eighteenth- and nineteenth-century fiction, which strongly focuses on the bizarre, mysterious, and grotesque. In a similar manner, Stahlmann's name connotes the delay, rather than the development, of humanity ("stall" and "man"), hinting that he hampers rather than helps Jed in his quest for amatory meaning and a masculinity sufficient to achieve it.

In this wavering fashion, medievalism enlightens yet obscures, inspires yet constrains, and it can offer only partial remedies against the queering force of southern history. In regard to Dante, who so inspires Jed's academic passion, Warren describes the ambiguity of his relationship with the author, outlining how his own "theology" is more world-centered than Dante's heavenly vision: "I am a creature of this world, but I am also a yearner, I suppose. . . . I think I put it as a close as I could in a poem called 'Masts at Dawn'—'We must try / To love so well the world that we may believe in the end, in God.' I am a man of temperament in the modern world who hasn't got any religion. Dante almost got me at one stage, but then I suddenly realized, My God, Dante's a good Protestant—he was!—Where have I gone? My poem reverses the whole thing, you see:

I would rather start with the world."[23] Although *A Place to Come To* is neither an autobiography nor a roman à clef, it parallels Warren's life in several ways, and Warren's ambiguous relationship with Dante mirrors that of his protagonist. Dante's medievalism inspires Jed to imagine a timeless view of life, to escape his grounding in a rigidly defined culture of coarse masculinity through a reimagined sense of self, but such an outlook contradicts Warren's view of the necessity of living within the present. For Warren, the contemporary world cannot escape the queering history that generated it, and Jed's escape from the U.S. South into medievalism must be balanced by a deeper understanding of their interrelationship.

QUEER HISTORY AND MAKING A MAN IN THE MEDIEVAL SOUTH

As much as medievalism assists Jed in separating himself from southern history and the example of his father's masculinity, Warren limits the redemptive powers inherent in his protagonist's embrace of the Middle Ages. In its most negative incarnation, medievalism in the novel symbolizes pain and torture: "I got up and began to pace about the house, and as I paced, the house seemed . . . to be contracting like some peculiarly ingenious and diabolical medieval device of torture" (227). For this man so tormented by southern history, medievalism promises pain as well as solace from history's afflictions, and Jed confronts the ways in which his vivifying intellectualism at times turns sterile: "I was reading, over and over, my long since battered copy of the *Divina Commedia*. . . . The trouble here was that though this was my program for keeping sane, the book's vision of all-embracing meaningfulness, in the midst of the incessant violence and perfidy depicted there, aggravated, by fundamental and ironic contrast, my awareness of the blankness of spirit that was then my way of life" (70). The thin line between timelessness and blankness, the contrast between an escape from history and a refuge into nothingness, traps Jed. Southern history must be eluded, but medievalism in itself cannot afford him access to the vision of blissful timelessness espoused by Stahlmann prior to his suicide. Condemnations of medievalism and intellectualism also provide moments of comic relief in an otherwise weighty and philosophical novel, such as when Jed mocks himself for his academic identity: "I asked myself if a man who was not afraid of reality would be hiding himself in the Middle Ages. My glance fell on my stack of lecture notes" (115). No longer an idyllic retreat into timelessness but merely a coward's escape from the pressures of life and love, medievalism corrupts masculinity more than enhancing it in scenes such as these. With a particularly biting yet humorous remark, Jed dismisses even the intellectual foundations of his life: "'Hell,' I said, 'I'm not a thinker, I'm a college professor'" (148).

Early in his graduate education, Jed sees his intellectual endeavors in medievalism as a performance parallel to his minstrel show of white southern masculinity, suggesting that both his familial history and his medieval career trap him in stultifying enactments of his identity: "The most obvious trouble seemed to be that my dissertation had become dust and ashes in my mouth. I began to regard it as little more than a trick performed by an idiot for the edification of fools, or vice versa" (84). His dissertation, which in many ways makes possible his search for meaning after Agnes's death, dwindles into little more than an intellectual parlor trick. It would be an exaggeration to label Jed's respected academic career an intellectual version of minstrelsy, yet its performance rings hollow at key points in the narrative. Medievalism distinguishes him from his father, but it cannot resolve the tensions inherent in escaping his southern roots because, in many ways, Jed's medievalism ironically mirrors his father's phallic masculinity.

Jed sees his sex drive and his intellectual medievalism at loggerheads with each other, as he struggles to establish a compromise between eros and intellectualism: "That creature now waking down there, in the darkness of the crotch, led, it seemed, a life of its own that had nothing to do with whatever had set Jediah Tewksbury in a chair in a room where curtains were drawn against a bright January afternoon, with his forehead leaning downward to press against written-on sheets of paper laid on a table" (168). The mind-body split, a hallmark of western philosophical inquiry, arises in a solipsistic skirmish between Jed's penis and his brain, with the Middle Ages serving as an ineffective mediator: it is unlikely that the paper on the table, representative of his academic endeavors and medievalism, will trump his persistent amatory desires. Although the Middle Ages grandly illustrates the passions inherent in romance and chivalry, this romantic past can never conquer the erotic forces of human sexuality. For as much as medievalism is tied to rarefied romance in *A Place to Come To,* Warren also delineates its connection to raw carnality. Notably, Jed's sexual encounter with Mrs. Jones-Talbot after witnessing an equine stud service removes them from the world of literary romance and places them in a world of sensual pleasures, and in such instances, Jed incarnates Buck's phallic manhood: he himself is a buck, a stud, with little to distinguish him from any other man with a functioning penis, and excessive sensuality thus denudes his medievalism of its illuminating potential. When Rose reconnects with Jed after a long separation, the iconography of Jed's position does not paint a tableau of ennobling romance; rather, it recalls Buck's fatal plunge and links Jed to his father's carnality and rejected model of masculinity: "[I]n other words, in that obscure and merciless logic that life is, as [Rose's] name came over the wire, out of time and distance, I was clutching my cock" (14).

Profane sexuality threatens the sacred nature of love, and even medieval literature—which, for Jed, expresses these ideals so purely, if at times contradictorily—cannot escape his disgust. In an acerbic scene of introspection, Jed expresses his loathing for medieval codes of courtly love: "I looked across at that table, with a twinge of ironic contempt for the self that had found pleasure and hope in scribbling those pages now locked in that darkness of the drawer. And more than once, in my weekly seminar on Love, Sacred and Profane, in the Middle Ages, as I heard my voice discussing the code of courtly love, I thought, with a scarcely suppressed irony, how all that posturing, that *courtoisie* and *foedelité,* that famous lyricism and bloated eloquence, those lies and gabblings, those complex rhymes, were nothing but bright scum and lacy froth on the dark stream" (183). Jed's diatribe against medieval poetry, for him now degraded into scum, ironically recalls Mrs. Jones-Talbot's desire to flee the scum of Nashville gossip through an idyllic retreat into Dante's literature. Scum now degrades the purity and rarefying aura of medievalism, as it also reveals Jed's descent into coarse carnality: "Even though I laid no claim to such thinking, I still had an argument for my existence: *debatuo ergo sum.* I fuck, therefore I am. This was, in a way, an argument, too, for the existence of at least one item in the external world: Rozelle" (184). This rejection of chivalric models of medieval masculinity, coupled with his turn to carnality, undoes the promise of the Middle Ages to imbue Jed's life with romantic meaning.

As chivalric codes of courtly love fail Jed, intercourse also fails to inspire him, and as he contemplates Rose and her body, he contrasts the potential for sexual pleasure to be found in her vagina and anus. Her vagina carries traces of the rose of medieval romance, but her "archetypal ass" promises nothing but dehumanizing emptiness: "Staring down at it, what I was aware of was not the poetry of the yearning, anonymous wound with the faint gleam of light caught there to give some hint of the roseate inwardness, but for the first time in my life, of the true, archetypal ass, the unbolted breech so simplistically and brutally designed for its blankly abstract function and the plunge into depersonalized, and depersonalizing, darkness" (167). The contrast between Rose's vagina, the inspiring locus of romance, and her anus, characterized as the sterile blankness of animalistic rutting, captures the omnipresent possibility of love descending into a bleak act of sensuality. In the end, Jed realizes, in conversing with an old friend, "The romance of youth is best put by" (300), and his romance with Rose falters (despite the possibility of their relationship rekindling in Italy). In the end, Rose, dehumanized synechdochically into her vagina and her anus, cannot advance his narcissistic ambitions of self-definition through her; she is a void and a cipher who functions, not as a woman, but merely as a masochistic reflection of male desire to be desired. One cannot overlook the misogyny of Rose's devolution into merely a symbol of female genitalia, yet despite this degrading vision of women, Jed begins to realize that his narcissistic masculinity has rendered her less than fully human.

Timelessness is an impossibility, and this theme is registered simply in that Jed's romance with Rose is marked by a beginning, a middle, and an end; it never evades time because it is mired in time. Furthermore, timelessness is a suspect goal for Jed, a theme that is underscored by its connection to empty sexuality. When Jed and Rozelle consider running off together, he discovers an instant of perfect timelessness: "For that one moment, outside the texture of actuality, outside of Time, we seemed, paradoxically, to be living in the meaningfulness of time" (224). Timelessness and meaningfulness merge despite the contradiction between a life outside of time and a life imbued with purpose, but it is only a momentary glimpse of a goal never to be achieved in a lasting manner. Jed later realizes that his years in Nashville have not been blessed but cursed by timelessness: "I don't know how much longer I could have lived the life I had been living in Nashville, all the intensities, lies, self-divisions, dubieties, duplicities, and blind and variously devised plummetings into timeless sexuality. *Timeless*—that is the word, for when I escaped Nashville, it was an escape into time, into its routines and nags, which make life possible after all" (269; italics in original). If readers consider Jed within the epic cast through which he views himself, he here assumes the position of Odysseus rejecting the timelessness (if not the indolence) of the island of the Lotos Eaters. Perfect bliss may be attainable in such an idle and idealized setting, but perfect bliss without work or effort bears the potential to become sickening and demoralizing. Jed engages in another paean to timelessness upon his return to Chicago: "It was a happiness based on a sense of pastlessness. If nothing has ever happened to you, then you can be happy" (271–72). Because Jed experiences much pleasure and pain throughout his years, such a realization is almost silly: his pastlessness and timelessness cannot shield him from an impending sense of history, and his momentary echo of Stahlmann's philosophy underscores his continual failure to understand his place in time and history.

Medievalism kindles romance and refurbishes Jed's tired southern masculinity, yet it also stultifies and deadens, and its only enduring aspect in *A Place to Come To* emerges in its inherent variability in relation to Jed's conception of himself and his manhood. As much as the passages above showcase the negative cast of medievalism, Jed continually returns to and revives himself in the distant past: "After breakfast I saw the notes on my desk and sat down, and as I sat there the first stirrings of an old excitement began. . . . Then I was thinking that I might—*might*—do a study, in the Provençal and Italian poets before Dante, of the relation of the concept of Love to that of Time" (217). In a sense, Jed's relationship with medievalism mirrors his relationship with women: both can lead either to enrichment and communion or to sterile retreats into solipsistic nothingness. Also, both continually force him to confront the meaning of his masculinity and history's queer pull on it. From the model of southern history, Jed rejects the brutish patriarchal masculinity that his father represents and loses his past; from the model of medieval literature, he constructs a masculinity predicated upon romantic ideals of chivalry, one that elides male privilege through the performances of submission in courtly love, but he still cannot find a core essence from a past so distant. Either way, he is a queered figure despite his heterosexuality, one who cannot determine a coherent sense of gendered identity and sexuality in regard to historical hermeneutics.

Medievalism does not serve as a stable signifier of timelessness or chivalric romantic values in *A Place to Come To,* but the narrative structure of the quest nonetheless underpins the novel. While traveling in Siena, Jed sees himself as a failed knight: "[T]he knight in the picture is moving in the logic of his unidentified mission. The dusty observer standing in that noble chamber to gaze up at him did not have any mission" (300). The paradox in this simple analogy emerges in that the knight's mission is unidentified (and thus how does the knight know what to seek on his quest?), yet Jed's mission is nonexistent. Such a difference is slight yet critical: even an unidentified mission stimulates a person to action; a nonexistent mission can never lead a protagonist to "a place to come to." Stahlmann describes Jed in a manner linking him to the legend of Perceval, the knight guilelessly ignorant both of his lineage and of how to proceed on his quest: "No—to put it differently—you want something and you do not know its name. Only that—that kind of ignorance, my dear boy—can ever lead to greatness" (60). Possessing detailed knowledge of the Middle Ages, Jed employs it to assert a new model of masculinity, yet ignorance may be of most use in his quest for a place to come to. Like Perceval, who undertakes his quest wholly unaware of his lineage, his goal, and even his name for a good part of the journey, Jed must learn the limits of his knowledge if he is to find any real answer to his questions.[24]

The moral of *A Place to Come To* is that history cannot be avoided and must be embraced, no matter its queering edges and the painfully masochistic potential of a suspect masculinity. In this regard, Jed learns the value of appreciating the past from Mrs. Jones-Talbot and his mother, Elvira, female characters who are jointly depicted as possessing uncanny wisdom. The two women share little in common in terms of their backgrounds or actions, yet they serve as prophetic figures who stress the necessity of appreciating one's personal history. Mrs. Jones-Talbot intimidates Jed to some degree, and he declares himself almost believing "the crazy notion that she could foretell everything" (238). He realizes that "the Dante sessions were . . . a ritual of appreciation" for her (126), and he must likewise learn to appreciate the quest as an experience unto itself rather than to expect any external fulfillment. She explicitly instructs Jed on this topic: "But what I was about to say is that I am one for appreciating to the best of my ability what is worth appreciating in life. . . . You know,—no, you wouldn't yet have had time enough to learn—that the faculty of appreciation, it's about the only thing that endures to the end" (240). When they discuss these matters again, he thanks her for helping him to remember the beauty of medieval literature: "To see how you loved the Dante—working at it. I guess it was the best thing around here for me. I'm grateful" (244). For Mrs. Jones-Talbot, the Middle Ages may not establish an amatory model for modern life, but Dante's poetry provides a means of speaking love, if not of escaping time. Her words help Jed to learn the significance of poetry, as does his friend Stephan Mostoki, who muses that poetry's value lies in love: "And I love you, dear friend. Our souls speak in understanding, for we know that love is the poetry of substance and that poetry is the only language of value. Poetry, and the beautiful mathematical statement of what otherwise might not be statable" (325). Here Jed's homosocial relationship with Stephan realizes what he fails to achieve through heterosexuality: a fully idealized conception of poetry and love that successfully unites two people (even if that union is asexual).

Similar to Mrs. Jones-Talbot in regard to her lessons on gratitude, Elvira Tewksbury recognizes the necessity of appreciating the past. Her second husband, Perk Simms, tells Jed, when he travels back to Alabama after his mother's death, about her sense of indebtedness to history: "She said, please, to understand, that if something in yore past time was good even a little time, it deserves you not to spit on it, no matter how bad it turned out, and she did not want to see anything good ever happened to her throwed away like dirt" (336). The past may not make people who they want to be, but it makes them who they are, and this dynamic of identity formation strips away the foundations of egotistical self-construction that posit the possibility of a self without history. Agency and personal identity are mediated through a queering historical process, yet one must accept the queerness of the past to realize one's self. It is ironic that Elvira sees the necessity of the past in constructing her self-identity. She earlier persuaded Jed to reject his roots, but by the novel's end, she teaches her son a final lesson, voiced from beyond the grave, contradicting her earlier stance on the meaning of southern masculinity.

In the final analysis, the beauty and aesthetic pleasure of *A Place to Come To* emerges in the appreciation of everything and the expectation of nothing. Jed's southern identity merges with medievalism when he muses, "I *am* the Lost Cause" (313; italics in original). This "Lost Cause" alludes to southern culture and its failure to win the Civil War, and it comprises the heartbreak and suffering of southern culture, along with its recalcitrant refusal throughout much of its subsequent history to accept responsibility for the conditions provoking the Civil War. The "Lost Cause" also bears a secondary meaning as a metaphor for all quests, in that romance quests are at times successful, but many are not, and the archetypal quest for the Holy Grail can never succeed. For Jed, the "Lost Cause" entailed running away from the U.S. South and its queering history of phallic manhood yet finally facing up to this past. In a conversation with Stephan Mostoki, Jed tells him the story of his father's death but no longer reenacts it by assuming the role of the phallic minstrel. He also realizes that his attempt to flee the South and its past has failed: "I told him how, hating the South, I had fled it, and ever afterwards blamed my solitude on that fact. I had fled but had found nowhere to flee to" (295). Not even fleeing deeper into history through the enactment of medievalism affords an escape from a person's roots.

The equipoise of the conclusion of *A Place to Come To* refuses easy interpretations about the text's meaning, yet queer history leads Jed to a sense of timelessness paradoxically incarnated in place. Stephan teaches Jed that "we are all accidents of history in accidental conjunction" (324), and Jed soon comes to a deeper understanding about his father's limitations: "[T]he only thing wrong with Buck was he was born out of phase" (340). History is both an accident and a terror: it bears little discernible purpose in its inexorable movement yet affects the present in unfathomable ways. Jed then feels sympathy for his rejected father: "Poor Buck, I thought" (341). As he accepts his southern roots at the novel's close and returns to Alabama, Jed decides to "come back and live alone in that house on Jonquil Street" (340). Warren could be obliquely criticizing Jed in this decision, in that the symbolism of Jonquil Street implicitly connotes Jed's narcissism, since the jonquil is also known as the narcissus. Nonetheless,

Jed's return to the U.S. South allows him to escape from the narcissism of his past and his headstrong rejection of his roots and to embrace a new identity denied throughout the narrative.

The U.S. South cannot serve as a panacea for Jed's existential loneliness, and he hopes for a reincarnation of medieval romance with Dauphine, whose name, like Rose's, conjures images of medieval femininity in its symbolic denotation of a future queen.[25] In his letter to her, Jed expresses his desire for romance to ameliorate the emptiness of his life: "I ask for your company because it is what I feel myself most deeply craving." The postscript then adds: "I ask for your company for what blessedness it is. But I say also that in it I may learn, even as the light fails, a little of what I need to know" (341). Unlike his view of Rose, whom he came to see as little more than her vagina, Jed appears to see Dauphine as a woman and as an equal, one whom he desires not solely for the pleasures of intercourse, nor for her narcissistic reflection of his worth, but for herself and the company and wisdom she can share with him. Chivalry's often brutal dismissal of women as little more than an appendage to masculine vainglory is here ameliorated, as Jed matures into a man capable of a meaningful relationship with a woman.

Jed also plans to reconcile himself to his southern roots and patriarchal heritage by teaching his son about his history: "I would be accompanied by Ephraim, and I could point out to him all the spots that I had dreamed of pointing to him" (341). The novel ends with Jed planning a history lesson, but one that must be predicated upon confronting his historical and southern queerness, for what else could Jed show Ephraim in Alabama if not the location of Buck's phallic death, or of Elvira's nasal castration of him? The trip home to Alabama must embrace the queering edges of the past if it is to offer any truth to his son. A medieval romance with a queen is coupled with a history lesson about the meaning of the U.S. South: unity emerges in this final vision, as Jed confronts his homeland to discover medieval poetic timelessness in a long-detested land.

For Warren, history and historiography blur reality, and Jed's quest away from and back to the U.S. South, as he ponders himself as an incarnation of the "Lost Cause," mirrors the author's belief that history seduces through its obscurity. The present generation must resist the tendency to gratify itself through those who came before, as Warren declares:

> [W]e should seek to end the obscene gratifications of history, and try to learn what the contemplation of the past, conducted with psychological depth and humane breadth, can do for us. What happens if, by the act of historical imagination—the historian's and our own—we are transported into the documented, re-created moment of the past and, in a double vision, see the problems and values of that moment and those of our own, set against each other in mutual criticism and clarification? What happens if, in innocence, we can accept this process without trying to justify the present by the past or the past by the present? We might, then, ask the question about inevitability in the only way that is fruitful—in the recognition that there can never be a *yes-or-no* answer, but the framing of perspectives of causality and context, as rigorously as possible even though provisionally, fulfills our urgent need to try to determine the limits of responsibility in experience.[26]

A Place to Come To thematically reflects Warren's view that history must transcend "yes-or-no" explications in order to reach deeper truths about how it affects present lives. In the contrasting depictions of the U.S. South and medievalism as damning and illuminating, constraining and freeing, Warren rewrites the meaning of the "Lost Cause" for white southern men as his protagonist affirms his identity as a "Lost Cause" so that he may finally move beyond it.

In *A Place to Come To* the quest for timelessness is a queering one that leads circularly to the history in which it is mired. Buck's penis, Jed's broken nose, and his quest for masculine conquest in academia and romance—these symbols and pursuits define Jed's life yet ultimately prove incapable of establishing his sense of masculinity. The quest challenges him not to escape the queer elements of the self that undermine timelessness, but to embrace masochistically the meaning of the queer in the foundational construction of the self—in time, in history, and always imperfect. Perhaps even more troubling for Jed in Buck's death was not its phallic aspect but its tragic finality. Warren describes how history paralyzes individuals due to its latent promise that everyone must eventually join history by dying: "The past is the tonic for self-pity, first by putting us in relation to the community of those who have conquered it, but also in another way, in a fundamental, primal way, one by which it mobilizes our deepest energies: it tells us that we, too, shall soon be part of the past."[27] The fear of death catalyzes no end of angst and empty activity for Jed, but embracing history entails embracing the realization that one can never escape time's inexorable march to the grave.

The myth of the U.S. South as a chivalric reincarnation of medieval romance is proved queerly true at the end of *A Place to Come To,* with Jed hoping to reunite with his lost queen in the southern landscape he fled. Malcolm Magaw declares that Jed's quest must fail to some degree, that he "has the good fortune of never finding *the* place to come to."[28] But the complementary valence to this view appears in Jed's coming to a place not of unity through false history but of queerness in real history—in the U.S. South, where myths of chivalry might indeed be proven true for an elderly man reuniting with his long-lost love before the inevitability that awaits us all, as we must enact the death of those who have come before and who created the history through which we must live.

6

"THE SIR WALTER DISEASE" AND QUEER QUESTS FOR MASCULINITY IN WALKER PERCY'S NOVELS

Walker Percy's novels share numerous key themes, including the search for love to escape solipsism and despair, the need for community in a fractured and spiritually enervated world, and the threat of malaise to undermine agency and social harmony; furthermore, much of his appeal as a writer lies in his ability to couple such grave themes with mordant irony, thus infusing a humorous streak into otherwise brooding and existential fiction.[1] Medieval themes and allusions, reflecting a narrative concern for the social repercussions of glorified visions of knightly masculinity, also recur frequently in Percy's novels, and these references to the past offer Percy a means to reflect on the present ills of society. Against a backdrop of southern gentility, medievalism offers his male protagonists both an escape from the pressures of modernity and alternative models of gendered identity as they quest to revitalize their lives with meaning. As in Flannery O'Connor's fictions, spiritual Catholicism and martial chivalry collide in Percy's constructions of southern manhood, leaving these men clinging to masculinities no longer available to them and useless for their spiritual quests.

Through its eponymous recasting of the quintessential Arthurian knight as a cuckolded southern lawyer, *Lancelot* (1977) most obviously models the ways in which medieval conceptions of masculinity martially inspire yet spiritually confuse Percy's protagonists, but his other novels—*The Moviegoer* (1960), *The Last Gentleman* (1966), *Love in the Ruins* (1970), *The Second Coming* (1980), and *The Thanatos Syndrome* (1987)—share this theme as well. This chapter begins with an analysis of *Lancelot,* Percy's most extensive consideration of medieval masculinities and the harmful spiritual side effects of exalting knighthood; the analysis then moves to Percy's first novel, *The Moviegoer,* next to the Will Barrett novels (*The Last*

Gentleman and *The Second Coming*), and last to the Thomas More novels (*Love in the Ruins* and *The Thanatos Syndrome*). Throughout his oeuvre, Percy pays close attention to the ways in which the medieval past colors the U.S. South, often in terms of the gendered identities of his questing protagonists.

Certainly, medieval, classical, and southern histories influenced Percy as a man and as a writer. Appropriately enough for an author who also trained as a physician, he diagnosed himself with "the Sir Walter disease"—Mark Twain's pejorative term for the tendency of southern men to view their culture through the lens of Walter Scott's novels. In his famed essay "Why Are You a Catholic?" Percy recalls his childhood hero-worship for Scott's vision of knightly heroism as incarnated in Richard the Lionhearted:

> My first hero and the hero of the South for a hundred years was Richard I of *Ivanhoe*, who with his English knights in the First Crusade stormed the gates of Acre to rescue the holy places from the Infidel. But, earlier than that, there was the Roman Emperor Marcus Aurelius. If one wished to depict the beau ideal of the South, it would not be the crucified Christ but rather the stoic knight at parade rest, both hands folded on the hilt of his broadsword, his face as grave and impassive as the Emperor's. In the South, of course, he came to be, not the Emperor or Richard, but R. E. Lee, the two in one.
>
> Bad though much of Southern romanticism may be, with Christianity and Judaism and Roman valor seen through the eyes of Sir Walter Scott, how could it have been otherwise with me?[2]

Rebuking southern romanticism for its replacement of Christ with the martial and imperial figures of medieval knights and Roman emperors, Percy centers his literature around this spiritual malaise of the U.S. South, and central to this project is his examination of how medieval ideals and "the Sir Walter disease" inhibit the development of spiritual and social maturity.

Percy criticizes Scott's heroic and medieval masculinities by depicting his characters following knightly perfection as their ideal gender performance yet failing to achieve its promises. In complementary contrast, the writings of such medieval authors as Augustine, Dante, and Chaucer espouse a view of gender in which sexual lapses remind humanity of its sinful nature and thus encourage penance. In his tongue-in-cheek self-help book *Lost in the Cosmos* (1983), Percy considers the nature of sexual sin by reviewing medieval authors and highlighting how sexual transgressions inspire greater sanctity for the faithful:

> *St. Augustine:* The triumph of the love of God in the City of God over lust in the city of man, but—"Grant me the gift of continence, but not just yet."
>
> *Dante:* Sexual sinners in the outermost, least punitive, circle of hell, storm-tossed, blown to and fro like birds on the winds of desire, yet still together and still in love. Cf. traitors and murderers in innermost circle, up to their necks in boiling pitch.
>
> *Chaucer's Miller and Wife of Bath:* The frankly erotic harmonized comically and humanely as earthy transgressions, committed and recognized as sins, but without neurotic guilt and to be forgiven by the loving Lord and Master, the goal of the Canterbury pilgrimage.[3]

Percy's analysis of Augustine, Dante, and Chaucer illustrates his view of their works as primarily comic in form. In medieval literature, the comic is not necessarily linked to humor, with such narratives ending as their protagonists experience a state of grace, redemption, or increased spiritual knowledge, as conclude such masterpieces as Dante's *Divine Comedy* and Chaucer's *Troilus and Criseyde*. In this regard, Percy's sense of the comic reflects Dante's influence, as is evident in the southerner's definition of the term: "Comic, in the old Dantean sense of the word, implying a happy outcome."[4] Such spiritual happiness ameliorates the malaise that Percy depicts as coincident with Scott's chivalric masculinities and other re-creations of martial masculinities in southern literature.

Writing his fictions in the U.S. South during the 1960s, 1970s, and 1980s, Percy observed notable shifts in gendered and religious identities, particularly in regard to the reforms to the Catholic Church effected by Vatican II, which profoundly altered the religious cultural landscape of Western society. In 1962 Pope John XXIII opened Vatican II, more formally known as the Second Ecumenical Council of the Vatican, which resulted in numerous changes to the Catholic Church, especially concerning issues of liturgy, religious liberty, and social justice. Paul Blanshard wryly opines that the changes brought about by Vatican II did not go far enough, declaring that "[i]n terms of twentieth-century velocity, the Council brought Catholicism from the thirteenth to the seventeenth century . . . but it still left this largest segment of world Christianity three hundred years behind the times."[5] In a 1986 interview, Percy reviews the cultural changes evident over the course of his lifetime and declares of the Catholic Church, "[W]e are obviously in a time of serious troubles" due to the "disturbing consequences of Vatican II." These words characterize Percy as a conservative reacting against social change, but he also mitigates his views in considering such issues. In the same interview he calls Vatican II "a valuable event" and characterizes the resistance of others as "a sign of insecurity when people are scandalized just because Latin is dropped and women distribute communion."[6] Percy sees change as not necessarily antithetical to his religious views but as an unleashed force disrespectful of important traditions. This double vision of cultural shifts—of change as necessary yet unsettling—inflects Percy's male protagonists, who no longer know what it means to be a man in the U.S. South.

Contemporary to these shifts in the Catholic Church, the women's and gay rights movements made marked advances in the 1960s and 1970s. Percy criticizes feminism both inside and outside of the Catholic Church, such as when he lambastes "radical feminist [nuns] who even put secular feminists to shame. From the Flying Nun to Bella Abzug in one generation. We have more than our share of viragos and barracudas." Given this hostility toward feminism, it is surprising that Percy claims to "defend as a proper cause . . . the virtues of feminism."[7] Such counterbalancing between strident and conciliatory statements characterizes much of Percy's criticism of contemporary culture, as is also apparent in his considerations of homosexuality. Within his fictions, most references to gay people carry a condemnatory, if satiric, valence. *Love in the Ruins* includes an ironic assessment of the state of American literature—"The Southern gothic novel yielded to the Jewish masturbatory novel, which in turn gave way to the WASP homosexual novel, which has nearly run its course" (*LR* 19)—before lamenting the lionization of a canonic gay author: "Gore Vidal is the grand old man of American letters" (*LR* 19). Even moments that appear to espouse a tolerant view of homosexuality—such as Lancelot's concern for his gay son—appear less approving when viewed within the wider context of the novel. Percy's reaction to feminists and homosexuals is best summarized in a self-interview in which he accuses himself of not having "much use for" such people as "fem-libbers" and homosexuals, to which he replies, "That's true—though, taken as individuals, they turn out to be more or less like oneself, i.e., sinners, and we get along fine."[8] Of course, Percy's white southern masculinity is not condemned in this statement in the same way that feminists and homosexuals are: it is the actions of a white southern man that cast him as a sinner, rather than an intrinsic part of one's being, as is the case with women and homosexuals.

Against this backdrop of spiritual and gendered shifts in Western society, Percy's protagonists undertake queer quests in which their masculinities are at stake. These quests do not reflect a submerged homosexuality latent in Percy's protagonists; for the most part, these men show no amorous tendencies other than heterosexual ones (although a strong case can be made for Lancelot in regard to his homoerotic attachment to his friend Percival). Percy's characters fortify their masculinities by overcoming sexual otherness, and these queer quests mark their shaky sense of masculine privilege in the modern U.S. South and their struggle to achieve heteronormativity. Given Percy's hesitations over religious reform, women's rights, and homosexuality, his depiction of men confused by their increasingly unfamiliar culture reflects his conservative view of the shifting genders of southern society. Medievalism offers alternate views of masculinity to guide his male protagonists in their quests, but such antiquated masculinities threaten to undermine their spiritual salvation.

LANCELOT

Lancelot trumpets its medievalism in its title, and the medieval past structures the narrative as its eponymous antihero seeks to return medieval values of courtliness and chivalry to southern society. As John Bugge points out, the appeal of Arthurian legends creates a compelling yet duplicitous narrative structure for the reader: "[W]e fall enthusiastically into Lance's mythographic way of seeing and thinking, only to be brought up short when we discover that Percy is . . . portraying [the Arthurian myth] as a distinctly negative force."[9] The recasting of Arthurian myth is foremost apparent in Percy's onomastics: he is often playfully allusive with the names he gives his characters; for example, the appellation "Lancelot" comments ironically on the protagonist's identity. If Percy is playfully allusive with his characters' names, he is playfully elusive as well, because they take on multiple significations beyond their apparent denotations. The name "Lancelot" denotes the knight of the Arthurian tradition, but this character recalls a conversation with his interlocutor that suggests another layer of meaning: "'Lancelot Andrewes Lamar,' you used to say. 'You were named after the great Anglican divine, weren't you? Shouldn't it have been Lancelot du Lac, King Ban of Benwick's son?'" (6). This question of identity runs throughout the novel, and readers must consider whether the name "Lancelot" reflects the values of the seventeenth-century Anglican minister instrumental in translating the King James Bible or of the valiant knight who betrays King Arthur through his clandestine affair with Guinevere.

Lancelot feels a deep kinship with medieval models of masculinity that continue to resonate in his present age and geography. Percy frequently conflates knightly masculinity with football heroes to stress the medievalized nature of southern life, and Lancelot recalls the glories of his youth as an epitome of this chivalric masculine ideal: "Here I was, a young Comus knight, the very one who had run 110 yards against Alabama" (213). The pageantry of a Mardi Gras masquerade, itself colored by medieval legends of knightly derring-do, merges with his legendary accomplishments on the gridiron, imbuing him with a heroic, if inflated, sense of masculinity. Describing the books in his father's library, Lancelot further outlines how southern models of military masculinity merge with visions of Arthurian knights: "I could detect no common denominator except a taste for the extraordinary and marvelous, the sentimental, the extraordinary experience, the extraordinary adventure undertaken by a brave few, . . . the extraordinary glory of a lost cause which becomes more extraordinary as it recedes in time and in fact Robert E. Lee and the Army of Northern Virginia had long since become for him as legendary and mythical as King Arthur and the Round Table. Do you think I was named Lancelot for nothing?" (116). Men of the U.S. South ascribe to themselves a chivalric and knightly masculinity in which they serve as the modern-day equivalents of Arthur's knights, and within this milieu, any previous confusion about whether Lancelot is named after Lancelot Andrewes or the Arthurian Lancelot is resolved, with the character assigning himself his name due to his father's passion for military masculinities dedicated to lost causes. Lancelot undermines the Arthurian masculinity inherent in his declaration of identity by linking it to "the extraordinary glory of a lost cause," which hints at the combined loss of martial and masculine pride through the defeat of the South in the Civil War.

In addition to the medieval masculinity of knighthood, Percy considers the ways in which medieval conceptions of sin and salvation affect his protagonist. The epigraph to *Lancelot*, taken from Dante's *Purgatorio*, asks readers to consider Lancelot's journey as one in which salvation remains accessible to him despite his violent crimes:

> He sank so low that all means
> for his salvation were gone,
> except showing him the lost people.
> For this I visited the region of the dead.[10]

The novel ponders the salvific repercussions of modeling one's life on southern chivalry, with Percy's Lancelot traveling through a southern landscape populated by the spiritually dead. Percy develops this depiction of his protagonist as mired in a spiritual purgatory through the novel's geographical setting in southern Louisiana, where Lancelot describes New Orleans in terms recalling Dante's purgatory: "This city's soul I think of as neither damned nor saved but eased rather, existing in a kind of comfortable Catholic limbo somewhere between the outer circle of hell, where sexual sinners don't have it all that bad, and the inner circle of purgatory, where things are even better" (23). For Dante and Percy, Purgatory is not a final destination but a midway point on the path to salvation, and the narrative question at the heart of *Lancelot* is whether the eponymous protagonist can progress through his chivalric solipsism into spiritual grace, or whether he will remain trapped in his archaic vision of southern masculinity.

Lancelot's vision of knightly masculinity sparks his desire for the past, and he describes himself as an anachronism suffering through the ills of modern society. Reliving the past, he believes, should cure the debilitating sexual and spiritual anomie of the present: "I cannot tolerate this age. . . . I would have felt at home at Mont-Saint-Michel, the Mount of the Archangel with the flaming sword, or with Richard Coeur de Lion at Acre. They believed in a God who said he came not to bring peace but the sword" (157). Lancelot sees himself as a crusader against immorality (and thus assumes yet another model of medieval masculinity), but this vision of masculinity as embodied through warriors of the past cannot hold in his fallen condition. Although he identifies powerful models of masculinity in the medieval past, his situation throughout the novel—in that he is imprisoned in a mental institution for failing to understand the nature of love—ironically parallels that of the Arthurian Lancelot, who suffered banishment for flaunting the codes of courtly love. The Arthurian Lancelot's troubles with courtly love arise largely due to his adultery with Guinevere, as depicted in such foundational Arthurian texts as Chrétien de Troyes's twelfth-century *Lancelot, ou le chevalier de la charette* and Thomas Malory's fifteenth-century *Morte d'Arthur.* Percy's Lancelot similarly must confront the repercussions of his amatory decisions.

Like the Arthurian Lancelot, Percy's protagonist fixates on the carnal rather than the spiritual aspects of love, but such a vision of romance misreads love in the Middle Ages. In the twelfth century, Andreas Capellanus penned the "rules" of courtly love, and he believed that chastity should elevate affection above carnal pursuits: "It is the pure love which binds together the hearts of two lovers with every feeling of delight. This kind consists in the contemplation of the mind and the affection of the heart; it goes as far as the kiss and the embrace and the modest contact with the nude lover, omitting the final solace, for that is not permitted to those who wish to love purely."[11] If Percy's Lancelot viewed love spiritually rather than physically, his sense of southern honor and masculinity would not need continual buttressing through sexual validation. Lancelot picks and chooses among the attributes expected of medieval knights, ignoring the chaste ideal of courtly love and focusing instead on the violence expected of crusading warriors.

Embodying such a medieval vision of masculinity proves deeply problematic for Lancelot and other men alienated from patriarchal privilege. Exposing his suspect masculinity, Lancelot outlines how his wife Margot, whom he describes oxymoronically as "mannish yet womanish" (186), usurps his sense of gendered identity. Narrating to Percival the story of their courtship, Lancelot recalls how she dominated him into effeminacy: "Strange: It was almost as if she were the man, I the woman, so much did she take the lead, work the radio, drive the car like a man, . . . I lumpish and docile in the seat beside her, hands in my lap, like a big dumb coed" (167–68). These inverted gender roles threaten Lancelot's vision of an ordered and meaningful world, and he turns to the medieval past to invigorate his enervated masculinity, which contemporary mores have undermined. In addition to her masculine characteristics, Margot also represents the enchantress figure of medieval romance; her name loosely resembles that of Morgan (le Fay), and Lancelot describes her as a "Texas magician" (82). Both within the gendered world of the U.S. South and within the novel's medievalized allegory, Margot proves herself an obstacle to Lancelot's quest by resisting his attempts to control her sexuality.

Beyond his effeminization in contrast to Margot, numerous queer aspects of Lancelot's character undermine a vision of him as heteronormative, such as the intimacy of his friendship with Percival that hums with homoeroticism. As there are many connotations of the name "Lancelot," this friend's appellation is also multiply signified. First, he is "simply Harry" but also "Harry Hotspur" and "Prince Hal" (9). Moving beyond the realm of late fourteenth- and early fifteenth-century England as depicted in Shakespeare's history plays, this friend's name suggests the Arthurian epithets of "Percival and Parsifal, who found the Grail and brought life to a dead land" (10). In addition, his name assumed spiritual connotations when he took the vows of priesthood: "[Y]ou took a religious name when you became a priest: John, a good name. But is it John the Evangelist who loved so much or John the Baptist, a loner out in the wilderness?" (10). In terms of the homosexual subtext inherent in Lancelot's relationship with this friend, the nickname "Pussy" effeminizes Percival, casting him as a vulgarly embodied vagina (10). Maria Hebert argues that these many nicknames signify Percival's multiple roles in Lancelot's struggle to understand his murderous actions: "He is all of these things to Lance: a peace-lover, a past whoremonger, an effeminate man, and a savior. He is Lance's mediator, his desired object of affection, and his more than friend."[12]

Given his deep friendship with Percival, Lancelot locates in him "a certain kinship of spirit" and concludes that Percival knows him with striking familiarity: "I knew you and saw that you knew me even better" (5). This deep friendship appears to be asexual, but its overarching asexuality merely submerges its homoerotic undertones. Mark Winchell observes that literary depictions of male friendships often carry traces of homosexuality: "The ideal of male companionship is one of the most enduring myths in American literature," yet such relationships assume a "scandalous, and ultimately subversive" flavor when the text calls into "doubt the 'innocence' of such a relationship."[13] Such is the case with Lancelot and Percival's friendship, as becomes evident when Lancelot extols Percival's femininity and ascribes his affection for him to it: "I think I loved you for equally curious reasons: that for all your saturninity, drinking, and horniness, there was something gracile and frail and feminine about you. Sometimes I wanted to grab you and hug those skinny bones—does that shock you?" (74). The two men seldom repeated this type of physical contact, which Lancelot regrets: "Later we never touched each other. Perhaps we were too close" (74). He soon returns to the question of why their friendship lacked physical intimacy: "Did it ever occur to you that after we went to college we never *touched* each other? Do you remember walking down Bourbon Street behind two Russian sailors who were holding hands? Do you remember sleeping in a motel bed in Jackson, Mississippi, with a whore between us? Why was it all right for us to simultaneously assault the poor whore between us but never once touch each other? Who is crazy, we or the Russians?" (94; italics in original). Hints of homosexual desire run through these lines, indicating that the taboo erotic energy between the two men can be acted on only through a female figure of no emotional importance to either of them. At the same time, the simple desire for such an innocent physical connection as hand-holding tempers the scene's homoeroticism while preserving a question of deep relevance to the unfolding narrative: why does modern society forbid intimacy between men, whether innocent or not? When recalling for Percival his climactic rampage of sex and murder, Lancelot again adumbrates the sexual undertones of their friendship: "Did it ever occur to you that we spent a lot of time naked, naked in the locker room, naked in the river swimming, naked taking sunbaths on the widow's walk?" (241–42). The merging of these two separate storylines of desire—the desire for murderous revenge in a sexually charged bedroom confrontation and the desire to relive his friendship with Percival that itself bears markers of subsumed sexuality—links them to each other, exposing that the shared carnality of both relationships handicaps Lancelot's capacity for spiritual maturation.

Lancelot's vision of masculine sexuality, in recognition both of his own muted desires for Percival and of his son's sexual orientation, includes the possibility of homosexuality. He describes his son as "a mild homosexual" (17), and, although one might well wonder what is intended by the adjective *mild*, Lancelot views homosexuality as a reaction against, rather than merely as a sign of, loosening sexual mores: "My son is a homosexual now and I can understand why. He told me he was terrified of all the pussy after him. All the girls want to fuck and it scared him. . . . He found it easier, the scared little prick, to be with other scared little pricks" (177). The characterization of gay men as a simpering mob of sexual cowards terrified by lusty girls is regressively homophobic; indeed, the adverb *now* in Lancelot's screed, through its latent suggestion that Lancelot's son was straight until sexually predatory women scared him into homosexuality, registers an archaic view of sexual orientation as a personal choice rather than as an inherent category of identity. Lancelot considers that, in following love and art, his son may have made a wise decision: "My son refused to go to Vietnam, went underground instead in New Orleans, lived in an old streetcar, wrote poetry, and made various sorts of love. Was he right, or was I right, or are you right?" (217). In this world of fallen love, it is as yet unclear whether the homosexual son, the murderous cuckold, or the celibate priest models the proper incarnation of sexual normativity. Lancelot's seductive musings lead the reader to defend his point of view, but given his murderous past, his words here should not be seen as an endorsement of homosexuality as much as another sign of his fallen nature. His sexuality is so fractured that even Margot's adulterous relationship with Merlin is imbued with an erotic frisson between the two men: "Somehow his offense against me was also an occasion of intimacy between us" (47).

Due to these queer chinks in his facade of heteronormative southern manhood, Lancelot casts himself as a knight questing to reincarnate his lost image as a southern hero: "I am reliving with you my quest. . . . It was a quest all right and a very peculiar one. But peculiar times require peculiar quests" (137). His quest inverts the spiritual valence typical of such journeys, and he pronounces that he quests not for good but for sin: "Sexual sin was the unholy grail I sought" (140). The quest provides an organizing principle for Lancelot to valorize his life, and this reinstitution of medieval chivalry stands as one of his chief goals. From his perspective, the loss of courtliness stripped men of their ability to interact with one another, as it correspondingly stripped women of their modesty: "[T]here will be a tight-lipped courtesy between men. And chivalry toward women. Women must be saved from the whoredom they've chosen" (158). The damsel-in-distress motif of medieval romance is here resignified, in that women no longer need to be rescued from ogres and dragons but from the loss of courtly love that leads them to sexual immodesty.

If knights of chivalric romances find worthy adversaries in fire-breathing dragons or sexually voracious giants (as occurs in Chrétien de Troyes's *Yvain: Le chevalier au lion*), for Percy's Lancelot, such an adversary appears in its modern (and humorous) incarnation as an overtly sexual woman disrupting southern decorum: "[A] lustful woman was as incredible as a fire-breathing dragon turning up at the Rotary Club" (130). In this reassessment of the meaning of chivalry and knighthood, Lancelot fights against lust, which he considers antithetical to southern culture: "What else is infinity but a woman become meat and drink to you, life and your heart's own music, the air you breathe? . . . The truth is, it never crossed my mind in my entire sweet Southern life that there was such a thing as a lustful woman" (129). The logical conclusion within Lancelot's worldview is that killing a lustful woman no more transgresses social mores than does a medieval knight's slaying a dragon. On the contrary, such an act not only defines the masculinity of the man who performs such a brave deed; it preserves the wider society from certain destruction. It is an appalling degradation of women, whose merit for Lancelot arises solely in their ability to narcissistically reflect his worth; once again, the bravado of southern chivalry is exposed as not a means of honoring women but of degrading them so that their utility to heterosexual men is their only value.

Throughout the novel Lancelot directs his quests outward—against Margot and Jacoby, against falling standards of personal morality—but in a key scene his words hint that his quest should be directed inward against his own rage: "Why was it so important for me to see them, Margot and Jacoby? . . . Was it a kind of voyeurism? Or was it a desire to feel the lance strike home to the heart of the abscess and let the pus out?" (236). The heavy irony of the word *lance* in this passage—suggesting that he needs to strike his heart to free himself from his struggles, that he is the metaphorical fire-breathing dragon that he must vanquish—indicates that Lancelot must embrace the salvific pain latent in his tortured view of sexuality. In terms of medieval masculinities, he needs to see himself not as a questing and chivalric knight but as a suffering and abased saint, not as a vengeful sadist but as an anguished masochist. Masochism frequently appears in male saints' lives of the Middle Ages, and the saint's exemplary suffering elevates him to his heavenly reward;[14] so too does Lancelot need to embrace the suffering that cuckoldry affords him as an opportunity to rise above earthly desires in favor of eternal ones.

Lancelot's medievalism inspires his sense of masculinity, yet he ironically detests the very history in which he is mired. If readers take seriously his diatribes against the past, including such dismissals as "The only thing I'm sure of is that the past is absolutely dead. The future must be absolutely new" (62), he must be seen as metaphorically dead in his incarnation of medieval values. As with many of his philosophical musings, Lancelot offers paradoxical viewpoints, and he describes the past as feeding off the future: "[T]he passage of time is nothing but the encroachment of the horrible banality of the past on the pure future. The past devours the future like a tape recorder, converting pure possibility into banality. The present is the tape head, the mouth of time" (106). Although he dismisses the past in passages such as this, he also regrets that the present lacks the possibility of epic achievement that marks history: "How strange it is that there are no longer any great historical events" (240). Past, present, and future—each marks Lancelot's conception of himself and his existential crisis, yet none defines him in his entirety. He incarnates an anachronistic view of masculinity divorced from the past, detached from the present, and inconceivable in the future.

For Lancelot, chivalry demands too idealized a form of love for it to function in a fallen world, and he therefore cannot gloss over the realities of his beloved's unfaithfulness. Beyond his murderous rampage resulting from his chivalric beliefs, Lancelot also enacts the dehumanizing qualities of chivalric love in his quasi-relationship with Anna, the woman in the cell next to his. He decides that she is imbued with grace due to the sexual violence inflicted upon her: "For she has . . . undergone the ultimate violation and come out of it not only intact but somehow purged, innocent. Who else might the new Virgin be but a gang-raped social worker?" (159). On a surface level, Lancelot realizes the depths of Anna's suffering, yet chivalry blinds him to her sense of agency as a woman. She rejects him bluntly, as he recounts: "Do you know that she took offense? In fact she flew into a rage. 'Are you suggesting,' she said to me, 'that I, myself, me, my person, can be violated by a *man*? You goddamn men. Don't you know that there are more important things in this world?'" (251; italics in original). Sex matters, but, in Percy's final analysis, it fails to define a person's sense of self, and Lancelot realizes this belatedly when he asks, "Why is it such an unspeakable thing for one creature to obtrude a small portion of its body into the body of another creature?" (16). His violent reaction to Margot's adultery showcases how Lancelot cannot abide the inconsequentiality of sex when it threatens his masculine and chivalric identity and depletes his pronouncements of normative identity of their signifying force.

Arthurian masculinity blinds Lancelot to the model of medieval masculinity valorized in the novel, which is not enacted in his desperately chivalric yet violent battles against sexuality but in his father's saintly masculinity that accommodates the sexual transgressions of others. In his surreal encounter with the Lady of the Camellias, Lancelot learns that his mother, Lily, despite the virtue encoded in her name, cuckolded his father. The Lady of the Camellias identifies Lancelot's father as the proper incarnation of genteel values: "Your father was such a perfect gentleman. What perfect tact and understanding!" She then transforms Lancelot's father from gentleman into saint: "He understood her relationship with Harry and accepted that. That man was a saint" (212). Despite his affection for heroic knights and the "Lost Cause" of the U.S. South, as evidenced by the books in his library, Lancelot's father shores up his masculinity through spiritual forbearance rather than through knightly violence. Unable to assume the saintly position of a cuckold who forgives the sexual failings of others, Lancelot proceeds with his plan to avenge Margot's adultery. Certainly, Percy's Lancelot represents a crippled version of the heroic Arthurian knight, as evidenced when the Lady of the Camellias bestows upon him not an honorable sword like Excalibur but a Bowie knife (226), a stunted representation of phallic masculinity that he uses to slit his rival's throat.

As the novel ends, this fallen knight becomes so mired in medieval models of masculinity and crippled by "the Sir Walter disease" that he is little better than the devil himself. In his description of the fiery conflagration that he unleashes, Lancelot recalls "wheeling slowly up into the night like Lucifer blown out of hell" (246), and Lancelot and Percival iconically assume the positions of Satan and Christ in a metaphorical reenactment of Christ's temptation, in which Lancelot attempts to seduce Percival into accepting his worldview: "Christ, you of all people should understand. . . . Why so wary? You act as if I were Satan showing you the kingdoms of the world from the pinnacle of the temple" (254). The interplay between *Christ* as mild oath and direct address—is Lancelot cursing at his God or calling to his friend?—deepens the allegorical nature of the scene, and Percy frequently exploits this possible confusion between mild curses and direct addresses, such as when Lancelot learns of his mother's infidelity and wonders about his parentage: "Jesus, was I also his son?" (214). Lancelot's questioning of his parentage merges with his spiritual crisis, as his words, on the surface level, address the issue of his earthly paternity but, on a deeper level, query his relationship with Christ.

The comic inversions of Lancelot's reenactment of Christ's encounter with Satan in the desert—in which a fallen medieval knight tempts a priest with the view from his cell—transform the spiritual gravitas of Christ's temptation into the petty enticements of a man gone mad through medievalism. The view from Lancelot's cell—"a patch of sky, a corner of Lafayette Cemetery, a slice of levee, and a short stretch of Annunciation Street" (3–4)—is laden with religious significance of death in the cemetery, resurrection in the levee, and the call to spirituality encoded in Annunciation Street. Lancelot's vision, however, does not recognize the spiritual possibilities so close at hand, instead fixating on an enigmatic sign he cannot decipher: "I have looked at that sign for a year. What does the sign say? Free and Easy Mac's Bowling? Free and Accepted Mason's Bar? Do Masons have bars?" (4). Donald and Sue Crowley interpret the sign as a statement of human free will: "The Gnostic Lance has missed the significance of the phonetic hieroglyph that would tell him what Percival 'knows,' that each of them—and Percy's reader as well—is free and may *be;* to 'be,' for Walker Percy, is both to become and to believe."[15] Again misreading the signposts on his spiritual path, Lancelot does not understand the significance of his offer to Percival, and thus his spiritual sickness cannot yet be cured.

In sum, medieval masculinity fails to function in modern America: it cannot undo the queering pressures of modernity upon an ostensibly chivalric man, and Lancelot's urgent cries for medieval values ring increasingly hollow. In his tirade against the values of contemporary culture, he again links his contumely for the modern world to its failure to celebrate his medieval ideals: "There are only three ways to go. One is their way out there, the great whorehouse and fagdom of America. I won't have it. The second way is sweet Baptist Jesus and I won't have that. Christ, if heaven is full of Southern Baptists, I'd rather rot in hell with Saladin and Achilles. There is only one way and we could have had it if you Catholics hadn't blown it: the old Catholic way. I Lancelot and you Percival, the only two to see the Grail if you recall. Did you find the Grail? You don't look like it. Then we knew what a woman should be like, your Lady, and what a man should be like, your Lord. I'd have fought for your Lady, because Christ had the broadsword. Now you've gotten rid of your Lady and taken the sword from Christ" (176–77). Lancelot's denouncement of whoredom shores up his call for chivalry, and his rejection of Baptists ironically evokes his identification with Saladin, the opponent of the Crusaders, which aligns him with another militaristic embodiment of medieval masculinity. Saladin (1137/38–1193) is known for his victories over Crusaders, including the recapture of Jerusalem for Islam; his subsequent loss to Richard the Lionhearted culminated in the truce of 1192, in which Saladin retained Jerusalem while the Kingdom of the Crusaders was reformed.[16] Lancelot's appeal to the concept of the Holy Grail ironically misses the meaning of Arthurian quests, in that such journeys are doomed to failure but that undertaking them nonetheless enables spiritual growth. As Richard Barber avows, "Even if we trace the different ways in which it has been envisaged over the centuries, the Grail functions ultimately as something beyond the reach of the ordinary world."[17] Lancelot defines exemplary gender roles in this passage through the respective ideals of Mary and Jesus, models that can never be attained due to their perfection and chastity.

If there is hope for this fallen knight to escape the Dantean purgatory in which he is trapped, it is in the possibility that the priestly Percival will teach him a new lesson about sin, gender, sexuality, and salvation. Lancelot queries, "Is there anything you wish to tell me?" and Percival replies simply, "*Yes*" (257; italics in original). The novel then ends without revealing Percival's lesson for Lancelot, yet this priestly voice is surely intended to help him find his way out of the purgatory induced by misunderstanding the relevance of historical genders to contemporary society. In *Lancelot,* medieval ideals of chivalric masculinity queer rather than fortify Lancelot's sense of his masculine self within the modern U.S. South, revealing the hollow bravado at his core, and such a dynamic—a questioning and reassessment of "the Sir Walter disease" and the ways in which it fractures chivalric masculinity—runs throughout Percy's other novels.

THE MOVIEGOER

In *The Moviegoer,* the medieval past colors the U.S. South in a myriad of mostly trivial ways. Notably, Percy sets his novel during the carnival season of Mardi Gras, and the costumes of the carousers take on a medieval flair: "The maskers look like crusaders with their nosepieces and their black eye sockets" (62). These revelers overlook the spiritual values celebrated in the carnival season as a preparation for the sacrifices of Lent, and even the traditions of pilgrimage are trivialized in the present-day U.S. South, as the spiritual journeys of yesteryear are reimagined as an effete celebration of architecture during "the Spring Pilgrimage, an annual tour of old houses and patios" (173). Pilgrimages have long provided fertile ground for satire, most notably in Chaucer's able hands, but the devolution of the ideal is laid bare in a conversation among Binx, Aunt Emily, Uncle Jules, Walter Wade, and Kate, in which pilgrimages now merely enable and excuse laissez-faire sexuality: "Several years ago, while Didi was married to her first husband, she is said to have attended the Natchez Pilgrimage with several other couples and 'swapped husbands'" (31). Percy further degrades medieval traditions of pilgrimage by alluding to Chaucer's *Canterbury Tales* in this context of loosening sexual mores when Walter remarks, "I didn't think the Pilgrimage came until April" (31), which points to the seasonal setting of Chaucer's famous opening line, "Whan that Aprill with his shoures soote."[18] With the novel's debased depiction of medieval values, chivalric masculinity can no longer inspire boys to acts of bravery, and the kitschy name of the local band, "Horace Heidt and His Musical Knights" (155), registers this etiolated brand of southern manhood.

Along with these carnal and trivial reenactments of southern medievalism, glimpses of chivalric masculinity surface. In a passage similar to *Lancelot*'s conflation of martial heroism and college sports, Binx remembers how Uncle Jules conflates southern football with Arthurian chivalry: "When he describes a goal-line stand against L.S.U. in 1932, it is like King Arthur standing fast in the bloodred sunset against Sir Modred and the traitors" (30). Arthurian military traditions illuminate southern masculinity, and Aunt Emily indoctrinated Binx into a southern vision of military manliness at a young age, after the death of his brother: "Scotty is dead. Now it's all up to you. It's going to be difficult for you but I know you're going to act like a soldier" (4). By naming Binx's brother "Scotty," Percy alludes to Walter Scott and his chivalric heroes but then dismisses this tradition as deceased. The Bolling family idealizes itself through its veneration of models of heroism and chivalry, as is evident in their display of family pictures of war heroes: "Only Alex Bolling is missing—he is in the third frame: an astonishingly handsome young man with the Rupert Brooke–Galahad sort of face you see so often in pictures of World War I soldiers" (24). The virtues inherent in medieval masculinity, as previously modeled by Arthurian knight and as contemporaneously incarnated by war heroes and football players, establish a model of masculinity for Binx, but one that he never successfully assumes.

Because Binx does not view himself within such a historical conception of heroic masculinity, whether medieval or modern, Kate attempts to inspire him with her paean to heroism: "How simple it would be to fight. What a pleasant thing it must be to be among people who are afraid for the first time when you yourself for the first time in your life have a proper flesh-and-blood enemy to be afraid of. What a lark! Isn't that the secret of heroes?" (58). Binx refuses to credit her assessment of heroism's glories and denies any affinity to heroic values: "I couldn't say. I wasn't a hero" (58). She then asks him about the happiest moment of his life, and

Binx replies that it "[w]as getting out of the army" (58), a clear rejection of the Rupert Brooke–Galahad model of military masculinity established as a Bolling clan tradition. Much of the dramatic tension in the novel revolves around whether Binx will accept his life as it is ("But there is much to be said for giving up such grand ambitions and living the most ordinary life imaginable, a life without the old longings" [9]) or whether he will infuse his life with meaning by undertaking a quest ("This morning, for the first time in years, there occurred to me the possibility of a search" [10]). Questing could open new avenues of masculinity for Binx, but such a possibility is immediately subverted by the nature of his first undertaking: seeking out film star William Holden. "It would be interesting to catch a glimpse of him" (12), Binx muses, but tracking down a Hollywood actor in New Orleans's French Quarter is hardly infused with the elevated spirituality of a grail quest.

Percy reimagines gendered models of historical masculinity in *The Moviegoer*, and Aunt Emily assumes the model of masculinity that Binx cannot incarnate, thus rendering his masculinity even more suspect. Here readers see the suppleness of gender as a social category, in that demarcations between the sexes can be readily transgressed, despite the apparently impermeable gender roles of the U.S. South. Binx frequently describes Aunt Emily with masculine terminology, such as when he observes that "[w]ith her blue-white hair and keen quick face and terrible gray eyes, she is somehow at sixty-five still the young prince" (27); moreover, Percy links her to medieval models of military masculinity when describing her: "as erect and handsome as the Black Prince" (221). The allusion to Edward the Black Prince, son of King Edward III and father of Richard II, connects Aunt Emily to a powerful avatar of masculinity, since the Black Prince is known primarily for his many successful excursions against France in the Hundred Years War.[19]

The gender play between male and female evident in Aunt Emily captures in fiction Percy's troubled reaction to homosexuality in his family. Lewis Lawson affirms that William Alexander Percy, Walker Percy's homosexual cousin who raised the Percy children after they were orphaned, serves as "the model for Aunt Emily,"[20] and Nikki Barringer, a close friend of Walker Percy, alludes to this connection between Aunt Emily and William Alexander Percy. She recalls Walker Percy's discomfort in acknowledging his cousin's homosexuality: "There is a suggestion that the aunt in *The Moviegoer* is an analogue for Uncle Will. I wouldn't have said anything like that to Walker. As a matter of fact, something happened to him one day where somebody came to Walker's house and suggested that Uncle Will was gay, and Walker threw him out of his house. I think it was pretty generally known that he was, but Walker had a real problem with that. . . . [T]here was a streak of homophobia in Walker. He never cottoned to the American Psychiatric Association's notion that homosexuals are not sick."[21] By basing Aunt Emily on his cousin William Alexander, Walker Percy acknowledges the permeability of gender in relation to male and female bodies, and he also addresses the ways in which his cousin's conceptions of masculinity influenced him. Along the lines of the "Rupert Brooke–Galahad" model of masculinity celebrated by the Bolling clan, William Alexander Percy's experiences fighting in World War I defined his conception of masculinity, and he recorded his belief in this masculine ideal in a letter to his mother, declaring that "[o]ne must be a soldier these days—there is no other part a man may play and be a man."[22] As much as he endorsed such heroic constructions of southern masculinity, William Percy also noted his ambivalence about the intersection of southern and medieval ideals of masculinity as a value system for raising his cousins: "I had no desire to send these youngsters of mine into life as defenseless as if they wore knights' armor and had memorized the code of chivalry. But what could I teach them other than what I myself had learned?"[23] By symbolizing through Aunt Emily the chivalric values of his homosexual cousin and foster-father William Alexander Percy, Walker Percy criticizes the value system in which he was raised and depicts narratively his cousin's own ambivalence about the masculine mores that he tacitly endorsed by teaching them.

Aunt Emily views history as an ennobling force for propagating the cultural values of the U.S. South, and this queerly reconstructed modern-day avatar of the Black Prince encourages Binx to align himself with a southern masculinity inflected with nobility and gentility: "More than anything I wanted to pass on to you the one heritage of the men of our family, a certain quality of spirit, a gaiety, a sense of duty, a nobility worn lightly . . . the only good things the South ever had and the only things that really matter in this life" (224). These qualities coincide with many of the symptoms of "the Sir Walter disease" as recorded in Scott's romances, but for Aunt Emily, they do not stand for archaic traditions divorced from reality but for transcendent values. Aunt Emily's sense of history bears transformative power, as Binx recalls: "She transfigures everyone. Mercer she still sees as the old retainer. Uncle Jules she sees as the Creole Cato, the last of the heroes. . . . All the stray bits and pieces of the past, all that is feckless and gray about people, she pulls together into an unmistakable visage of the heroic or the craven, the noble or the ignoble. So strong is she that sometimes the person and the past are in fact transfigured by her. They become what she sees them to be" (49). Aunt Emily embodies the values associated with the Black Prince and transforms those around her into antiquated masculine figures of dutiful serfs, noble rulers, and, in Binx's case, military heroes, with the lure of medieval history galvanizing her view of the U.S. South and her family's position in it. History matters in *The Moviegoer:* it envelops the South and bears the potential to metamorphose its citizens into avatars of yesteryear's values.

In Binx's climactic confrontation with Aunt Emily, she insults his masculinity, revealing that she is disappointed by the disjunction between her expectations for him and his actions: "It is like leaning on what seems to be a good stalwart shoulder and feeling it go all mushy and queer" (221). "Queer" need not mean homosexual here, but a strong shoulder turning queer surely adumbrates a loss of masculinity.[24] Depicting Binx as a "mushy and queer" man, Percy further builds the ironically masculine iconography of this scene by putting a "sword" in Aunt Emily's hands, as Binx narrates: "We both gaze down at the letter opener, the soft iron sword she has withdrawn from the grasp of the helmeted figure on the inkstand" (221). Aunt Emily's "sword" is a minor detail in this encounter, yet it mesmerizes Binx—"I cannot tear my eyes from the sword" (224)—suggesting his inability to match his aunt in performing a credibly heroic masculinity.

As Binx learns the malleability of gender roles through his aunt's masculinity, Aunt Emily must correspondingly learn to accept both the limits of history's transformative powers and her inability to transmute Binx into a hero: "My aunt has become fond of me. As soon as she accepted what she herself had been saying all those years, that the Bolling family had gone to seed and that I was not one of her heroes but a very ordinary fellow, we got along very well" (237). Chivalric and medieval masculinities cannot cure Binx of his suspect heroism, and he thus represents the inverse of Percy's Lancelot: Binx fails to incarnate medieval masculinity yet achieves reconciliation with his family through a more modest performance of manhood, whereas Lancelot obsessively pursues his medieval chivalric masculinity yet murders his wife.

Although Binx undoubtedly plays the role of the protagonist in *The Moviegoer,* the novel's medievalism encourages the reader to see Aunt Emily's evolution as well. As enigmatic and strangely likable a character as Binx is, his quest does not stimulate heroism; rather, he is a nonheroic man who considers questing at the novel's beginning, trails a movie star, and then finds love, yet never transforms into any recognizable incarnation of heroism in this faltering and existential world. For Percy, Binx's conquering of his "habitual disposition" to despair marks a quest of deeper heroism than that of a typical knight, and he succeeds both by embracing his family and, although the character declares that he "naturally sh[ies] away from the subject of religion" (237), by infusing his life with a deeper religious sensibility. He may never cure himself of a queered earthly masculinity, as evidenced by his "mushy" shoulders, but a chivalric model of masculinity would not lead him to the spiritual growth he experiences and that provides the metaphysical climax of the novel.

In realizing the limitations of her medievalism and historically modulated consciousness, Aunt Emily undergoes a transformation as profound as her nephew's. Like Lancelot, she must learn that medieval history and its reenactments provide a limited (and ultimately ineffective) model for negotiating the present; also similar to Lancelot, she must accept that her medievally inflected masculinity cannot resolve the complex moral and interpersonal crises of the modern world. If Aunt Emily initially succumbs to the masculine narcissistic vision of southern culture that she proudly represents, she finally surpasses the traditional role of many women in southern narratives by no longer transforming men into the narcissistic roles that southern culture demands of them. Medievalism inspires yet constrains many of Percy's characters, and nowhere is this dynamic more apparent than in the dying medieval masculinity of this southern matriarch, who was modeled on Percy's homosexual cousin and surrogate father.

THE LAST GENTLEMAN AND *THE SECOND COMING*

Similar to Lancelot and Binx, Williston Bibb Barrett, protagonist of *The Last Gentleman* and *The Second Coming*, undertakes a quest to imbue his disorienting life with meaning. Will's journey in *The Last Gentleman* initially necessitates returning home so that he can assert the type of royal masculinity that should stand as his birthright: "After twenty-three years he could retire and go home, where, if the ranks of old ladies had thinned out, he could let out rooms and live like a king" (*LG* 19). Aspiring to such a regal and courtly position, Will assumes the role of a questing knight, and when he tells Mrs. Vaught that he comes from "Ithaca . . . Over in the Delta" (*LG* 54), this allusion also casts him as a metaphorical incarnation of Odysseus, one who must overcome numerous dangers and seductions on the journey home to his family. If the allegorical cast of Will as Odysseus were not apparent in the declaration of his hometown, Percy reiterates this thematic register by naming the white truck that Rita offers him "Ulysses" (*LG* 95). A hybrid figure of questing knight of romance and war-spent hero of epic, Will must negotiate his spiritual development while tending to his southern identity and masculinity, which are buffeted by the conflicting demands of Kitty's romantic affections, Rita's overweening jealousy, Val's calm spirituality, and Sutter's familial alienation.

In regard to his family (and in a pattern similar to Binx's relationship with Aunt Emily), Will believes that he has failed to adhere to the high standards of military masculinity established by his patriarchal lineage. He tells Kitty of one of his ancestors—"My kinsman took part in the siege of Richmond and later of Petersburg. . . . He was exactly my age and a colonel in the infantry" (*LG* 111)—but in his quest for a loving home life, Will eschews fortifying his masculinity by becoming a soldier. He cannot match his forebears in terms of their militarism, and he also fails to equal their intellectual accomplishments. He briefly attended Princeton, but his ambiguous position in society and his need for a quest arise in large part because he left his education incomplete: "Like his father and grandfather and all other male forebears, save only those who came of age during the Civil War, he was sent up to Princeton University. But unlike them he funked it" (*LG* 13). Some of Will's troubles at Princeton resulted from his reenacting the Civil War by sabotaging memorials to northern soldiers—

"When I was at Princeton, I blew up a Union monument" (*LG* 267)—but this prank does not match the elevated martial acts of his ancestors who fought in the war. Despite the nonheroic times in which he lives, Will attempts to foster his self-image of masculine strength, but he fails repeatedly in his attempts.

In *The Second Coming*, the weight of chivalric masculinity further cripples Will's understanding of his family and his relationship with them. His family's southern chivalry alienates him from their values, bringing him face-to-face with the solace they found in death: "[The gun] was one of the four things he had saved from Mississippi. The other three were the Luger, his grandfather's *Ivanhoe*, and his father's *Lord Jim*. It figured. Both his grandfather and his father had enemies. One, like Ivanhoe, had enemies he hated. The other had the guilts like Jim and an enemy he hated, himself. And one had the shotgun, the other the Luger. What do you do when you are born with a love of death and death-dealing and have no enemies?" (*SC* 146). Because most acts of violence require someone against whom to direct such displays of masculine aggression, Will's father and grandfather needed their enemies to define themselves. This patrilineal bequeathal of weapons and literature paradoxically—yet, in the final analysis, beneficially—isolates Will from his family's ancestral masculinity. Percy most powerfully denounces a culture of death in *The Thanatos Syndrome*, but in this depiction of Will's fatally minded family, death's destructive force degrades medieval chivalric masculinity because it enervates rather than inspires men, despite the honor accorded such chivalrous fantasies of male identity in Walter Scott's *Ivanhoe* and by his grandfather.

Will's southern heritage catalyzes his existential crises in both novels. He must determine what it means to be a man when his role models embody both chivalry and death. In his conversation with Lewis Peckham, Peckham lauds the importance of heritage for a man: "I've decided the worst thing that can happen to a man is to lose his heritage" (*SC* 153). Will, in contrast, wonders about the meaning of heritage and whether people imbue it with undue value: "What heritage? Tidewater unbeliever who had read Dante six times for the structure, could draw the circles of hell, the platforms of purgatory, and the rose of heaven? When you came down to it, Lewis took Erich Fromm more seriously than God, Dante, or Virginia. Was this not madness pure and simple, to come from Tidewater

Virginia, read about Dante and God, read the *terza rima* aloud with such admiration that tears came to his eyes—and top it off with Erich Fromm?" (*SC* 153). Looking to the Middle Ages for models of masculinity, Percy sees great spiritual worth in Dante's pilgrim, in contrast to the knightly figures pilloried throughout his corpus; also, as is evident in Will's dismissal of Peckham for his concentration on the *Divine Comedy*'s structure rather than its message, Peckham's reading of Dante leads him only to the sterile musings of Erich Fromm. Kieran Quinlan documents Percy's distaste for Fromm—"[H]is many references both to the theories of Fromm and to Freudian analysis . . . strongly suggest that he found these procedures problematic, if not altogether incapable of producing a successful outcome"[25]—which reveals that Peckham's vision of Dante's pilgrim fails to inspire him to spiritual growth. By rejecting Fromm in this passage, Percy suggests the necessity for his protagonist to reject Peckham's example: Will must choose the spiritual lineage trail-blazed by Dante in his salvific journey through hell, purgatory, and paradise rather than psychoanalytic musings that lead only to a solipsistic vacuum.

Will finds himself alienated from his family and its dominant ethos of honor, academic achievement, and militarism, and Percy criticizes these sterile values through his depiction of Will's father's fate: "In the end he was killed by his own irony and sadness and by the strain of living out an ordinary day in a perfect dance of honor" (*LG* 10). This brief passage argues that performances of masculine chivalry and honor inevitably sap a man of his vigor, with the debilitating force of honor sabotaging his daily encounters. Will rejects the U.S. South and its traditions as a result of his familial and spiritual alienation: "In short, he became an Ohioan and for several weeks walked like a cat with his toes pointed in, drank beer, forgot the old honorable quarrels of the South, had not a thought in his head nor a care in the world" (*LG* 21). The U.S. South's brand of masculinity, humorously contrasted to that of a drunken midwesterner, cannot be assumed without the accompanying threat of chivalry degraded into a hollow embodiment of honor.

For the most part, Will's half-hearted attempts at heroic and chivalric masculinity invite ridicule from those around him. Rita repeatedly refers to him with such mock-genteel epithets as "lance corporal" (*LG* 95 and passim) and "my lordly young sir" (*LG* 97). If Will were to incarnate a modern-day version of knightly heroism, his "slide rule, which he wore in a scabbard like a dagger" (*LG* 201) would likely not intimidate his foes. Percy's critique of medieval chivalric values becomes further apparent in Will's misunderstanding of the nature of his quest throughout the U.S. South. When he meets photographer Forney Aiken ("fornication") and writer Mort Prince ("death prince"), he falls under the sway of medieval modes of thought. Aiken invites Will to join them in his hometown, the site of their fall festival: "Some of the biggest names in Hollywood and Broadway are coming down. What it is, is like the old morality plays in the Middle Ages" (*LG* 132). Again Percy asperses medieval ideals, as he resignifies medieval morality plays into modernist musings of existential and erotic angst rather than dramatic enactments of transcendent Christian truths. A play written by one of the company members valorizes homosexuality and reenvisions the Mass as sodomitic intercourse: "It was about an artist who has gone stale, lost his creative powers, until he musters the courage to face the truth within himself, which is his love for his wife's younger brother. He puts a merciful end to the joyless uncreative marriage in favor of a more meaningful relationship with his friend. . . . 'It has been a long time since I was at Mass,' says the youth, looking at the church. 'Let's have our own Mass' replies the artist as softly as Pelleas and, stretching forth a shy hand, touches the youth's golden hair" (*LG* 322). The scene ends with the two men establishing their sexual relationship, and the medieval overtones of the play—its allegorical import as a morality play and its recasting of the Arthurian knight Pelleas as a homosexual—exposes how modern society denigrates the values of the Middle Ages. The danger to Will in this scene arises in the possibility of succumbing to such a queer vision of medievalism. He must carefully avoid slipping into an ostensibly perverted version of chivalric and medieval manhood. Percy's homophobia is rather striking here, in that love between two men registers as the ultimate debasement of spiritual values, yet within his fictions, this is precisely the trap that Will must evade.

In both *The Last Gentleman* and *The Second Coming*, homosexual aspects of Will's character further indicate that sexuality threatens his salvific journey, that the plot line of the "morality play" in *The Last Gentleman* could parallel his life. Like the gay coloring of Lancelot in *Lancelot*, although less pronounced, hints of homosexuality inflect Will's character.

Sutter wonders about his new friend's sexual orientation, asking him directly, "Are you a homosexual?" (*LG* 220), and various men accost Will in a confrontational yet eroticized manner. In a chance encounter in *The Last Gentleman*, "[Lamar Thigpen] held him close as a lover and gazed hungrily at his cheek" (231); a similar moment occurs in *The Second Coming* when Vance Battle "came close as a lover, breath strong and sweet, sniffed at him, looked into his eyeballs" (306). These moments do not resonate with as much homoerotic potential as the relationship between Lancelot and Percival in *Lancelot*, but they highlight the ubiquitous possibility for Percy's protagonists to fall into any manner of sexual sin.

Hints of homosexuality in *The Last Gentleman* and *The Second Coming* are not the only threats to Will's masculinity, and his heterosexual infatuation with Kitty likewise imperils his spiritual journey. Will is momentarily lured in by romantic and chivalric thinking when he decides to pursue Kitty according to dating principles of yesteryear—"I shall court her henceforth in the old style" (*LG* 166)—but his true challenge in the narrative is not winning Kitty's hand in marriage but saving Jamie's soul through baptism. Even if Forney Aiken and Mort Prince cannot seduce him into depraved medievalism, Will's mistaking of sexual passion with Kitty for spiritual solace leads him into other medievally inflected perils to his masculinity. The past, as Will must learn, is not an escape but a snare, and the idyllic trappings of life with the Vaughts almost capture him. The reader sees that "The Vaughts lived in a castle fronting on golf links," and its subdivision was "built in the 1920's, a time when rich men still sought to recall heroic ages" (*LG* 189). Will's quest, although it is inflected with allusions to Odysseus's epic journey, centers more on his struggle to save Jamie than to marry Kitty, and these medievally inspired settings of romance place additional roadblocks on his journey.

"Mr. Barrett, Jamie's salvation may be up to you" (*LG* 212), urges Jamie's sister Val, and these words underscore the spiritual—not amatory—nature of Will's quest. In contrast to Val's concern for Jamie's soul, Rita hopes to convince Will to travel with Jamie by painting an image of the boy as a lost knight bereft of love. Rita's antagonistic position toward Will explains why she would lead him away from his quest, and her dislike for him arises in response to Will's affection for Kitty. Certainly, Rita's relationship with Kitty carries undertones of lesbianism, as is evident when Kitty tells Will,

"Rita and I are going to Fire Island" (*LG* 72, cf. 96); this destination hints strongly at her homosexual desires.[26] Likewise, Kitty later confesses that she "led [Rita] on" (*LG* 113). To lure Will from Kitty, Rita depicts Jamie as erotically, and therefore emotionally, unfulfilled: "Jamie was standing in front of me in the lovely, careless way he gets from you or from somebody, like young golden-haired Sir Tristram, leaning on his sword, and all at once the dreadful thought occurred to me: what must it be like to live and die without ever having waked in the morning and felt the warm mouth of one's beloved on his?" (*LG* 160). As poignant as this picture is, *The Last Gentleman* focuses on the fact that Jamie is bereft of God's grace through baptism, not that his sex life will be cut short by his untimely death. Likewise, Will's spiritual journey necessitates resisting the allure of medieval and carnal masculinity by concentrating on a mission of grace. Even Rita's use of Tristram as a model for Jamie underscores the undesirability of such masculine models, since Tristram's unrestrained passion for Isolde leads to their untimely deaths and the betrayal of their many loved ones, including Mark, Brangwen, and Isolde of the White Hands.

With medieval identities rejected, Will must discover a masculinity that is not knightly but Christly. When he encourages Sutter to help him baptize Jamie, Sutter wonders why he should participate in such an extraordinary undertaking: "Why should I answer you? What are you to me? Christ, if you recall I never solicited your company in the first place" (*LG* 381). Percy's conflation of a mild exclamation with an allegorical direct address imbues this scene with religious meaning. Like Percival in *Lancelot*, Will assumes a Christological coloring in this scene, suggesting a Christian capacity for undertaking spiritual action rather than a knightly propensity for militarism. Will succeeds in having Jamie baptized, and the novel's closing scenes feature his homosocial yet chaste union with Sutter. Medieval chivalry and southern honor are meaningless in light of spiritual salvation, and even Kitty—the lovely wellspring of heterosexual devotion in *The Last Gentleman*—is surpassed as an object of desire in Will's spiritual quest. She is reimagined as a middle-aged frump in *The Second Coming*, rendering her an unwelcome reward should Will have continued his pursuit of her over an asexual yet homosocial bond with the Sutton men, a bond that leads them closer to the divine and farther from the tired chivalric roles of southern masculinity. In this instance, women are again depicted as little more than sexual objects that must be discarded if a man is to mature into his spiritual potential.

In complementary contrast, Will finds heterosexual companionship with Allison at the close of *The Second Coming*. Here he achieves a heteronormatively masculine sexuality in his romantic relationship, a goal that eluded him throughout both novels. Uniting sexuality with spirituality, his vision of romantic union coincides with his union with God: "What is it I want from her and him, he wondered, not only want but must have? Is she a gift and therefore a sign of a giver? Could it be that the Lord is here, masquerading behind this simple silly holy face? Am I crazy to want both, her and Him? No, not want, must have. And will have" (*SC* 360). The love that Will finds does not merely pronounce his masculinity but fulfills his life spiritually. In his queer quest beyond the borders of normative southern masculinity, he achieves a spiritual grace alien to the aggressive forms of masculinity enacted by his family and thus escapes the despair that doomed his father and grandfather to hollow suicides. An aging man faces vast difficulties in demonstrating a virile embodiment of southern manhood, but such a vision of manliness, in the end, isolates one from love, both human and divine. Despite his advanced years, Will achieves a spiritual virility at the end of his adventures, one that coincides with his eventual success as a lover freed from tired models of historical masculinity.

LOVE IN THE RUINS AND *THE THANATOS SYNDROME*

Love in the Ruins and *The Thanatos Syndrome* address the meaning of love and community in apocalyptic times, and, as in Percy's other novels, the Middle Ages provides a historical touchstone to consider how the present rereads the past. Similar to Percy's other medievalized figures, numerous characters in these novels allude directly to figures of the Middle Ages and the Renaissance. The protagonist Thomas More most obviously denotes his namesake, the author of *Utopia* (1516) and the famed defender of marriage against Henry VIII's revolutionary divorce plans, and he claims a blood kinship with this illustrious ancestor: "Sir Thomas More, in fact, is a collateral ancestor. Our name anyhow is More" (*LR* 22). An array of minor characters likewise contribute to the novels' medieval flair. In *Love in the Ruins*, fleeting mention is made of a minor character's classical and medieval forebears ("And here is golden-haired golden-limbed Chuck looking like Phoebus Apollo or Sir Lancelot in hip-huggers" [48]), and in Gene Sarazen, More finds an antagonist with whom he can metaphorically reenact the medieval Crusades in which believers are pitted against infidels (i.e., Saracens). Mickey LaFaye, More's patient and early omen of the approaching sexual anomalies in *The Thanatos Syndrome*, suggests Morgan le Fay, the traditional villainess of the Arthurian tradition, and Vergil Bon alludes both to the author of the *Aenead* and to Dante's depiction of Vergil in his *Divine Comedy*, especially since Percy's Vergil frequently guides other characters to their destinations. Even such a minor character as Leroy Ledbetter, who appears in both books, takes on a medieval cast, because his name adumbrates a longing for a simpler monarchical system ("the king lead better"). Most strikingly, Thomas More's journey throughout these novels resembles that of Dante in the *Divine Comedy*, as Percy remarked: "*Love in the Ruins* begins with a very conscious allusion to Dante, at the beginning of the *Inferno*, losing his way in the midst of his life and finding himself in the woods."[27] Like Dante, More must undertake an arduous journey for spiritual salvation, during which his soul faces continual temptation.

Beyond the ways in which characters resonate with allegorical significance, disease and plague also define the medieval landscapes of *Love in the Ruins* and *The Thanatos Syndrome*. In *Love in the Ruins*, Max Gottlieb discloses to More that his invention has sparked widespread psychoses among the populace: "Your device has triggered a mass hysteria. Like the St. Vitus's dance in the Middle Ages. These are strange times" (241). The reader learns early in *The Thanatos Syndrome* that the Black Death, the scourge of the Middle Ages, has not been eradicated but reemerges in southern ports: "The plague does in fact turn up from time to time in New Orleans, the nation's largest port" (4). The devious Van Dorn sees a threat in the "three social plagues" of crime, teenage suicide–drug abuse, and AIDS, which he believes will destroy modern society: "[These plagues] are going to wreck us just as surely as the bubonic plague wrecked fourteenth-century Europe." He relies on his plague metaphor to smooth over the ethical ramifications of his solution: "[I]n time of plague you have to be Draconian" (*TS* 218). The medieval past signifies the possibility of apocalyptic chaos and destruction through a new outbreak of the plague, yet modern society accords itself the possibility of inflicting suffering in ways unimaginable to the medieval imagination: "[I]f there's a war, [it's] going to make the Somme look like Agincourt" (*TS* 90), More ponders, indicating his belief that modern times bear exponentially more destructive power than the past.

Southern communities suffer from long-standing cases of "the Sir Walter disease" in these novels, and More points to Walter Scott as the cultural mediator between the modern U.S. South and the medieval past: "Sir Walter in every plantation house as inevitable as the King James Bible and the Audubon prints; Sir Walter sending all these English-Americans to war against the Yankees as if they were the Catholic knights in *Ivanhoe* gone off to fight the infidel" (*TS* 181). Similar to the gendered paradigms depicted in *Lancelot,* this model of heroic masculinity inspires men to greatness yet offers them little real guidance in modern times. Even More's favorite drink, his "Early Times" bourbon whiskey that metaphorically represents his relationship with history, establishes a framework for viewing the past suspiciously. In a humorous aside collapsing the distinction between whiskey and history, More acknowledges that "[t]he Early Times is not sitting well" (*LR* 140), and at the conclusion of *Love in the Ruins,* he confesses that he has given it up entirely: "No drink for six months. One reason is willpower. The other is that Ellen would kill me" (*LR* 390). More forgets his abstinence from Early Times in *The Thanatos Syndrome,* such as when he takes "a nip of Early Times both in celebration and for worry" (*TS* 336). Following the logic of this symbolism, certain aspects of medievalism generate spiritually soporific effects, leaving More incapable of action and alienated from his community.

In *Love in the Ruins,* More incarnates a historical masculinity incapable of facing the troubled times of social decay and violence, and he ponders contrasting models of historical masculinity:

> Consider this though: would Richard Coeur de Lion have let Saladin have it in the back, heathen though he was?

> The trouble is that my grandfather set more store by Sir Walter Scott than he did by Thomas More.
>
> What would Thomas More have done? Undoubtedly he would have—(295)

Percy abruptly cuts off these ruminations before More reaches a decision, but it is nonetheless apparent that More evaluates competing models of masculinity: those of Richard the Lionhearted, Sir Walter Scott (and his medievally inflected protagonists such as Richard the Lionhearted), and St. Thomas More. Richard the Lionhearted and Walter Scott are aligned with military models of medieval masculinity but not a heroic model, if shooting an enemy in the back is a viable salvo in a holy war. Beyond the grandfather who prefers Scott to More, other members of More's family likewise reject their spiritual connection to St. Thomas More. More's mother ignores the saint's ancestral claim on the family: "My mother, who sets no store at all by our connection with Sir Thomas More, speaks often of her ancestor Sieur de Marigny, who was a rascal but also, she says, an aristocrat" (*LR* 276). Bernard Xavier Philippe de Marigny de Mandeville (1785–1868), notorious rake and roué, is famous for proudly proclaiming his transgressions to his wife: "Madame, I wish to inform you that I possess in the highest degree every vice of a gentleman!" He is also credited with "introduc[ing] the game of craps to America" and reported to have enjoyed dueling.[28] More's challenge is to surpass his family's veneration for fallen models of masculinity by emulating his namesake, but as the break in his line of thought indicates, his alliance with St. Thomas More is tentative at this moment, and the lure of de Marigny, so captivating to his family, could seduce him as well.

More desires to merge militarism and spirituality by incarnating medieval knightly masculinity. Through his prayer for guidance he seeks to improve on the primarily martial incarnation of such masculinity by linking it to Christianity: "Dear God . . . [w]hy can I not be merry and loving like my ancestor, a gentle pure-hearted knight for our Lady and our blessed Lord and Savior? Pray for me, Sir Thomas More" (*LR* 109). The plea for God's blessing concludes with the name "Sir Thomas More," but is this a valedictory or a direct address? Is the character More ascribing to himself the position of a knightly supplicant before his God, or he is appealing to St. Thomas More as an intercessor in his prayer to the divine? The protagonist More identifies the More of this prayer as a "sir," but because he is an American in an ostensibly classless society, the protagonist could not be a lorded member of the aristocracy, except in an ironic sense. (Prayers, as a genre, are not particularly conducive to irony.) If the name that concludes protagonist More's prayer indicates an intercessory appeal to St. Thomas More, the title "sir" bespeaks the confusion More confronts on his spiritual journey, preferring his namesake's courtly, rather than saintly, identity. Given Percy's attention to deflating medieval models of courtly masculinity, More's reverence for a knightly identity in this passage bespeaks his desire to transcend earthly concerns; his solecism, evident in the word "sir," lies in adopting the wrong kind of role model, even when St. Thomas More himself figures as the paradigm of masculinity.

With St. Thomas More as his role model of saintly masculinity, More is nonetheless often targeted as an object of homosexual desire in brief scenes that recall the homoerotic posturings in *Lancelot* and the Will Barrett novels, such as when he describes Bob Comeaux's approach as that of a failed lover: "Bob shrugs and turns away, his eyes suddenly distant and preoccupied, like an unsuccessful suitor" (*TS* 36). After the climactic showdown at the child-care center, the Sheriff approaches More aggressively and sexually: "He comes up close as a lover, actually touching me with his stomach, like an enraged coach bumping an umpire—but more erotically" (*TS* 319).[29] More's sexual relationships with women often emasculate him, such as when Lucy dominates him sexually: "Her mouth is on mine. She, Alabama-German-Lucy-Alice, is under the comforter and I under her, she a sweet heavy incubus but not quite centered" (*TS* 163; cf. 348). The woman is quite literally on top in this scene, and its queer potential emerges in that incubi are male demons, in contrast to their female counterparts, the succubi. Percy clearly understood the difference between succubi and incubi, as is evident in More's assault by succubi in *Love in the Ruins:* "It was during the following week . . . that I became ill, suffering simultaneous depressions and exaltations, assaulted at night by longings, succubi, and the hideous shellfire of Verdun" (97). The fact that More is assaulted by succubi in *Love in the Ruins* and by an (oxymoronically) female incubi in *The Thanatos Syndrome* indicates strongly that his encounter with Lucy emasculates him. Even More's musings over his personal identity—"And who am I? the last of the Mohicans? the fag end of the English Catholics here, queer birds indeed in these parts" (*TS* 181)—carry inflections of homosexuality. With his sexual manhood under duress and in need of fortification, medieval chivalric manhood appears as a panacea to his gendered ills, but, as in Percy's other novels, the cure carries unexpected side effects detrimental to spiritual growth.

As engaging and quirky a protagonist as Thomas More reborn in the modern age may be, he is not a knight, despite his muted inclination to incarnate this model of manhood. More's struggles with medievalism convey his desire, not to return to the past, but to transfigure the present into a more meaningful and spiritually coherent age. He averts apocalyptic ends in both novels, but these victories do not arise from succumbing to "the Sir Walter disease" and emerging as a triumphantly chivalric hero. In contrast, *The Thanatos Syndrome* proffers yet another model of medieval masculinity, one given greater latitude in achieving moral victories and one that subverts knighthood by parodying its claims to heroic action. The model of medieval masculinity most venerated in the novels is that of Father Smith, the priest who ensconces himself up in a tree in an act generally perceived as a sign of his insanity (*TS* 111) and who is associated with the great madman of chivalric literature, Don Quixote. Foremost, many of the characters see Father Smith as ridiculous, if not altogether demented: "'He could be doing vicarious penance for the awful state of the world. It is, after all, good Catholic practice,' says Jan sarcastically. 'The Carmelites and the Desert Fathers have been doing it for centuries. . . . After all, how . . . do you think Lucca was saved from the Black Plague in the fourteenth century?'" (*TS* 113). In an age of doubt, Jan's sarcasm punctures Father Smith's actions, deflating their emotional and salvific resonance, but Percy addresses the complexities of faith in the priest's inscrutable actions, not their surface appearance. Jan's rhetorical questions linger hauntingly in the air, but the impossibility of understanding prayer in earthly terms does not therefore undo the spiritual impact of Smith's actions.

Percy modeled Father Smith on St. Simon Stylites (c. 390–459 CE), a hermit who built a ten-foot-high pillar and then lived on it for the rest of his life to seclude himself from the troubles of the world and to devote himself to prayer.[30] For Percy, St. Simon allegorically captures Father

Smith's efforts to speak Catholic truth through signs: "[T]he parallel is [to] St. Simon Stylites who went up as an act of penance and to escape the sinful world—to do penance and to worship on top of the tower, which admittedly is a little odd, odd behavior. . . . I don't think most readers picked up on 'signs' but the underlying, very lightly stressed idea, was that the present day world is almost without signs. The signs have, as Smith would say, been evacuated . . . and the words are worn out by . . . Satan. So naturally Father Smith is in the sign business—in a fire tower you look for signs."[31] Father Smith, as priest and prophet, sees through the haze of moral doubt to act oddly yet passionately for the good of humanity. In a world in which spiritual signs pass unnoticed, his dedication to interpreting them elevates him both literally (in the tower) and figuratively (as a role model for salvation).

In terms of Father Smith's medieval coloring, he believes that his lessons in Germany were a core part of his introduction to southern culture, which he links to "the Sir Walter disease": "Do you recall that being a student at Heidelberg was as much a part of the Southern tradition as reading Sir Walter Scott?" (*TS* 240).[32] Much as reading Scott's novels of Crusaders and knights errant inculcated values of masculinity within southern youth, Smith sees his education in Germany as a formative part of his education. The seductive appeal of knightly medievalism almost ensnared him due to his admiration for his friend Helmut. This young man, who wore an "SS Officer's cap with its German eagle and death's head" (*TS* 247), symbolically represents Nazism and genocide, but Smith found both Nazism and his friendship with Helmut so alluring that he envisioned himself as "a young English Crusader signing up with Richard to rescue the holy places from the infidel" (*TS* 248). The priest later realized the horrors of Nazism, but Helmut so mesmerized him that he almost succumbed to the temptations of military masculinity: "I would have gone to the Junkerschule, sworn the solemn oath of the Teutonic knights at Marienberg, and joined the Schutzstaffel. Listen. Do you hear me? *I would have joined him*" (*TS* 248–49; italics in original). Here is Percy's strongest denunciation of "the Sir Walter disease," as he creates a menacing network of crusading, medieval heroism, southern masculinity, and Nazism, an intoxicating brew for young men to imbibe but one that leads to the horrors of the Holocaust.

If knightly masculinities are at best empty statements of bravado and at worst seductive fantasies that lead men to commit genocide, the comic inversions of parody nonetheless exalt a positive form of chivalric identity. When More notices Father Smith's hand, he perceives a carnivalesque model of medieval masculinity as embodied in Cervantes' delusional cavalier: "I look at his hand, which is still on the azimuth. It is as withered as Don Quixote's, yet, when he clasped mine, as strong as the Don's too" (*TS* 237). Don Quixote, the lunatic knight on a crazed yet delightfully human quest, provides a powerful metaphor for responding to the fallen world. As Montserrat Ginés describes, "Don Quixote embodies an ideal as chimerical as it is indestructible—that the knightly function can be revived in a crass present. It is chimerical because, by definition, it belongs to the world of fantasy, and as such is unattainable in historical reality."[33] To love life so strongly, to fight against death so tirelessly, may be a mark of madness, and Father Smith's actions indeed border on the bizarre. In the interlude entitled "Father Smith's Confession," the reader learns that Smith respects Cervantes because he was known for tending to the infirm; the priest recalls a lesson from his mentor Dr. Heyde, who "mentioned Cervantes's description of the mental hospital in Seville, also noted for its humane treatment of patients" (*TS* 246). For Percy, in his eloquent rebuttal against a culture of death, Smith's manic manliness models the only viable escape from despair.

The Thanatos Syndrome condemns death as an easy answer to difficult problems, especially abortion and euthanasia, and Father Smith enjoys the company of the dying over that of the living: "Yes, I took in the dying. Do you want to know why? Because dying people were the only people I could stand. They were my kind" (*TS* 244). Tending to the needs of the dying represents, in some measure, a quest as mad as Don Quixote's because death can never be escaped: fighting death is quixotic, but like medieval quests for the Holy Grail, embarking on such a journey sparks spiritual growth, even if the object of the quest always eludes discovery. It is nonetheless a meaningful act, one that celebrates life while acknowledging the limits of human power to transcend death. More's admiration for Father Smith allows him to surpass his concern for medieval military masculinities, to shake off the powerful allure of "the Sir Walter disease," and to incorporate a deeper sense of spiritual masculinity. Earlier in this novelistic diptych, Percy aligns More with Don Quixote both when his protagonist "hum[s] the *Don Quixote* theme in [Lola's] ear" (*LR* 91; cf. 181) and when he expresses admiration for Cervantes for overcoming incarceration to create his fiction: "It is easy to understand how men do their best work in prison or exile, men like Dostoevsky, Cervantes, Bonhoeffer, Sir Thomas More, Genet, and I, Dr. Thomas More" (*LR* 106). A precursor of Don Quixote in *Love in the Ruins,* More comes to a deeper respect for this parodically chivalric figure through his incarnation in Father Smith, Percy's model of Catholic virtue in a morally lost world. As models of masculinity for the U.S. South, knights mislead the men who follow them, but within the Thomas More novels, Don Quixote—the carnivalesque inversion of these paragons of military masculinity—inspires an insane yet redemptive lust for life and the living.

Percy's reformed image of Don Quixote as savior rather than madman finds an intriguing precursor in the words of Mark Twain. Prefiguring Percy's distaste for southern medievalism, Twain lambasted the U.S. South for its affection for Sir Walter Scott, but like Percy, he saw Cervantes' *Don Quixote* as a cure for the malady: "A curious exemplification of the power of a single book for good or harm is shown in the effects wrought by *Don Quixote* and those wrought by *Ivanhoe.* The first swept the world's admiration for the mediaeval chivalry-silliness out of existence; and the other restored it. As far as our South is concerned, the good work done by Cervantes is pretty nearly a dead letter, so effectually has Scott's pernicious work undermined it."[34] Twain's analysis springs to life in Percy's fictions, as these two authors, remarkably different in styles, temperaments, and themes, unite in their opinion of Sir Walter Scott's destructive fictions and Cervantes' salutary antidote to them.

It is frequently a shaky critical practice to interpret literature with the author's biography as a hermeneutic, but many of Percy's critics succumb to this enticement. As William O'Brien laments, "[t]here are few writers today who have been so persistently misunderstood as Walker Percy" due to the "inclination of many critics to find Mr. Percy's voice in that of one or another of his protagonists."[35] John Blair argues in regard to *Lancelot,* "In some ways, Percy does clearly identify with his murderous and misogynous protagonist," and then he specifies, "The point at which Lance's beliefs intersect with Percy's own is not at Lance's hatred of women, but at his disgust with the secularization of modern society and its consequent moral decay."[36] As is evident in the quotation from "Why Are You a Catholic?" at the beginning of this chapter, Percy saw himself moving from a childlike fascination with medieval heroism into an adult skepticism about the possibility that these models of manliness lead men to overlook deeper spiritual truths. Percy's fictions should not be read as autobiographies or romans à clef, but he does ask readers to join him in rejecting medieval knightly and heroic masculinities as false models of manliness, ones that contribute to an aggrandized sense of self with little corresponding spiritual growth. For Percy, the famed author-physician, "the Sir Walter disease" is a deadly and queering corruption of the spirit and of southern masculinity, and his fiction puts forth the cure.

7

CONCLUSION

Ellen Gilchrist's The Annunciation *and the Queer Future of Chivalric Masculinities*

As Twain, O'Connor, Toole, Warren, and Percy demonstrate in their vastly different fictions, the masculine chivalric ideal invites deep questions about what it means to be a white man in the U.S. South. The promise of chivalric manhood establishes a cultural goal for men to esteem, venerate, and follow, but this hollow fantasy can never shield them from queer fissures disrupting otherwise normative identities. A masculinity based upon the idea of imperviousness and perfect honor will eventually crack under external pressures, and chivalry, by painting over the internal incoherencies of white masculinity and heterosexuality as triumphantly normative, ironically reveals the inherent challenges in maintaining ideological purity. For these great authors of the U.S. South, the narrative utility of southern and medieval chivalry arises in its potential to goad their male protagonists (and thus their readers as well) into reassessing the ideologically normative status of white heterosexual masculinity and thus to see the masochistic play at its heart.

For these reasons, as has been addressed throughout this monograph, women are frequently shunted to the sides in men's quests for chivalric masculinity, despite their ostensible preeminence in proving a man's desirability. The creation of heterosexual masculinity necessitates the rejection not only of homosexuality but of any trace of femininity as well. Judith Butler outlines how the psychological construction of heterosexuality requires a series of repudiations: "Becoming a 'man' . . . requires repudiating femininity as a precondition for the heterosexualization of sexual desire and its fundamental ambivalence. If a man becomes heterosexual by repudiating the feminine, where could that repudiation live except in an identification which his heterosexual career seeks to deny? Indeed, the desire for the feminine is marked by that repudiation: he wants the woman he would never be. He wouldn't be caught dead being her: therefore he wants her."[1] Despite the variety of masculine experience in Twain's, O'Connor's, Toole's, Warren's, and Percy's fictions, their male protagonists share this repudiation of femininity in acts ranging from hesitation to aversion: the transformation of Hank's intense dislike of Sandy into rapturous love in Twain's *A Connecticut Yankee in King Arthur's Court;* Thomas's fear of Sarah Ham in O'Connor's "The Comforts of Home" and General Sash's imaginary re-creations of sexual experiences with nonexistent women in "A Late Encounter with the Enemy"; Ignatius's antagonistic relationships with Lana and Myrna in Toole's *A Confederacy of Dunces,* which masks the pseudohomosexuality at the character's core; Jed's debilitating love for Rozelle in Warren's *A Place to Come To,* which consistently undermines his assumption of southern masculinity; and Lancelot's murderous revenge against Margot for stripping the facade of his chivalric pretense in Percy's *Lancelot.* Such treatments of women further expose the queer foundations of southern chivalric masculinity, for these women are simply treated as appendages to the male protagonists seeking to prove their masculinity.

As women serving in the role of lovers must be simultaneously pursued and repudiated for the assumption of southern chivalric masculinity, women as mothers must be likewise denigrated. Twain does not depict Hank's mother in *A Connecticut Yankee,* yet readers see a mostly uniform portrayal of southern motherhood in the works of O'Connor, Toole, Warren, and Percy. Despite the variations in their personalities and their relationships with their sons, Julian's mother in O'Connor's "Everything That Rises Must Converge," Thomas's mother in "The Comforts of Home," Mrs. Reilly in *A Confederacy of Dunces,* Elvira Tewksbury in *A Place to Come To,* and Aunt Emily in *The Moviegoer* hinder their sons (in Aunt Emily's case, her nephew) from assuming the masculinity they assume to be their southern birthright. Gilles Deleuze posits that masochists must confront their mother and maternal desires: "The masochist experiences the symbolic order as an intermaternal order in which the mother represents the law under certain prescribed conditions; she generates the symbolism through which the masochist expresses himself."[2] And so once again women are experienced as a masochistic prohibition, as a symbol rather than as an individual, one who allows the male protagonist to accede into masculinity through the queer prohibitions at her fantastic core. To perpetuate the masculine fantasy of chivalry, men must reject women as lovers and as mothers to revel in the devastatingly narcissistic aloneness inherent in chivalric masculinity.

Chivalric and medieval themes will undoubtedly maintain their privileged position in the mythology of southern literature, but as new writers engage with past traditions, the trope will develop in unexpected ways. This monograph has focused on the queering effect of medieval masculinities in southern literature, but it would be remiss to overlook the ways in which medieval and gendered tropes are shifting profoundly. One writer deploying chivalric and medieval tropes in her writing while reimagining their ideological weight is Ellen Gilchrist, who examines the U.S. South from a woman's perspective in much of her fiction. Gilchrist's appreciation of medieval literature is evident throughout her corpus; she referred to T. H. White's *The Once and Future King*, the greatest of the twentieth-century retellings of the Arthurian legend, as "perhaps my single favorite piece of writing."[3] For Gilchrist, knightly chivalry does not serve as an exclusively male trait, and she imbues her female characters with this mythic edge. One of Gilchrist's recurring characters is Nora Jane Whittington, a young woman who disguises herself as a nun to rob a bar in *In the Land of Dreamy Dreams* (1981). From such a humorous yet ignominious beginning, Nora Jane develops into a chivalric heroine. Later in her narrative career as recorded in *The Courts of Love* (1996), her husband Freddy compares her to a questing knight: "'Three knights were allowed to see the Grail,' Freddy said. 'Bors and Percival and Galahad. They were pure of heart. You're pure of heart, Nora Jane'" (11–12).[4]

Beyond describing female characters as Arthurian knights, Gilchrist considers the meaning of quests for southern women, notably in *The Annunciation* (1983), and, in so doing, reinvents chivalric themes in the U.S. South. The novel's feminist themes arise in its matrilineal introduction to protagonist Amanda McCamrey: "These were the people of Esperanza Plantation. These were the ones who taught Amanda everything she would always know. There were three generations of women, not counting Amanda, who made it four" (6).[5] Despite Gilchrist's focus on a woman's world, Amanda's models of identity are molded through the constrictive force of archaic and medieval gender roles. As a child, Amanda is described as a "little princess" (8), and this terse characterization puts her in the passive narrative position of the female in need of rescue rather than in the active role of the rescuer. The plot of *The Annunciation* addresses Amanda's metamorphosis from a princess awaiting a knightly savior into a woman relying on herself, rather than her lover, to solve the problems she faces in life and love.

In contrast to the initial depictions of Amanda as a passive child in need of a hero, her cousin and lover Guy initially plays the narrative role of the dashing hero. The name *Guy* suggests that he represents a generic form of masculinity, and Gilchrist's portrayal of him accentuates his strategies for exploiting the gendered expectations of chivalric male behavior. He plans to take Amanda away from her college for a tryst, but the house mother balks, and so he wins this woman over by charmingly performing southern gentility: "'She has to be back by nine, you know,' the fat old headmistress said, going all coy and girlish in the face of Guy's marvelous shoulders and the elegant manners that well-raised Mississippi boys wield like rapiers" (34). When Gilchrist depicts Guy's reputation in this southern landscape hinging on his gridiron accomplishments, one can detect a tone similar to that of Walker Percy's depiction of southern men playing football to prove their modern-day heroism. Amanda's hero-worship of Guy as a "knight-in-shining-armor" figure of romance devolves as she realizes that he is incapable of assisting her in any concrete manner after she becomes pregnant. By the novel's end, she does not need a knightly hero reborn in the U.S. South as much as she needs herself.

As Gilchrist refuses to idealize history and the romanticized past it represents, this dynamic overwrites both the mythologized history of the U.S. South and the fairy-tale image of the Middle Ages. Although Amanda desires to escape her nightmarish present by figuratively fleeing into a remote history, the depiction of the past in *The Annunciation* highlights its funereal qualities, such as when she laments her social life in New Orleans: "I know there's something better to do in the world than hang around doing numbers on each other in this fucking dead old anachronistic world" (89). Not merely dismissing the historically inflected culture of present-day New Orleans, she also rejects the romanticized "princess" identity of her childhood when she leaves her husband Malcolm: "I was the Wasp princess and [our marriage] didn't work out" (93). History traps

Amanda in both its contemporary reenactments and its sugar-coated idealism, and her narrative struggle involves freeing herself from history so that she may live in the present.

Despite the promises of southern chivalry to venerate and protect women, the U.S. South does not nurture women into any sense of well-being in Gilchrist's novel. Amanda's doctor, observing the damage done to her body by her pregnancy at such a young age, condemns its social mores: "Every stupid and pointless thing in the outworn gothic mores of the Deep South was in the garbled story she was telling him" (39). The gothicism assigned to the U.S. South, in its frequent depiction as aggressively antimodern and thus mysterious and backward, reveals the ways in which history traps its citizens. "Goddamn their crazy outworn used-up terror and ignorance and hypocrisy and fear. Imagine letting that child carry a baby to term. She'll probably never conceive again," Amanda's doctor further fulminates (41). Condemning the U.S. South for its treatment of women and its regressive maintenance of their sexuality, the doctor implies that history destroys women: its traditions, quite simply, are poisonous.

Due to history's thematic toxicity in *The Annunciation*, and also due to Amanda's antihistorical stance in regard to southern culture, it is surprising that she immerses herself in the Middle Ages as an escape from the stultifying environs of New Orleans. Gilchrist's deployment of medieval themes in *The Annunciation* overarchingly criticizes constructions of southern male chivalry and its accompanying marginalization of women's agency, yet she complicates the novel's medievalism by also highlighting the allure of a romanticized and escapist vision of the past. While living with nuns as she awaits the birth of her and Guy's child, Amanda embraces the fantasy of the Middle Ages: "She saved the sweets to eat while she read herself to sleep at night, her mind far away in fifteenth-century England, taking sides in the War of the Roses" (16). In her youth (and despite the maturity of the situation in which she finds herself), Amanda views the medieval past as an escape route from her struggles in the modern U.S. South, where young girls are rigorously disciplined for their perceived sexual transgressions. Through such medieval daydreams, Amanda flees the pressures of her southern landscape, at least imaginatively.

In abandoning her loveless marriage to Malcolm, Amanda asserts her independence, as well as her intellectual gifts, by turning again to the

Middle Ages. Her professional ambition to translate *Les chansons mystiales perdues d'Helene Renoir* (The lost wedding songs of Helene Renoir) frees her through her literary accomplishments, and she promises herself that she will "be the best translator of Middle French that ever walked the face of the earth" (113).[6] The narrator soon reiterates Amanda's determination in this regard: "She meant to devote the rest of her life to a dead poet's imagination" (150). Here the romanticized past of the Middle Ages elicits Amanda's passion. This view of the past contrasts sharply with her rejection of the poetry of the present, which she condemns as "just words. . . . There isn't any heart in any of it. It's all either surreal or nihilistic. . . . I want something that means something. I want something with a moral heart to it, or some passion, or something worth passing on" (119–20). Here the Middle Ages relieves the existential angst of modernism, yet such a contrast muddies interpretations of history's meaning for Gilchrist's protagonist.

Further complicating the thematic deployment of medievalism in *The Annunciation* is that Amanda's relationship with her young lover Will incarnates numerous medieval ideals in a manner similar to her relationship with Guy. Like Guy, Will represents the romance of the medieval past, but in contrast, he appears mostly free from the burdens of southern history. On a date with Will, Amanda imagines him crowned like a Plantagenet king (185–85), and she compares him to Richard the Lionhearted in retelling "the story of his golden lion-hearted youth" (187). He is described as a troubadour (270), and while planning future vacations together, Amanda reveals her desire to share with him the defining symbol of medieval regal masculinity: "I want to show you The Sword in the Stone. Oh, Will, I want to give you The Sword in the Stone" (233). Also, Will's last name is Lyons (142), which links him to the setting of Helene Renoir's poetry (148). Building this theme, Will refers to himself as a "romantic" (227), and a minor character likewise says of Amanda, "She speaks romance" (138). These aspects of Will's character and the romance he shares with Amanda "re-romanticize" the novel and foreshadow that Amanda will discover true love with a chivalric figure of medieval masculinity. Even a friend's dog named Carl Orff (235), in honor of the composer of the *Carmina Burana*, contributes to Amanda's aesthetic delight in medievalism.

For Amanda, then, history is both alluring and constricting. It is powerfully attractive in its seductive vision of romance, yet such romance threatens her freedom and sense of agency. She forthrightly rejects the past of the U.S. South: "I'm through with the past and the terrible decadent south and everything it represents" (206). Gilchrist also delineates the limitations of the Middle Ages to guide Amanda's present. Although her literary relationship with Helene Renoir liberates her from her shallow life in New Orleans, she also discovers that translating this dead poet's work cannot fully help her to establish her own identity. Initially infatuated with Helene's life and travails, Amanda loses her literary adulation for this author: "Goddammit, she was twenty-one years old. I don't know about all this romantic suicide stuff." Her friend Marshall Jordan queries her about this shift in her views, but Amanda has now lost her romanticized opinion of the medieval past:

> "I thought you were in sympathy with Helene. Because they took her baby away."
>
> "She should have gone and found the baby instead of killing herself. She was twenty-one years old. I'll tell you one thing. If I'd been that old no one could have taken my child from me. The United States government couldn't have taken it from me." (297–98)

Unlike the male characters of much southern fiction who uncritically assume the mantle of chivalrous manhood, Amanda reassesses her relationship with Helene Renoir, and thus reassesses her relationship with history. Toward the novel's end, she still prides herself on her identity as the "oldest pregnant translator of Middle French in the Western Hemisphere, maybe the world" (310), but she does so with a sharply critical eye regarding her forebear's limitations both as a mother and as a poet.

The mythologies of the Middle Ages purport to offer an escape from life's vicissitudes, but Amanda realizes that she does not need to escape: she can resist the ideological force of southern culture within its geographical milieu while remaining true to her convictions. When Amanda considers the meaning of her life in Arkansas, she thinks to herself, "What a place to make my stand" (299). Here Gilchrist plays against the agrarian traditions of southern literature, notably those expressed by Robert Penn Warren, John Crowe Ransom, Allen Tate, and other southern commentators in the influential volume *I'll Take My Stand* (1930), and the tenacity of spirit evident in her words underscores that she no longer needs to escape the U.S. South, as historically defined by white men, to prosper. Margaret Bauer interprets *The Annunciation* as a subversion of William Faulkner's *The Sound and the Fury*, in which "Gilchrist unmistakably provides the reader with a more optimistic view of the future of the nonconforming southern woman than Faulkner chose to offer."[7] Tackling the masculine edge of southern literary history, Gilchrist rewrites the past by reimagining women's relationship to it and depicting their ability to resist its sway.

To underscore her protagonist's independence in the narrative's denouement, Gilchrist does not portray a tidy romantic ending in which Amanda and Will marry and then raise their child together as a homey nuclear family. Rather, Will appears to die in a car accident, leaving Amanda alone at the novel's close to contemplate her life on her own terms.[8] With this stark rejection of the expected end of a romance narrative, Gilchrist upends the typical tropes of the genre by illustrating a woman content in herself. Rather than reliving the medieval past or remaining trapped in southern history, Amanda realizes her potential by creating a new future for herself and her child. Pregnancy and childbirth thematically dominate *The Annunciation*, and Gilchrist contrasts Amanda's pregnancy with her grandmother's death to highlight the constricted possibilities afforded women of prior generations. When Amanda's grandmother dies, the household attendant Duke, whose name plays on medieval tropes of courtly privilege, reports the circumstances of her final moments: "She just making a noise like trying to push a baby out. Big old sucking noise" (51). In a novel so thematically focused on children and childbirth, Amanda's grandmother's final moments take on the imagery of death in labor, both that of the would-be mother and of the stillborn child. For Amanda, liberated from the archaisms of the U.S. South, pregnancy and childbirth free her to create the future, and she assumes divine characteristics with her child's birth, thus fulfilling the novel's eponymous prophecy. Her friend Katie observes how her pregnancy illuminates her divinity: "She willed [her child] into being, all by herself, out of light and air. Well, I swear I think she's starting to believe it" (315). In her assessment of her life and its vagaries, Amanda rewrites the Lord's Prayer as a paean to her sense of self: "My will be done, goddammit. My will be done" (325).

It is easy to accuse Amanda (or Gilchrist, for that matter) of a solipsistic viewpoint in such self-deification, but to read Amanda as an egotist dismisses the strength of her accomplishments. Writing against the weight of southern literature, in which, in Robert Penn Warren's words, southerners are "frozen" and "trapped in history,"[9] Gilchrist reimagines the meaning of history and allows a female character to triumph over the regressively medieval qualities of her culture. Despite history's weight, Amanda learns that she can free herself of its burdens: "I used to believe the past was the present, that we could never live it down, never leave it behind. Bullshit. The past is the past. You can dwell in it or you can move forward" (293). Comparing Gilchrist's stance on the weight of the past with the beliefs of such southern writers as Warren, who see history monolithically bearing down on the present, readers perceive that history can be as momentous or as trivial as one allows it to be. Amanda McCamrey shrugs off the weight of mythic history as if it were gossamer and forges a new life for herself through her actions, which are in part inspired by her medieval forebears but in no manner limited by them.

Amanda McCamrey provides a model for the future of southern chivalry, and through her Gilchrist illustrates the ways in which current writers grope with the weight of the U.S. South's defining cultural fantasies. The masochistic allure inherent in chivalry, of proclaiming an identity defensively as a result of lost causes and fractured white masculinities, bespeaks both the impossibility and the painful undesirability of archaic genders triumphing in the modern world. Chivalry is nonetheless an attractive fiction, one that southerners and southern writers turn to repeatedly for limning the contours of this region and its recalcitrant march into modernity. Readers can expect that this most persistent of tropes will persist, but Gilchrist's Amanda McCamrey highlights the gendered shifts under way as southern chivalry progressed into the late twentieth century and now into the twenty-first.

Notes

1. INTRODUCTION: SOUTHERN HISTORY, MYTHIC WHITE MASCULINITY, AND QUEERING THE MEDIEVAL CHIVALRIC IDEAL

1. James Boswell, quoting Samuel Johnson, *Boswell's Life of Johnson*, by James Boswell, ed. George Birbeck Hill (Oxford: Clarendon, 1964), 5.403, the entry dated Saturday, November 20, 1773.

2. Hayden White, *The Content of the Form* (Baltimore: Johns Hopkins University Press, 1987), 14; see also his *Tropics of Discourse: Essays in Cultural Criticism* (Baltimore: Johns Hopkins University Press, 1978), esp. 51. For an overview of historiographical theories, see Stefan Berger, Heiko Feldner, and Kevin Passmore, eds., *Writing History: Theory and Practice* (London: Hodder Arnold, 2003).

3. Mary Midgley, *The Myths We Live By* (London: Routledge, 2003), 1.

4. Claude Lévi-Strauss, *The Raw and the Cooked*, trans. John Weightman and Doreen Weightman (1964; New York: Harper & Row, 1969), 12.

5. C. Vann Woodward, *The Burden of Southern History*, 3rd ed. (Baton Rouge: Louisiana State University Press, 1993), 12–13. It is ironic that Woodward concentrates on mythological and iconoclastic historians in this dichotomy, thus apparently overlooking the potential for a historian engaged in neither mythmaking nor myth-busting. Here we see hints of the ideological colorings of historiography, as outlined by Hayden White.

6. Eugene Genovese, *The Southern Tradition* (Cambridge: Harvard University Press, 1994), 4–5.

7. For a study of the mythic nature of southern history, see Patrick Gerster and Nicholas Cords, eds., *Myth and Southern History*, 2nd ed. (Urbana: University of Illinois Press, 1989). Garvin Davenport, *The Myth of Southern History: Historical Consciousness in Twentieth-Century Southern Literature* (Nashville: Vanderbilt University Press, 1967), explores romanticized constructions of history in the southern literary record.

8. Craig Friend and Lorri Glover, "Rethinking Southern Masculinity," *Southern Manhood: Perspectives on Masculinity in the Old South*, ed. Craig Friend and Lorri Glover (Athens: University of Georgia Press, 2004), vii–xvii, at viii.

9. Stephen Berry, ed., *Princes of Cotton: Four Diaries of Young Men in the South, 1848–1860* (Athens: University of Georgia Press, 2007), xiii.

10. Alan Nolan, "The Anatomy of the Myth," *The Myth of the Lost Cause and Civil War History*, ed. Gary Gallagher and Alan Nolan (Bloomington: Indiana University Press, 2000), 11–34, at 12. Nolan's essay provides an excellent overview of the tenets of the "Lost Cause" and their historical veracity.

11. Charles Wilson, *Baptized in Blood: The Religion of the Lost Cause, 1865–1920* (Athens: University of Georgia Press, 1980). Bertram Wyatt-Brown similarly observes the propensity of the antebellum U.S. South to theologize its principles: "[I]n slaveholding societies, honor may be seen as a people's theology, a set of prescriptions endowed with an almost sacred symbolism." *Honor and Violence in the Old South* (New York: Oxford University Press, 1986), vii.

12. Judith Butler, *Undoing Gender* (New York: Routledge, 2004), 48. See also her *Bodies That Matter: On the Discursive Limits of "Sex"* (New York: Routledge, 1993); and *Gender Trouble: Feminism and the Subversion of Identity* (New York: Routledge, 1990). It is well beyond the scope of this study to conclude definitively about the respective roles of biology and ideology in the formation of gender, but Anne Fausto-Sterling intriguingly points to the interconnections between the two forces: "Our cultural conceptions will change the way our bodies grow, and how our bodies grow will change the way our culture views them." *Myths of Gender: Biological Theories about Women and Men* (New York: Basic, 1985), 220.

13. Susan Donaldson and Anne Goodwyn Jones, "Haunting Bodies: Rethinking the South through Gender," *Haunted Bodies: Gender and Southern Texts*, ed. Susan Donaldson and Anne Goodwyn Jones (Charlottesville: University Press of Virginia, 1997), 1–19, at 2.

14. Robert Penn Warren, *Jefferson Davis Gets His Citizenship Back* (Lexington: University Press of Kentucky, 1980), 15. On the ideological function of interpellation, see Louis Althusser, "Ideology and Ideological State Apparatuses," *Lenin and Philosophy and Other Essays*, trans. Ben Brewster (New York: Monthly Review, 1971), 85–126.

15. George Tindall, *Natives and Newcomers: Ethnic Southerners and Southern Ethnics* (Athens: University of Georgia Press, 1995), 4–5.

16. Stanley Aronowitz, "My Masculinity," *Constructing Masculinity*, ed. Maurice Berger, Brian Wallis, and Simon Watson (New York: Routledge, 1995), 307–20, at 307.

17. Holly Crocker, *Chaucer's Visions of Manhood* (New York: Palgrave Macmillan, 2007), 3.

18. Julian Carter, *The Heart of Whiteness: Normal Sexuality and Race in America, 1880–1940* (Durham, NC: Duke University Press, 2007), 3–4.

19. Sally Robinson, *Marked Men: White Masculinity in Crisis* (New York: Columbia University Press, 2000), 1.

20. Umberto Eco, *Travels in Hyperreality: Essays*, trans. William Weaver (San Diego: Harcourt, 1983), 68.

21. This definition of medieval romance captures the primary characteristics of the genre, especially in regard to the traits that surface in southern re-creations of these narratives. Admirable studies of medieval romance include W. R. J. Barron, *English Medieval Romance* (New York: Longman, 1987); Derek Pearsall, *Arthurian Romance: A Short Introduction* (Oxford: Blackwell, 2003); and Roberta Krueger, ed., *The Cambridge Companion to Medieval Romance* (Cambridge: Cambridge University Press, 2000).

22. Maurice Keen, *Chivalry* (New Haven: Yale University Press, 1984), 16. Additional studies of chivalry include the classic studies of Richard Barber, *The Knight and Chivalry* (Woodbridge, Suffolk: Boydell, 1995); and *The Reign of Chivalry* (Woodbridge, Suffolk: Boydell, 2005); as well as Mark Girouard, *The Return to Camelot: Chivalry and the English Gentleman* (New Haven: Yale University Press, 1981).

23. Eugene Genovese, "The Southern Slaveholders' View of the Middle Ages," *Medievalism in American Culture,* ed. Bernard Rosenthal and Paul Szarmach (Binghamton, NY: Medieval and Renaissance Texts and Studies, 1989), 31–52, at 32.

24. Gregory VanHoosier-Carey, "Byrhtnoth in Dixie: The Emergence of Anglo-Saxon Studies in the Postbellum South," *Anglo-Saxonism and the Construction of Social Identity,* ed. Allen Frantzen and John Niles (Gainesville: University Press of Florida, 1997), 157–72, at 170.

25. Michael Alexander, *Medievalism: The Middle Ages in Modern England* (New Haven: Yale University Press, 2007), xxii.

26. Tara McPherson, *Reconstructing Dixie: Race, Gender, and Nostalgia in the Imagined South* (Durham, NC: Duke University Press, 2003), 1.

27. For a study of Scott's medievalism, see Jerome Mitchell, *Scott, Chaucer, and Medieval Romance* (Lexington: University Press of Kentucky, 1987).

28. Sigmund Freud, "On Narcissism: An Introduction," *The Standard Edition of the Complete Psychological Works of Sigmund Freud,* trans. James Strachey (London: Hogarth, 1959), 14.67–102, at 73–74.

29. Julia Kristeva, *Tales of Love,* trans. Leon Roudiez (New York: Columbia University Press, 1987), 43.

30. Kaja Silverman, *Male Subjectivity on the Margins* (New York: Routledge, 1992), 326.

31. Scott Bravmann, *Queer Fictions of the Past: History, Culture, and Difference* (Cambridge: Cambridge University Press, 1997), 129.

32. Carolyn Dinshaw, "Chaucer's Queer Touches / A Queer Touches Chaucer," *Exemplaria* 7.1 (1995): 75–92, at 76–77.

33. Eve Sedgwick, *Tendencies* (Durham, NC: Duke University Press, 1993), 8; her italics.

34. John Howard, *Men like That: A Southern Queer History* (Chicago: University of Chicago Press, 1999), xiv. See also Howard, ed., *Carryin' on in the Lesbian and Gay South* (New York: New York University Press, 1997); as well as the essays in Carlos Dews and Carolyn Law, eds., *Out in the South* (Philadelphia: Temple University Press, 2001).

35. Michael Bibler, *Cotton's Queer Relations: Same-Sex Intimacy and the Literature of the Southern Plantation, 1936–1968* (Charlottesville: University of Virginia Press, 2009), 3.

36. Gary Richards, *Lovers and Beloveds: Sexual Otherness in Southern Fiction, 1936–1961* (Baton Rouge: Louisiana State University Press, 2005), 28.

37. Richards 2.

38. Jane Gallop, *The Daughter's Seduction: Feminism and Psychoanalysis* (Ithaca, NY: Cornell University Press, 1982), xii.

39. *Gone with the Wind,* dir. Victor Fleming, perf. Vivien Leigh and Clark Gable, DVD (1939; Burbank, CA: Warner, 1999).

40. See in particular Andreas's "rules" of courtly love, in his *The Art of Courtly Love,* trans. John Jay Parry (New York: Columbia University Press, 1960), 184–86.

41. Maud Wilder Goodwin, *The Colonial Cavalier* (1894; New York: Arno, 1975), 9.

42. Margaret Mitchell, *Gone with the Wind* (1936; New York: Warner, 1993), 238.

43. Florence King, *He: An Irreverent Look at the American Male* (New York: Stein & Day, 1978), 4.

44. Paul Jones, *Unwelcome Voices: Subversive Fiction in the Antebellum South* (Knoxville: University of Tennessee Press, 2005), 1–2.

45. Henry Clay Lewis, *Odd Leaves from the Life of a Louisiana Swamp Doctor* (1850; Baton Rouge: Louisiana State University Press, 1997), esp. 157–64.

46. Mark Twain, *Life on the Mississippi* (1883; New York: Oxford University Press, 1996), 467–68.

47. Henry Seidel Canby, *American Memoir* (Boston: Houghton Mifflin, 1947), 94 and 96; qtd. in John Fraser, *America and the Patterns of Chivalry* (Cambridge: Cambridge University Press, 1982), 9.

48. William Alexander Percy, *Lanterns on the Levee: Recollections of a Planter's Son* (1941; Baton Rouge: Louisiana State University Press, 1996), 56.

49. For more on the allegorical interplay between the Civil War and the Norman invasion in the southern imaginary, see Ritchie Watson, *Normans and Saxons: Southern Race Mythology and the Intellectual History of the American Civil War* (Baton Rouge: Louisiana State University Press, 2008).

50. Harriet Beecher Stowe, *Uncle Tom's Cabin* (1852; New York: Modern Library, 1996). For the legend of St. George, see "St. George," *Saints' Lives in Middle English Collections*, ed. E. Gordon Whatley (Kalamazoo: Medieval Institute, 2004), 71–102.

51. Caroline Lee Hentz, *The Planter's Northern Bride* (1854; Irvine, CA: Reprint Services, 1992).

52. Thomas Dixon Jr., *The Clansman: An Historical Romance of the Ku Klux Klan* (1905; Lexington: University Press of Kentucky, 1970). *The Clansman* is the basis of D. W. Griffith's early film masterpiece *Birth of a Nation* (1915). This film's controversial reception likewise highlights the historical vagaries attached to depictions of southern manhood.

53. James Avirett, "Knights and Courtly Ladies: The Romantic Ultimate," *The Romantic South*, ed. Harnett Kane (New York: Coward-McCann, 1961), 182–85, at 182. See also Rollin Osterweis, *Romanticism and Nationalism in the Old South* (New Haven: Yale University Press, 1949), for an overview of southern medievalism.

54. Ritchie Watson, *The Cavalier in Virginia Fiction* (Baton Rouge: Louisiana State University Press, 1985), 269.

55. For Warren's defense of segregation, see "The Briar Patch" in *I'll Take My Stand*, by Twelve Southerners, ed. Susan Donaldson (1930; Baton Rouge: Louisiana State University Press, 2006), 246–64. Susan Donaldson emphasizes the distressed masculinity of these authors in her edition of the text, demonstrating how they "proclaimed their intention to retrieve and rehabilitate the 'discredited' Old South and its defeated traditions, and that goal revealed not just their central preoccupation with taking hold of what they viewed as their rightful cultural heritage by their own sense of besieged white manhood in a time of bewildering and threatening change" (xi–xii).

56. If the reader is wondering why a chapter of this monograph is not dedicated to Cabell's *Jurgen*, it is simply because *Jurgen* is set in a fairy-tale wonderland rather than in the U.S. South, and therefore it is difficult to draw definitive conclusions about Cabell's consideration of southern masculinity within this work.

57. Walker Percy, "Why Are You a Catholic?" *Signposts in a Strange Land*, ed. Patrick Samway (New York: Farrar, Straus & Giroux, 1991), 304–15, esp. 313–14.

58. William Faulkner, *Requiem for a Nun* (New York: Random House, 1950), 92; Robert Penn Warren, *All the King's Men* (1946; San Diego: Harcourt Brace, 1974), 435.

59. William Gilmore Simms, *Southward Ho! A Spell of Sunshine* (1885; New York: AMS Press, 1970), 3. For the definitive study of Simms, see Mary Ann Wimsatt, *The Major Fiction of William Gilmore Simms: Cultural Traditions and Literary Form* (Baton Rouge: Louisiana State University Press, 1989).

60. C. Vann Woodward, *Origins of the New South, 1877–1913* (Baton Rouge: Louisiana State University Press, 1951), ix.

2. DIALECTICAL HISTORY, WHITE INDIANS, AND QUEER ANXIETY IN MARK TWAIN'S *A CONNECTICUT YANKEE IN KING ARTHUR'S COURT*

1. Quotations and parenthetical citations are taken from Mark Twain, *A Connecticut Yankee in King Arthur's Court* (1889; New York: Oxford University Press, 1996).

2. Richard Pressman, "A Connecticut Yankee in Merlin's Cave: The Role of Contradiction in Mark Twain's Novel," *American Literary Realism* 16 (1983): 58–72, at 65.

3. Mark Twain, *The Innocents Abroad* (1869; New York: Oxford University Press, 1996).

4. Letter to Orion Clemens, March 18, 1861, *Mark Twain's Letters*, vol. 1, *1853–1866*, ed. Edgar Branch et al. (Berkeley: University of California Press, 1987), 117; letter to Olivia Langdon, March 2, 1869, *Mark Twain's Letters*, vol. 3, *1869*, ed. Victor Fischer and Michael Frank (Berkeley: University of California Press, 1992), 132–33.

5. For Lecky's influence on *A Connecticut Yankee in King Arthur's Court*, see Mark Twain, *Mark Twain's Notebooks and Journals*, vol. 3, *1883–1891*, ed. Robert Pack Browning, Michael Frank, Lin Salamo, and Frederick Anderson (Berkeley: University of California Press, 1979), 502–6.

6. Letter to Olivia Langdon, January 10, 1870, *Mark Twain's Letters*, vol. 4, *1870–1871*, ed. Victor Fischer and Michael Frank (Berkeley: University of California Press, 1995), 15–16.

7. Letter to Brander Matthews, May 4, 1903, *Mark Twain's Letters*, ed. Albert Paine (New York: Harper, 1917), 2.738.

8. Letter to Olivia Langdon, August 2–6, 1873, *Mark Twain's Letters*, vol. 5, *1872–1873*, ed. Lin Salamo and Harriet Smith (Berkeley: University of California Press, 1997), 428.

9. *Mark Twain's Letters*, ed. Salamo and Smith 430n10.

10. Letter to Brander Matthews, June 1910, *Mark Twain's Letters*, ed. Paine 2.738–39.

11. Linda Morris, *Gender Play in Mark Twain* (Columbia: University of Missouri Press, 2007), 1. See also Peter Stoneley, *Mark Twain and the Feminine Aesthetic* (Cambridge: Cambridge University Press, 1992).

12. Frederick Jameson, "Marxism and Historicism," *New Literary History* 11 (1979): 41–73, at 43–44.

13. Bruce Michelson, "Realism, Romance, and Dynamite: The Quarrel of *A Connecticut Yankee in King Arthur's Court*," *New England Quarterly* 64 (1991): 609–32, at 625.

14. Lesley Kordecki, "Twain's Critique of Malory's Romance: *Forma tractandi* and *A Connecticut Yankee,*" *Nineteenth-Century Literature* 41 (1986): 329–48, at 329–30.

15. Sigmund Freud, *Civilization and Its Discontents,* trans. James Strachey (New York: Norton, 1961), 99.

16. Slavoj Žižek, *The Puppet and the Dwarf: The Perverse Core of Christianity* (Cambridge: MIT Press, 2003), 56.

17. Nancy Oliver, "New Manifest Destiny in *A Connecticut Yankee in King Arthur's Court,*" *Mark Twain Journal* 21 (1983): 28–32, at 30.

18. Mary Shanley and Peter Stillman, "Mark Twain: Technology, Social Change, and Political Power," *The Artist and Political Vision,* ed. Benjamin Barber and Michael McGrath (New Brunswick, NJ: Transactions, 1982), 267–89, at 273–74.

19. Edmund Reiss, afterword to *A Connecticut Yankee in King Arthur's Court,* by Mark Twain (New York: Signet, 1963), 321–31, at 325; qtd. in Shanley and Stillman 274.

20. Bruce Michelson, *Printer's Devil: Mark Twain and the American Publishing Revolution* (Berkeley: University of California Press, 2006), 175.

21. Shari Huhndorf, *Going Native: Indians in the American Cultural Imagination* (Ithaca, NY: Cornell University Press, 2001), 6. Huhndorf analyzes the tension between whiteness and American Indians in her study, yet her words are also apropos of Hank Morgan, who paradoxically "goes native" among whites, in that he deems them the savage equivalent to American Indians.

22. Ralph Waldo Emerson, "Friendship," *The Essential Writings of Ralph Waldo Emerson,* ed. Brooks Atkinson (1841; New York: Modern Library, 2000), 201–14, at 206.

23. Leila Rupp, *A Desired Past: A Short History of Same-Sex Love in America* (Chicago: University of Chicago Press, 1999), 47–48. For additional studies of romantic friendships, see Martin Duberman, *About Time: Exploring the Gay Past,* rev. ed. (New York: Meridian, 1991); Jonathan Katz, *Love Stories: Sex between Men before Homosexuality* (Chicago: University of Chicago Press, 2001); Carolyn Oulton, *Romantic Friendship in Victorian Literature* (Aldershot, Eng.: Ashgate, 2007); and Anthony Rotundo, "Romantic Friendship: Male Intimacy and Middle-Class Youth in the Northern United States, 1800–1900," *Journal of Social History* 23 (1989): 1–25. For primary sources detailing literary romantic friendships, see Axel Nissen, *The Romantic Friendship Reader: Love Stories between Men in Victorian America* (Boston: Northeastern University Press, 2003).

24. Chris Packard, *Queer Cowboys and Other Erotic Male Friendships in Nineteenth-Century American Literature* (New York: Palgrave Macmillan, 2005), 96–97.

25. Andrew Hoffman, "Mark Twain and Homosexuality," *American Literature* 67.1 (1995): 23–49, at 23–24, 27. For Fiedler's asexually allegorical reading of homoeroticism in *Huckleberry Finn,* see his "Come Back to the Raft Ag'in, Huck Honey," *Partisan Review* 15 (1948): 664–71.

26. Mark Twain, "A Medieval Romance," *Sketches, New and Old* (1875; New York: Oxford University Press, 1996), 171–79.

27. Mark Twain, *How Nancy Jackson Married Kate Wilson and Other Tales of Rebellious Girls and Daring Women,* ed. John Cooley (Lincoln: University of Nebraska Press, 2001). For

the story of "How Nancy Jackson Married Kate Wilson," 105–23; for the Cooley quotation, 105. Twain wrote the story circa 1902, but it was not published until 1987 (105).

28. Fred Kaplan, *The Singular Mark Twain* (New York: Doubleday, 2003), 450. See also Ron Powers, *Mark Twain: A Life* (New York: Free Press, 2005), who quotes one of Susy's letters to Louise: "Please come in to me and let me lie down in your arms, and forget everything but the joy of being near you" (560).

29. Foucault cites Carl Westphal's "famous article of 1870 on 'contrary sexual sensations'" and suggests that it "can stand as [homosexuality's] date of birth." *The History of Sexuality,* vol. 1, *An Introduction,* trans. Robert Hurley (New York: Vintage, 1990), 43.

30. Calvin Thomas, *Male Matters: Masculinity, Anxiety, and the Male Body on the Line* (Urbana: University of Illinois Press, 1996), 16.

31. As quoted in Henry Smith, *Mark Twain's Fable of Progress* (New Brunswick, NJ: Rutgers University Press, 1964), 8.

32. One woman, the wife of the poacher who refuses to confess his crime to Morgan le Fay, is invited to join the Man-Factory (212). Despite the apparent egalitarianism of this moment, readers never see a woman in the Man-Factory, and only males are among its members in the end. Viewing Hank Morgan as a protofeminist is difficult, given his sexist views of women's suffrage: "[U]pon Arthur's death unlimited suffrage should be introduced, and given to men and women alike—at any rate to all men, wise or unwise, and to all mothers who at middle age should be found to know nearly as much as their sons at twenty-one" (514).

33. Justin Kaplan, *Mr. Clemens and Mark Twain* (New York: Simon & Schuster, 1966), 300.

34. Betsy Bowden, "Gloom and Doom in Mark Twain's *Connecticut Yankee,* from Thomas Malory's *Morte Darthur,*" *Studies in American Fiction* 28 (2000): 179–202, at 193.

35. Justin Kaplan, introduction to Mark Twain's *A Connecticut Yankee in King Arthur's Court* (1889; London: Penguin, 1971), 9–23, at 18.

36. Bruce Michelson, "Mark Twain, 'Foreigners,' and the American Self," *The Insular Dream: Obsession and Resistance,* ed. Kristiaan Versluys (Amsterdam: VU University Press, 1995), 86–98, at 90.

37. William Dean Howells, *My Mark Twain: Reminiscences and Criticisms* (New York: Harper, 1910), 145.

38. Mark Twain, *Personal Recollections of Joan of Arc* (1896; New York: Oxford University Press, 1996), xxxiii.

3. MEDIEVAL MASCULINITY, SOUTHERN CHIVALRY, AND REDEMPTIVE HOMOSEXUALITY IN FLANNER O'CONNOR'S FICTION

1. The range of narratives selected from O'Connor's corpus for analysis in this chapter may strike some readers as somewhat haphazard, but within her oeuvre, these stories most insistently place men within a historically modulated milieu. Many of O'Connor's other narratives, such as "The Barber," "Parker's Back," and *Wise Blood,* focus on male protagonists,

but these men are not as frozen in history as the protagonists of the narratives examined in this chapter.

2. In regard to O'Connor's treatment of race, Nicholas Crawford argues that "American Africanism . . . serves as a locus for the protagonists' unresolved personal associations with home and heritage," an observation that harmonizes with this chapter's assessment of the historical ramifications of sexuality on O'Connor's characters. "An Africanist Impasse: Race, Return, and Revelation in the Short Fiction of Flannery O'Connor," *South Atlantic Review* 68.2 (2003): 1–25, at 1. See also Beauty Bragg, "Intersections: Race and Gender Ideologies, Flannery O'Connor and Alice Walker," *Flannery O'Connor Review* 6 (2008): 56–58.

3. D. H. Lawrence, *Lady Chatterley's Lover* (1928; New York: Modern Library, 1959), 343.

4. Jack Lait and Lee Mortimer, *U.S.A. Confidential* (New York: Crown, 1952), 45; qtd. in Leo Braudy, *From Chivalry to Terrorism: War and the Changing Nature of Masculinity* (New York: Knopf, 2003), 506.

5. Arthur Schlesinger, "The Crisis of American Masculinity (1958)," *The Politics of Hope* (Boston: Houghton Mifflin, 1962), 237–46, at 237, 241.

6. Lynne Segal, "Looking Back in Anger: Men in the Fifties," *Male Order: Unwrapping Masculinity*, ed. R. Chapman and J. Rutherford (London: Lawrence & Wishart, 1988), 68–96, at 69.

7. James Gilbert, *Men in the Middle: Searching for Masculinity in the 1950s* (Chicago: University of Chicago Press, 2005), 65.

8. Flannery O'Connor, *Mystery and Manners*, ed. Sally Fitzgerald and Robert Fitzgerald (New York: Farrar, Straus & Giroux, 1969).

9. Flannery O'Connor, *The Habit of Being: Letters*, ed. Sally Fitzgerald (New York: Farrar, Straus & Giroux, 1979).

10. Frank Lawrence Owsley, "The Irrepressible Conflict," *I'll Take My Stand*, by Twelve Southerners, ed. Susan Donaldson (1930; Baton Rouge: Louisiana State University Press, 2006), 61–91, at 69–70.

11. Allen Tate, *The Man of Letters in the Modern World* (London: Thames, 1955), 312.

12. John Desmond, *Risen Sons: Flannery O'Connor's Vision of History* (Athens: University of Georgia Press, 1987), 104.

13. Anthony di Renzo, *American Gargoyles: Flannery O'Connor and the Medieval Grotesque* (Carbondale: Southern Illinois University Press, 1993), 167.

14. Mikhail Bakhtin, *Rabelais and His World*, trans. Hélène Iswolsky (Bloomington: Indiana University Press, 1984), 256.

15. Richard H. Wilmer, *In Memoriam: A Sermon in Commemoration of the Life and Labors of the Rt. Rev. Stephen Elliott, D.D., Late Bishop of Georgia* (Mobile, AL: Farrow & Dennett, 1867), 17. Wilmer was the bishop of Alabama.

16. Quotations from O'Connor's short stories are taken from Flannery O'Connor, *The Complete Stories of Flannery O'Connor* (1971; New York: Farrar, Straus & Giroux, 1988).

17. Jason Goldman, "Subjects of the Visual Arts: St. Sebastian," *Queer Encyclopedia of the Visual Arts*, ed. Claude Summers (San Francisco: Cleis, 2004), 321–22, at 321.

18. Flannery O'Connor, *Wise Blood* (1949; New York: Farrar, Straus & Giroux, 2007), unnumbered page, entitled "Author's Note to the Second Edition." In terms of O'Connor's play with medievalism beyond the influence of saints, Scott Daniel sees the influence of

medieval mystics such as Meister Eckhart (1260–1328): "O'Connor's gender-bending mysticism works in the manner of a dirty joke. O'Connor's subversive sexual rhetoric provides her with an avenue in which to explore the liberating Christology mystically available to the soul." "Gender-Bending Innuendo and Mystical Theology in O'Connor's *Wise Blood*," *Flannery O'Connor Review* 4 (2006): 110–21, at 112. In regard to *Wise Blood*, O'Connor notes Hazel Motes's mystical nature: "All H. Motes had to sacrifice was his sight but then . . . he was a mystic and he did it" (*HB* 116).

19. John Delaney, *Dictionary of Saints* (New York: Doubleday, 1980), 65. For the story of Antony of Egypt, see Robert Meyer, *St. Athanasius: The Life of St. Antony* (New York: Newman, 1978).

20. Meyer 23.

21. Jeremy Tambling, *Allegory and the Work of Melancholy* (New York: Rodopi, 2004), 186.

22. The shared thematic deployment of New York City in "The Geranium" and "Judgement Day" also reflects the connection between the two stories, in that the latter is a revision of the former that O'Connor completed not long before her death.

23. I do not address "The Barber" in this chapter, but it bears potential for a queer reading. Rayber imagines that his response to the barber's allegation would be: "I am neither a Negro- nor a white-lover" (15). This story focuses on political affiliations and disenfranchisement within a predominantly white male community, yet O'Connor hints that Rayber feels an attraction to the barber's employee George: "Rayber wondered what George's leanings were. He was a trim-looking boy" (16). "Leanings" refers primarily to George's political beliefs, but the latent homoeroticism in this scene surfaces with the appreciative appraisal of George's physique. Certainly, Rayber is alienated from his wife, which indicates that his marriage does not fulfill his needs for emotional or sexual connection: "He didn't know but what she was for Hawkson herself" (22).

24. O'Connor's historical models for General Sash and the Atlanta premiere of *Gone with the Wind* are addressed by Elizabeth Evans, "A Note on 'A Late Encounter with the Enemy,'" *Flannery O'Connor Bulletin* 26–27 (1998–2000): 136–38.

25. Katherine Prown, *Revising Flannery O'Connor: Southern Literary Culture and the Problem of Female Authorship* (Charlottesville: University Press of Virginia, 2001), 76.

26. Ted Spivey, *Flannery O'Connor: The Woman, the Thinker, the Visionary* (Macon, GA: Mercer University Press, 1995), 31.

27. J. O. Tate, "The Essential Essex," *Flannery O'Connor Bulletin* 12 (1983): 47–49, at 49.

28. Thomas of Aquinas, *Summa Theologica*, trans. Fathers of the English Dominican Province (1912–36; Westminster, MD: Christian Classics, 1981), second part of the second part, question 154, articles 1, 12; quotation from article 1. The primary study of O'Connor as a Thomist is Marion Montgomery, *Hillbilly Thomist: Flannery O'Connor, St. Thomas, and the Limits of Art* (Jefferson, NC: McFarland, 2006).

29. Christopher Craft, "Alias Bunbury: Desire and Termination in *The Importance of Being Earnest*," *Representations* 31 (1990): 19–46, at 28. Joel Fineman likewise posits that the name "was not only British slang for a male brothel, but is also a collection of signifiers that straightforwardly express their desire to bury in the bun." "The Significance of Literature: *The Importance of Being Earnest*," *October* 15 (1980): 79–90, at 89.

30. The music and lyrics of "Hallelujah, I'm a Bum" are recorded in Olin Downes and Elie Siegmeister, eds., *A Treasury of American Song*, 2nd ed. (New York: Knopf, 1943), 386–87; the title also refers to a 1933 film starring Al Jolson.

31. John Duvall, *Race and White Identity in Southern Fiction* (New York: Palgrave Macmillan, 2008), 64.

32. Robert Donahoo, "Tarwater's March toward the Feminine: The Role of Gender in O'Connor's *The Violent Bear It Away*," *CEA Critic* 56.1 (1993): 96–106, at 97.

33. The *Oxford English Dictionary* defines "buggery" as "unnatural intercourse of a human being with a beast, or of men with one another, sodomy" and dates this usage to the fourteenth century.

34. Cole Porter, *The Complete Lyrics of Cole Porter*, ed. Robert Kimball (New York: Da Capo, 1992), 114.

4. "IT'S PROLLY FULLA DIRTY STORIES": QUEER MASCULINITY AND MASTURBATORY ALLEGORY IN JOHN KENNEDY TOOLE'S *A CONFEDERACY OF DUNCES*

1. John Kennedy Toole, *A Confederacy of Dunces*, foreword by Walker Percy (Baton Rouge: Louisiana State University Press, 1980; reprint, New York: Wings Books, 1996; published by arrangement with LSU Press). It should be noted that although Toole's book was published in 1980, it was written in the 1960s and thus reflects the cultural shifts of that period rather than of a later era.

2. Lee Edelman, *No Future: Queer Theory and the Death Drive* (Durham, NC: Duke University Press, 2004), 6–7.

3. John Kennedy Toole to Robert Gottleib, January 15, 1965, qtd. in *Ignatius Rising: The Life of John Kennedy Toole*, by René Pol Nevils and Deborah Hardy (Baton Rouge: Louisiana State University Press, 2001), 139.

4. After receiving his M.A., Toole was accepted as a Ph.D. student in Renaissance literature at the University of Washington. See Nevils and Hardy 52 and 63.

5. Wesley Britton, "Two Visions of Medievalism and Determinism: Mark Twain and John Kennedy Toole's *A Confederacy of Dunces*," *Southern Quarterly* 34.1 (1995): 17–23, at 17.

6. I take the term *pseudohomosexuality* from Barbara Ehrenreich and her analysis of 1950s U.S. masculinity, *The Hearts of Men: American Dreams and the Flight from Commitment* (Garden City, NY: Anchor, 1983). In positing the penumbral fear surrounding homosexuality in the mid-twentieth-century United States, *pseudohomosexuality* is a useful term for delineating the sociotemporal murkiness of sexual categories. It should be noted, however, that the word *pseudohomosexual* predates Ehrenreich's use of it considerably: Magnus Hirschfeld describes pseudohomosexuals, using his synonymous term *urianasters*, as situational homosexuals—such as "uranized soldiers of the French Foreign Legion"—who engage in homosexual acts despite preferring sex with women. *The Homosexuality of Men and Women*, trans. Michael Lombardi-Nash (1914; Amherst, New York: Prometheus, 2000), 40. As with many taxonomical issues, the term *pseudohomosexual* is not without its limitations as well, since

the prefix *pseudo* denotes that the (homo)sexuality in question is somehow a false one. The "truth" or "falsity" of a given pseudohomosexual's sexuality is thus always in question, yet the term elucidates more than obscures the hazy significations of midcentury sexualities.

7. Norman Mailer, "The Homosexual Villain," *Sexual Revolution*, ed. Jeffery Escoffier (New York: Thunder's Mouth, 2003), 477–85, at 483; qtd. in Ehrenreich 129.

8. Ehrenreich 14–15.

9. Gerald Clarke, *Capote: A Biography* (1988; New York: Carroll & Graf, 2005), 62–63.

10. James Keller, "Tennessee Williams Doesn't Live Here Anymore: Hypocrisy, Paradox, and Homosexual Panic in the New/Old South," *Out in the South*, ed. Carlos Dews and Carolyn Law (Philadelphia: Temple University Press, 2001), 144–56, at 155.

11. Florence King, *Southern Ladies and Gentlemen* (New York: St. Martin's, 1975), 141–54, at 154.

12. Dalt Wonk, "John Kennedy Toole's Odyssey among the Dunces," *New Orleans Times-Picayune*, October 25, 1981, Dixie 7+, at 15 and 17.

13. For details of this case, see Jonathan Katz, ed., *Gay American History* (New York: Crowell, 1976), 127–28.

14. John Howard, *Men like That: A Southern Queer History* (Chicago: University of Chicago Press, 1999), 117.

15. Keith Miller, "The Conservative Vision of John Kennedy Toole," *Conference of College Teachers of English Proceedings* 48 (1983): 30–34; William Nelson, "The Comic Grotesque in Recent Fiction," *Thalia: Studies in Literary Humor* 5.2 (1982–83): 36–40; David McNeil, "*A Confederacy of Dunces* as Reverse Satire: The American Subgenre," *Mississippi Quarterly* 38.1 (1984–85): 33–47, at 35; Elizabeth Bell, "The Clash of World Views in John Kennedy Toole's *A Confederacy of Dunces*," *Southern Literary Journal* 21.1–2 (1988): 15–22; Robert Regan, "The Return of *The Moviegoer*: Toole's *A Confederacy of Dunces*," *Delta* 13 (1981): 169–76; Pat Gardner, "Midst Great Laughter," *Southern Quarterly* 34.2 (1996): 78–90, at 87; and Hugh Ruppersburg, "The South and John Kennedy Toole's *A Confederacy of Dunces*," *Studies in American Humor* 5.2–3 (1986): 118–26, at 125.

16. Carmine Palumbo, "John Kennedy Toole and His *Confederacy of Dunces*," *Louisiana Folklore Miscellany* 10 (1995): 59–77, at 62. See also Nevils and Hardy 55–56. Dalt Wonk describes Byrne as "a portly medievalist who wore a 'sensible' rain hat with ear flaps, played the lute and criticized erroneous opinions for a lack of 'geometry and theology.'" "Odyssey among the Dunces" 17.

17. Toole partially models the relationship between Ignatius and Mrs. Reilly on his relationship with his mother. See Nevils and Hardy 147–58. Joel Fletcher, *Ken and Thelma: The Story of "A Confederacy of Dunces"* (Gretna, LA: Pelican, 2005), primarily recounts Thelma Toole's efforts to publish her son's book after his suicide but also includes biographical details of Toole's life (13–40).

18. Gordon Teskey, *Allegory and Violence* (Ithaca, NY: Cornell University Press, 1996), 2; Angus Fletcher, *Allegory* (Ithaca, NY: Cornell University Press, 1964), 69.

19. For studies of Ignatius's limited understanding of Boethian thought, see Noel Kaylor, "Fortune's Wheel, *The Consolation of Philosophy*, Boethius, and Recent American and British Fiction," *Carmina Philosophiae* 10 (2001): 73–81; and Britton.

20. Mary Purcell, *The First Jesuit: St. Ignatius Loyola* (Chicago: Loyola University Press, 1981), 260–62.

21. Walker Percy, foreword to Toole viii.

22. For the pedagogical valence of medieval tragedies, see Henry Kelly, "The Lessons of Tragedy," *Chaucerian Tragedy* (Cambridge, UK: D. S. Brewer, 1997), 65–79.

23. Larry Scanlon, *Narrative, Authority, and Power: The Medieval Exemplum and the Chaucerian Tradition* (Cambridge: Cambridge University Press, 1994), 243.

24. Richard Patteson and Thomas Sauret, "The Consolation of Illusion: John Kennedy Toole's *A Confederacy of Dunces*," *Texas Review* 4.1–2 (1983): 77–87, at 80. Lloyd Daigrepont likewise observes, "Two final effects of the dunces' defining themselves in economic terms are the degradation of religion and escapism." "Ignatius Reilly and *A Confederacy of Dunces*," *New Orleans Review* 9.3 (1982): 74–80, at 79.

25. Ignatius's affection for Dante is also apparent in his envisioning of an allegorically and ironically appropriate punishment for Officer Mancuso, whom he views as his nemesis: "In my private apocalypse he will be impaled upon his own nightstick" (58).

26. William Clark, "All Toole's Children: A Reading of *A Confederacy of Dunces*," *Essays in Literature* 14.2 (1987): 269–80, at 276.

27. Jon Whitman, *Allegory: The Dynamics of an Ancient and Medieval Technique* (Cambridge: Harvard University Press, 1987), 2.

28. Carolynn Van Dyke, *The Fiction of Truth: Structures of Meaning in Narrative and Dramatic Allegory* (Ithaca, NY: Cornell University Press, 1985), 27; and Frederick Jameson, *The Political Unconscious: Narrative as a Socially Symbolic Act* (Ithaca, NY: Cornell University Press, 1982), 28–29.

29. See Steven Justice, *Writing and Rebellion: England in 1381* (Berkeley: University of California Press, 1994).

30. Dalt Wonk proposes that Myrna was modeled on the students of "a progressive girls' school in Manhattan with a student body that was predominately Jewish. These intense, liberated girls with their endless social causes intrigued [Toole]. 'Every time the elevator opens at Hunter,' [Toole] once said, 'you are confronted by 20 pairs of burning eyes, 20 sets of bangs, and everyone waiting for someone to push a Negro.'" "Odyssey among the Dunces" 17.

31. Madhavi Menon, *Wanton Words* (Toronto: University of Toronto Press, 2004), 129–30.

32. Hrotsvit is likely an obscure reference for a general reader of *A Confederacy of Dunces*, which underscores how Ignatius's medievalism alienates him from his family and community. For studies of Toole's deployment of Hrotsvit, see Katharina Wilson, "Hrotsvit and the Tube: John Kennedy Toole and the Problem of Bad TV Programming," *Germanic Notes* 15.1 (1984): 4–5; and Karl Zaenker, "Hrotsvit and the Moderns: Her Impact on John Kennedy Toole and Peter Hacks," *Hrotsvit of Gandersheim*, ed. Katharina Wilson (Ann Arbor, MI: Marc, 1987), 275–85.

33. One might argue that a range of bodily fluids other than semen could stain Ignatius's undergarments and bedsheets; however, the narrator never mentions any troubles that Ignatius might have with incontinence, and given the detailed attention paid to his autoerotic avocation, it is more likely that the stains result from discharges of semen.

34. This passage highlights Toole's skillful deployment of dialect to illuminate his various characters. Barbara Fennell and John Bennett argue that Toole uses dialects and speech communities to "characterize [Ignatius] as an outsider who flouts the regular conventions of discourse and sets himself up in a speech community of one." "Sociolinguistic Concepts and Literary Analysis," *American Speech* 66.4 (1991): 371–79, at 371.

35. Thomas Laqueur, *Solitary Sex: A Cultural History of Masturbation* (New York: Zone, 2003), 306.

36. Bell 20–21.

5. "I *AM* THE LOST CAUSE": QUEER HISTORY, THE SOUTHERN PHALLUS, AND THE QUEST FOR MEDIEVAL TIMELESSNESS IN ROBERT PENN WARREN'S *A PLACE TO COME TO*

1. Robert Penn Warren, *A Place to Come To* (New York: Random House, 1977).

2. Floyd Watkins and John Hiers, eds., *Robert Penn Warren Talking: Interviews, 1950–1978* (New York: Random House, 1980), 198. Warren's thoughts on the meaning of history are also presented in his famous essay "The Use of the Past," *New and Selected Essays: Robert Penn Warren* (New York: Random House, 1989), 29–53.

3. Robert Penn Warren, "Mark Twain," *Southern Review* 8.3 (1972): 459–92, at 459–60.

4. For Warren's early views of race, see "The Briar Patch," *I'll Take My Stand*, by Twelve Southerners, ed. Susan Donaldson (1930; Baton Rouge: Louisiana State University Press, 2006), 246–64, in which he presents discriminatory views against African Americans: "In the past the Southern negro has always been a creature of the small town and farm. That is where he still chiefly belongs, by temperament and capacity; there he has less the character of a 'problem' and more the status of a human being who is likely to find in agricultural and domestic pursuits the happiness that his good nature and easy ways incline him to as an ordinary function of his being" (260–61).

5. Robert Penn Warren, *The Legacy of the Civil War: Meditations on the Centennial* (New York: Random House, 1961), 54.

6. Robert Penn Warren, *Who Speaks for the Negro?* (New York: Random House, 1965), 428.

7. Christina Greene, "'We'll Take Our Stand': Race, Class, and Gender in the Southern Student Organizing Committee, 1964–1969," *Hidden Histories of Women in the New South*, ed. Virginia Bernhard et al. (Columbia: University of Missouri Press, 1994), 173–203, at 179–80.

8. Robert Penn Warren, *Jefferson Davis Gets His Citizenship Back* (Lexington: University Press of Kentucky, 1980), 94. Although *A Place to Come To* predates *Jefferson Davis Gets His Citizenship Back* by three years, the events described in *Jefferson Davis Gets His Citizenship Back* occurred contemporaneously with Warren's penning of *A Place to Come To.*

9. Warren, *Jefferson Davis* 112.

10. Warren, *Legacy of the Civil War* 82.

11. David Eng, "Introduction: What's Queer about Queer Studies Now?" *Social Text* 23.3–4 (2005): 1–17, at 1.

12. William Clark, ed., *Selected Letters of Robert Penn Warren*, vol. 2, *The "Southern Review" Years, 1935–1942* (Baton Rouge: Louisiana State University Press, 2001), 225, 227, and 229. For Dante's influence on Warren's fictions, see Joseph Millichap, "Robert Penn Warren's Divine Comedy," *Kentucky Philological Review* 8 (1992): 34–40; and Linda Westervetl, "Robert Penn Warren's *A Place to Come To:* An *Altersroman* Inspired by Dante," *Genre* 34 (2001): 101–24.

13. Lucy Ferriss, "Gynocritics and the Masculine Writer: Opportunities in Warren Criticism," *The Legacy of Robert Penn Warren*, ed. David Madden (Baton Rouge: Louisiana State University Press, 2000), 84–96, at 96.

14. Judith Butler, *Bodies That Matter: On the Discursive Limits of "Sex"* (New York: Routledge, 1993), 60; her italics.

15. Jerry Mills, "Equine Gothic: The Dead Mule as Generic Signifier in Southern Literature of the Twentieth Century," *Southern Literary Journal* 29 (1996): 2–17, at 4–5; his italics. Mills finds dead mules in many southern classics, including such masterworks as William Faulkner's *As I Lay Dying* (1930); Zora Neale Hurston's *Their Eyes Were Watching God* (1937); Truman Capote's *Other Voices, Other Rooms* (1948); and Cormac McCarthy's *Child of God* (1973).

16. Margaret Mitchell, *Gone with the Wind* (1936; New York: Warner, 1993), 458. As much as swords represent southern masculinity, it would be remiss not to mention that southern women are also depicted with swords and sword imagery. Also in *Gone with the Wind*, Melanie Wilkes appears with Charles's saber to help Scarlett kill an invading Yankee (434); in a similar vein, Scarlett thinks of Melanie as a sword protecting her from public contumely: "But now, with the memory of Melanie standing between her and social ruin, standing like a thin, shining blade, with trust and a fighting light in her eyes, there seemed nothing to do but confess" (935).

17. Diane Bonds, "Vision and Being in *A Place to Come To*," *Southern Review* 16 (1980): 816–28, at 816.

18. Randy Hendricks, *Lonelier than God: Robert Penn Warren and the Southern Exile* (Athens: University of Georgia Press, 2000), 167.

19. Watkins and Hiers 53.

20. Gary Engle, ed., *This Grotesque Essence: Plays from the American Minstrel Stage* (Baton Rouge: Louisiana State University Press, 1978), xxviii.

21. For a study of Rose Hardcastle, see Lucy Ferris, *Sleeping with the Boss: Female Subjectivity and Narrative Pattern in Robert Penn Warren* (Baton Rouge: Louisiana State University Press, 1997), 75–92.

22. For Warren's views of race, see Anthony Szczesiul, *Racial Politics and Robert Penn Warren's Poetry* (Gainesville: University Press of Florida, 2002).

23. Gloria Cronin and Ben Siegel, eds., *Conversations with Robert Penn Warren* (Jackson: University Press of Mississippi, 2005), 120.

24. As with much Arthurian literature, the Perceval legend has numerous incarnations, some that complement and others that contradict one another. My description of the legend follows Chrétien de Troyes's version.

25. The word *dauphin* refers to the eldest son of the King of France and thus the presumed inheritor to the throne. A dauphine, as the wife of a dauphin, is therefore likely to assume the role of queen.

26. Warren, *Legacy of the Civil War* 99–100; italics in original.

27. Warren, "Use of the Past" 52–53.

28. Malcolm Magaw, "Pilgrimage to Ambivalence: A Reinterpretation of Robert Penn Warren's *A Place to Come To*," *Midwest Quarterly* 29 (1988): 469–86, at 486; italics in original.

6. "THE SIR WALTER DISEASE" AND QUEER QUESTS FOR MASCULINITY IN WALKER PERCY'S NOVELS

1. Quotations from Percy's novels are taken from the following editions: *The Moviegoer* (1960; New York: Vintage, 1998); *The Last Gentleman* (New York: Picador, 1966); *Love in the Ruins* (New York: Picador, 1970); *Lancelot* (New York: Picador, 1977); *The Second Coming* (New York: Picador, 1980); and *The Thanatos Syndrome* (New York: Picador, 1987).

2. Walker Percy, "Why Are You a Catholic?" *Signposts in a Strange Land*, ed. Patrick Samway (New York: Farrar, Straus & Giroux, 1991), 304–15, at 313.

3. Walker Percy, *Lost in the Cosmos: The Last Self-Help Book* (New York: Noonday, 1983), 189–90; italics in original.

4. Lewis Lawson and Victor Kramer, eds., *More Conversations with Walker Percy* (Jackson: University Press of Mississippi, 1993), 61.

5. Paul Blanshard, *Paul Blanshard on Vatican II* (Boston: Beacon, 1966), 33. See also John Miller, ed., *Vatican II: An Interfaith Appraisal* (Notre Dame, IN: University of Notre Dame Press, 1966), for an overview of contemporary reactions to Vatican II.

6. Lawson and Kramer 114–17.

7. Lawson and Kramer 115.

8. Percy, *Signposts in a Strange Land* 418.

9. John Bugge, "Arthurian Myth Devalued in Walker Percy's *Lancelot*," *Lancelot and Guinevere: A Casebook*, ed. Lori Walters (New York: Garland, 1996), 181–91, at 183.

10. The passage is taken from *Purgatorio*, canto 30, lines 136–39, in which Beatrice reveals her spiritual work on Dante's behalf. For an excellent edition and translation, see Dante Alighieri, *Purgatorio*, ed. and trans. Jean Hollander and Robert Hollander (New York: Doubleday, 2003).

11. Andreas Capellanus, *The Art of Courtly Love*, trans. John Jay Parry (New York: Columbia University Press, 1960), 122. It should be noted that Andreas's text has proved remarkably difficult for scholars to pin down to a particular ethos, since it appears in some passages to be sincere and in others ironic. Nonetheless, medieval romances typically—although by no means entirely—concentrate on the chaste nature of courtly love.

12. Maria Hebert, "Between Men: Homosocial Desire in Walker Percy's *Lancelot*," *Mississippi Quarterly* 56.1 (2002–3): 125–45, at 140. Hebert gives an insightful reading of the ways in which homosociality functions in the narrative.

13. Mark Winchell, *Reinventing the South: Versions of a Literary Region* (Columbia: University of Missouri Press, 2006), 176. Winchell's argument focuses on the homoerotic subtext of Tennessee Williams's *Cat on a Hot Tin Roof*, and a similar dynamic unfolds in Percy's *Lancelot*.

14. For an exemplary study of this dynamic in medieval literature, see Robert Mills, "'Whatever you do is a delight to me!': Masculinity, Masochism, and Queer Play in Representations of Male Martyrdom," *Exemplaria* 13 (2001): 1–37.

15. Donald Crowley and Sue Crowley, "Walker Percy's Grail," *King Arthur through the Ages II*, ed. Valerie Lagorio and Mildred Day (New York: Garland, 1990), 255–77, at 273; italics in original.

16. For an account of Saladin's accomplishments, see Hamilton Gibb, *The Life of Saladin: From the Works of Imad ad-Din and Baha' ad-Din* (Oxford: Clarendon, 1973).

17. Richard Barber, *The Holy Grail: Imagination and Belief* (Cambridge: Harvard University Press, 2004), 5. See also Emma Jung and Marie-Louise von Franz, *The Grail Legend*, trans. Andrea Dykes (London: Hodder & Stoughton, 1971).

18. Geoffrey Chaucer, *The Riverside Chaucer*, ed. Larry Benson, 3rd ed. (Boston: Houghton Mifflin, 1987), 23, line 1.

19. In terms of southern literature, "The Black Prince" is also the title story of Shirley Ann Grau's collection *The Black Prince and Other Stories* (1955; New York: Knopf, 1972), but in this instance, the eponymous prince represents the devil.

20. Lewis Lawson, *Following Percy: Essays on Walker Percy's Work* (Troy, NY: Whitston, 1988), 122.

21. David Harwell, ed., *Walker Percy Remembered: A Portrait in the Words of Those Who Knew Him* (Chapel Hill: University of North Carolina Press, 2006), 38.

22. William Alexander Percy, *Lanterns on the Levee: Recollections of a Planter's Son* (1941; Baton Rouge: Louisiana State University Press, 1996), 201.

23. Percy, *Lanterns on the Levee* 312.

24. In most of his uses of the word *queer*, Percy employs its nonsexual denotations, as in the title of his *The Message in the Bottle: How Queer Man Is, How Queer Language Is, and What One Has to Do with the Other* (1975; New York: Noonday, 1997). As Percy himself notes, however, language perpetually confuses its meanings: "Language is a living organism and, as such, is subject to certain organic ailments." "Why Are You a Catholic?" 306. Percy's use of *queer* captures this type of "organic ailment" endemic to language, in that its nonsexual denotations of "odd," "unusual," "eccentric," and "peculiar" at times collapse into subversive assessments of a man's masculinity and/or sexuality.

25. Kieran Quinlan, *Walker Percy: The Last Catholic Novelist* (Baton Rouge: Louisiana State University Press, 1996), 29.

26. For Fire Island's place in gay American history, see Esther Newton, *Cherry Grove, Fire Island: Sixty Years in America's First Gay and Lesbian Town* (Boston: Beacon, 1993).

27. Lawson and Kramer 30.

28. Tyler Bridges, *Bad Bet on the Bayou* (New York: Farrar, Straus & Giroux, 2001), 7–8. For Marigny's penchant for dueling as a manifestation of southern honor, see Liliane Crété,

Daily Life in Louisiana, 1815–1830, trans. Patrick Gregory (Baton Rouge: Louisiana State University Press, 1981), 101–3.

29. Homosexual sheriffs are a recurring theme in Percy's fiction. In *Lancelot,* Merlin details how the protagonist of his film catalyzes emotional growth in the local law enforcement: "He even gets to the sheriff . . . actually there's a strong hint here of Southern sheriff homosexuality, right?" (148).

30. John Delaney, *Dictionary of Saints* (New York: Doubleday, 1980), 523.

31. Lawson and Kramer 196–97.

32. For a detailed reading of Father Smith's confession, and for parallels between this scene and *Lancelot,* see William Allen, "Father Smith's Confession in *The Thanatos Syndrome,*" *Walker Percy: Novelist and Philosopher,* ed. Jan Gretlund and Karl-Heinz Westarp (Jackson: University Press of Mississippi, 1991), 189–98.

33. Montserrat Ginés, *The Southern Inheritors of Don Quixote* (Baton Rouge: Louisiana State University Press, 2000), 1. For Ginés's account of Percy's medievalism, see the chapter "Walker Percy and the Last Gentleman of Southern Literature," 147–67.

34. Mark Twain, *Life on the Mississippi* (1883; New York: Oxford University Press, 1996), 470.

35. William O'Brien, "Walker Percy's *Lancelot:* A Beatrician Visit to the Region of the Dead," *Southern Humanities Review* 15.2 (1981): 153–64, at 153. The most detailed study in this line of inquiry is Edward Dupuy, *Autobiography in Walker Percy: Repetition, Recovery, and Redemption* (Baton Rouge: Louisiana State University Press, 1996).

36. John Blair, "Southern Honor and Sexual Violence: The Case of Walter Percy's *Lancelot,*" *Southern Studies* 5 (1994): 83–94, at 93. Biographies of Percy include Jay Tolson, *Pilgrim in the Ruins: A Life of Walker Percy* (New York: Simon & Schuster, 1992); and Patrick Samway, *Walker Percy: A Life* (New York: Farrar, Straus & Giroux, 1997).

7. CONCLUSION: ELLEN GILCHRIST'S *THE ANNUNCIATION* AND THE QUEER FUTURE OF CHIVALRIC MASCULINITIES

1. Judith Butler, *The Psychic Life of Power* (Stanford, CA: Stanford University Press, 1997), 135.

2. Gilles Deleuze, *Masochism: Coldness and Cruelty* (New York: Zone, 1991), 63.

3. Ellen Gilchrist, *Falling through Space: The Journals of Ellen Gilchrist* (Boston: Little, Brown, 1987), 161.

4. Ellen Gilchrist, *In the Land of Dreamy Dreams* (Boston: Little Brown, 1981); and *The Courts of Love* (Boston: Little Brown, 1996). Among the short stories of *In the Land of Dreamy Dreams,* Nora Jane first appears in "The Famous Poll at Jody's Bar" (49–59).

5. Ellen Gilchrist, *The Annunciation* (Boston: Little Brown, 1983).

6. The reader later learns that Helene Renoir wrote her poems in 1733 (124). This date runs late for the Middle Ages, since most scholars date the Middle French period roughly between 1340 and 1610. Gilchrist's supple use of medieval themes demonstrates the fluidity

of the Middle Ages as a construct in southern narratives, in which historical accuracy is less important than narrative development.

7. Margaret Bauer, *The Fiction of Ellen Gilchrist* (Gainesville: University Press of Florida, 1999), 128.

8. In the description of Will's car accident, Gilchrist writes, "The car filled with light. It was all right. It was all perfectly all right. He even had time to regret the borrowed car" (351). These lines seem to indicate Will's final thoughts before his death, but in Gilchrist's story collection *Light Can Be Both Wave and Particle* (Boston: Little, Brown, 1989), she includes a four-page story entitled "Life on the Earth" (109–12) that continues from where *The Annunciation* concludes; there she reveals that Will survives the accident.

9. Robert Penn Warren, *The Legacy of the Civil War: Meditations on the Centennial* (New York: Random House, 1961), 56.

Bibliography

Alexander, Michael. *Medievalism: The Middle Ages in Modern England.* New Haven: Yale University Press, 2007.

Allen, William. "Father Smith's Confession in *The Thanatos Syndrome.*" *Walker Percy: Novelist and Philosopher.* Ed. Jan Gretlund and Karl-Heinz Westarp. Jackson: University Press of Mississippi, 1991. 189–98.

Althusser, Louis. "Ideology and Ideological State Apparatuses." *Lenin and Philosophy and Other Essays.* Trans. Ben Brewster. New York: Monthly Review, 1971. 85–126.

Andreas Capellanus. *The Art of Courtly Love.* Trans. John Jay Parry. New York: Columbia University Press, 1960.

Aronowitz, Stanley. "My Masculinity." *Constructing Masculinity.* Ed. Maurice Berger, Brian Wallis, and Simon Watson. New York: Routledge, 1995. 307–20.

Asals, Frederick. *Flannery O'Connor: The Imagination of Extremity.* Athens: University of Georgia Press, 1982.

Avirett, James. "Knights and Courtly Ladies: The Romantic Ultimate." Kane 182–85.

Bakhtin, Mikhail. *Rabelais and His World.* Trans. Hélène Iswolsky. Bloomington: Indiana University Press, 1984.

Barber, Richard. *The Holy Grail: Imagination and Belief.* Cambridge: Harvard University Press, 2004.

———. *The Knight and Chivalry.* Woodbridge, Suffolk: Boydell, 1995.

———. *The Reign of Chivalry.* Woodbridge, Suffolk: Boydell, 2005.

Barron, W. R. J. *English Medieval Romance.* New York: Longman, 1987.

Bauer, Margaret. *The Fiction of Ellen Gilchrist.* Gainesville: University Press of Florida, 1999.

Bell, Elizabeth. "The Clash of World Views in John Kennedy Toole's *A Confederacy of Dunces.*" *Southern Literary Journal* 21.1–2 (1988): 15–22.

Berger, Stefan, Heiko Feldner, and Kevin Passmore, eds. *Writing History: Theory and Practice.* London: Hodder Arnold, 2003.

Berry, Stephen, ed. *Princes of Cotton: Four Diaries of Young Men in the South, 1848–1860.* Athens: University of Georgia Press, 2007.

Bibler, Michael. *Cotton's Queer Relations: Same-Sex Intimacy and the Literature of the Southern Plantation, 1936–1968.* Charlottesville: University of Virginia Press, 2009.

Blair, John. "Southern Honor and Sexual Violence: The Case of Walter Percy's *Lancelot*." *Southern Studies* 5 (1994): 83–94.

Blanshard, Paul. *Paul Blanshard on Vatican II*. Boston: Beacon, 1966.

Blues, Thomas. *Mark Twain and the Community*. Lexington: University Press of Kentucky, 1970.

Bonds, Diane. "Vision and Being in *A Place to Come To*." *Southern Review* 16 (1980): 816–28.

Boswell, James. *Boswell's Life of Johnson: Together with Boswell's "Journal of a Tour to the Hebrides" and Johnson's "Diary of a Journey into North Wales."* Ed. George Birbeck Hill. 6 vols. Oxford: Clarendon, 1964.

Bowden, Betsy. "Gloom and Doom in Mark Twain's *Connecticut Yankee*, from Thomas Malory's *Morte Darthur*." *Studies in American Fiction* 28 (2000): 179–202.

Bragg, Beauty. "Intersections: Race and Gender Ideologies, Flannery O'Connor and Alice Walker." *Flannery O'Connor Review* 6 (2008): 56–58.

Brantley, Will. *Feminine Sense in Southern Memoir: Smith, Glasgow, Welty, Hellman, Porter, and Hurston*. Jackson: University Press of Mississippi, 1993.

Brattain, Michelle. *The Politics of Whiteness: Race, Workers, and Culture in the Modern South*. Princeton, NJ: Princeton University Press, 2001.

Braudy, Leo. *From Chivalry to Terrorism: War and the Changing Nature of Masculinity*. New York: Knopf, 2003.

Bravmann, Scott. *Queer Fictions of the Past: History, Culture, and Difference*. Cambridge: Cambridge University Press, 1997.

Bridges, Tyler. *Bad Bet on the Bayou*. New York: Farrar, Straus & Giroux, 2001.

Brinkmeyer, Robert. *Three Catholic Writers of the Modern South*. Jackson: University Press of Mississippi, 1985.

Britton, Wesley. "Two Visions of Medievalism and Determinism: Mark Twain and John Kennedy Toole's *A Confederacy of Dunces*." *Southern Quarterly* 34.1 (1995): 17–23.

Bugge, John. "Arthurian Myth Devalued in Walker Percy's *Lancelot*." *Lancelot and Guinevere: A Casebook*. Ed. Lori Walters. New York: Garland, 1996. 181–91.

Butler, Judith. *Bodies That Matter: On the Discursive Limits of "Sex."* New York: Routledge, 1993.

———. *Gender Trouble: Feminism and the Subversion of Identity*. New York: Routledge, 1990.

———. *The Psychic Life of Power*. Stanford, CA: Stanford University Press, 1997.

———. *Undoing Gender*. New York: Routledge, 2004.

Canby, Henry Seidel. *American Memoir*. Boston: Houghton Mifflin, 1947.

Carter, Julian. *The Heart of Whiteness: Normal Sexuality and Race in America, 1880–1940*. Durham, NC: Duke University Press, 2007.

Caruso, Teresa, ed. *"On the subject of the feminist business": Re-reading Flannery O'Connor.* New York: Peter Lang, 2004.

Casper, Leonard. *The Blood Marriage of Earth and Sky: Robert Penn Warren's Later Novels.* Baton Rouge: Louisiana State University Press, 1997.

Chaucer, Geoffrey. *The Riverside Chaucer.* Ed. Larry Benson. 3rd ed. Boston: Houghton Mifflin, 1987.

Chrétien de Troyes. *Arthurian Romances.* Ed. D. D. R. Owen. London: Everyman, 1993.

Clark, William. "All Toole's Children: A Reading of *A Confederacy of Dunces.*" *Essays in Literature* 14.2 (1987): 269–80.

———, ed. *Selected Letters of Robert Penn Warren.* Vol. 2, *The "Southern Review" Years, 1935–1942.* Baton Rouge: Louisiana State University Press, 2001.

Clarke, Gerald. *Capote: A Biography.* 1988. New York: Carroll & Graf, 2005.

Coles, Robert. *Flannery O'Connor's South.* Athens: University of Georgia Press, 1993.

Cox, James. *Mark Twain: The Fate of Humor.* Columbia: University of Missouri Press, 2002.

Craft, Christopher. "Alias Bunbury: Desire and Termination in *The Importance of Being Earnest.*" *Representations* 31 (1990): 19–46.

Crawford, Nicholas. "An Africanist Impasse: Race, Return, and Revelation in the Short Fiction of Flannery O'Connor." *South Atlantic Review* 68.2 (2003): 1–25.

Crété, Liliane. *Daily Life in Louisiana, 1815–1830.* Trans. Patrick Gregory. Baton Rouge: Louisiana State University Press, 1981.

Crocker, Holly. *Chaucer's Visions of Manhood.* New York: Palgrave Macmillan, 2007.

Cronin, Gloria, and Ben Siegel, eds. *Conversations with Robert Penn Warren.* Jackson: University Press of Mississippi, 2005.

Crowley, Donald, and Sue Crowley. "Walker Percy's Grail." *King Arthur through the Ages II.* Ed. Valerie Lagorio and Mildred Day. New York: Garland, 1990. 255–77.

Cullick, Jonathan. *Making History: The Biographical Narratives of Robert Penn Warren.* Baton Rouge: Louisiana State University Press, 2000.

Daigrepont, Lloyd. "Ignatius Reilly and *A Confederacy of Dunces.*" *New Orleans Review* 9.3 (1982): 74–80.

Daniel, Scott. "Gender-Bending Innuendo and Mystical Theology in O'Connor's *Wise Blood.*" *Flannery O'Connor Review* 4 (2006): 110–21.

Dante Alighieri. *Purgatorio.* Ed. and trans. Jean Hollander and Robert Hollander. New York: Doubleday, 2003.

Davenport, Garvin. *The Myth of Southern History: Historical Consciousness in Twentieth-Century Southern Literature.* Nashville: Vanderbilt University Press, 1967.

Delaney, John. *Dictionary of Saints.* New York: Doubleday, 1980.

Deleuze, Gilles. *Masochism: Coldness and Cruelty.* New York: Zone, 1991.

Dempsey, Terrell. *Searching for Jim: Slavery in Sam Clemens's World.* Columbia: University of Missouri Press, 2003.

Desmond, John. *Risen Sons: Flannery O'Connor's Vision of History.* Athens: University of Georgia Press, 1987.

DeVoto, Bernard. *Mark Twain's America.* Boston: Houghton Mifflin, 1967.

Dews, Carlos, and Carolyn Law, eds. *Out in the South.* Philadelphia: Temple University Press, 2001.

Dinshaw, Carolyn. "Chaucer's Queer Touches / A Queer Touches Chaucer." *Exemplaria* 7.1 (1995): 75–92.

Di Renzo, Anthony. *American Gargoyles: Flannery O'Connor and the Medieval Grotesque.* Carbondale: Southern Illinois University Press, 1993.

Dixon, Thomas, Jr. *The Clansman: An Historical Romance of the Ku Klux Klan.* 1905. Lexington: University Press of Kentucky, 1970.

Donahoo, Robert. "Tarwater's March toward the Feminine: The Role of Gender in O'Connor's *The Violent Bear It Away.*" *CEA Critic* 56.1 (1993): 96–106.

Donaldson, Susan, and Anne Goodwyn Jones. "Haunting Bodies: Rethinking the South through Gender." *Haunted Bodies: Gender and Southern Texts.* Ed. Susan Donaldson and Anne Goodwyn Jones. Charlottesville: University Press of Virginia, 1997. 1–19.

Downes, Olin, and Elie Siegmeister, eds. *A Treasury of American Song.* 2nd ed. New York: Knopf, 1943.

Duberman, Martin. *About Time: Exploring the Gay Past.* Rev. ed. New York: Meridian, 1991.

Dupuy, Edward. *Autobiography in Walker Percy: Repetition, Recovery, and Redemption.* Baton Rouge: Louisiana State University Press, 1996.

Duvall, John. *Race and White Identity in Southern Fiction.* New York: Palgrave Macmillan, 2008.

Eco, Umberto. *Travels in Hyperreality: Essays.* Trans. William Weaver. San Diego: Harcourt, 1983.

Edelman, Lee. *No Future: Queer Theory and the Death Drive.* Durham, NC: Duke University Press, 2004.

Ehrenreich, Barbara. *The Hearts of Men: American Dreams and the Flight from Commitment.* Garden City, NY: Anchor, 1983.

Emerson, Ralph Waldo. "Friendship." *The Essential Writings of Ralph Waldo Emerson.* Ed. Brooks Atkinson. 1841. New York: Modern Library, 2000. 201–14.

Eng, David. "Introduction: What's Queer about Queer Studies Now?" *Social Text* 23.3–4 (2005): 1–17.

Engle, Gary, ed. *This Grotesque Essence: Plays from the American Minstrel Stage.* Baton Rouge: Louisiana State University Press, 1978.

Evans, Elizabeth. "A Note on 'A Late Encounter with the Enemy.'" *Flannery O'Connor Bulletin* 26–27 (1998–2000): 136–38.

Faulkner, William. *Requiem for a Nun*. New York: Random House, 1950.

Fausto-Sterling, Anne. *Myths of Gender: Biological Theories about Women and Men*. New York: Basic, 1985.

Fennell, Barbara, and John Bennett. "Sociolinguistic Concepts and Literary Analysis." *American Speech* 66.4 (1991): 371–79.

Ferriss, Lucy. "Gynocritics and the Masculine Writer: Opportunities in Warren Criticism." *The Legacy of Robert Penn Warren*. Ed. David Madden. Baton Rouge: Louisiana State University Press, 2000. 84–96.

———. *Sleeping with the Boss: Female Subjectivity and Narrative Pattern in Robert Penn Warren*. Baton Rouge: Louisiana State University Press, 1997.

Fiedler, Leslie. "Come Back to the Raft Ag'in, Huck Honey." *Partisan Review* 15 (1948): 664–71.

Fineman, Joel. "The Significance of Literature: *The Importance of Being Earnest*." *October* 15 (1980): 79–90.

Fletcher, Angus. *Allegory*. Ithaca, NY: Cornell University Press, 1964.

Fletcher, Joel. *Ken and Thelma: The Story of "A Confederacy of Dunces."* Gretna, LA: Pelican, 2005.

Foucault, Michel. *The History of Sexuality*. Vol. 1, *An Introduction*. Trans. Robert Hurley. New York: Vintage, 1990.

Fraser, John. *America and the Patterns of Chivalry*. Cambridge: Cambridge University Press, 1982.

Freud, Sigmund. *Civilization and Its Discontents*. Trans. James Strachey. New York: Norton, 1961.

———. "On Narcissism: An Introduction." *The Standard Edition of the Complete Psychological Works of Sigmund Freud*. Trans. James Strachey. London: Hogarth, 1959. 14.67–102.

Friend, Craig, and Lorri Glover. "Rethinking Southern Masculinity." *Southern Manhood: Perspectives on Masculinity in the Old South*. Ed. Craig Friend and Lorri Glover. Athens: University of Georgia Press, 2004. vii–xvii.

Gallop, Jane. *The Daughter's Seduction: Feminism and Psychoanalysis*. Ithaca, NY: Cornell University Press, 1982.

Gardner, Pat. "Midst Great Laughter." *Southern Quarterly* 34.2 (1996): 78–90.

Genovese, Eugene. "The Southern Slaveholders' View of the Middle Ages." *Medievalism in American Culture*. Ed. Bernard Rosenthal and Paul Szarmach. Binghamton, NY: Medieval and Renaissance Texts and Studies, 1989. 31–52.

———. *The Southern Tradition*. Cambridge: Harvard University Press, 1994.

Gentry, Marshall. "Gender Dialogue in O'Connor." Rath and Shaw 57–72.

Gerster, Patrick, and Nicholas Cords, eds. *Myth and Southern History*. 2nd ed. Urbana: University of Illinois Press, 1989.

Gibb, Hamilton. *The Life of Saladin: From the Works of Imad ad-Din and Baha' ad-Din*. Oxford: Clarendon, 1973.

Gilbert, James. *Men in the Middle: Searching for Masculinity in the 1950s*. Chicago: University of Chicago Press, 2005.

Gilchrist, Ellen. *The Annunciation*. Boston: Little, Brown, 1983.

———. *The Courts of Love*. Boston: Little, Brown, 1996.

———. *Falling through Space: The Journals of Ellen Gilchrist*. Boston: Little, Brown, 1987.

———. *In the Land of Dreamy Dreams*. Boston: Little Brown, 1981.

———. *Light Can Be Both Wave and Particle*. Boston: Little, Brown, 1989.

Ginés, Montserrat. *The Southern Inheritors of Don Quixote*. Baton Rouge: Louisiana State University Press, 2000.

Girouard, Mark. *The Return to Camelot: Chivalry and the English Gentleman*. New Haven: Yale University Press, 1981.

Goldman, Jason. "Subjects of the Visual Arts: St. Sebastian." *Queer Encyclopedia of the Visual Arts*. Ed. Claude Summers. San Francisco: Cleis, 2004. 321–22.

Gone with the Wind. Dir. Victor Fleming. Perf. Vivien Leigh and Clark Gable. 1939. DVD. Burbank, CA: Warner, 1999.

Goodwin, Maud Wilder. *The Colonial Cavalier*. 1894. New York: Arno, 1975.

Grau, Shirley Ann. *The Black Prince and Other Stories*. 1955. New York: Knopf, 1972.

Greene, Christina. "'We'll Take Our Stand': Race, Class, and Gender in the Southern Student Organizing Committee, 1964–1969." *Hidden Histories of Women in the New South*. Ed. Virginia Bernhard, Betty Brandon, Elizabeth Fox-Genovese, Theda Perdue, and Elizabeth Hayes Turner. Columbia: University of Missouri Press, 1994. 173–203.

Gwin, Minrose. *The Woman in the Red Dress: Gender, Space, and Reading*. Urbana: University of Illinois Press, 2002.

Hale, Grace. *Making Whiteness: The Culture of Segregation in the South, 1890–1940*. New York: Pantheon, 1998.

Harwell, David, ed. *Walker Percy Remembered: A Portrait in the Words of Those Who Knew Him*. Chapel Hill: University of North Carolina Press, 2006.

Hebert, Maria. "Between Men: Homosocial Desire in Walker Percy's *Lancelot*." *Mississippi Quarterly* 56.1 (2002–3): 125–45.

Hendricks, Randy. *Lonelier than God: Robert Penn Warren and the Southern Exile*. Athens: University of Georgia Press, 2000.

Hentz, Caroline Lee. *The Planter's Northern Bride*. 1854. Irvine, CA: Reprint Services, 1992.

Hirschfeld, Magnus. *The Homosexuality of Men and Women.* Trans. Michael Lombardi-Nash. 1914. Amherst, NY: Prometheus, 2000.

Hoffman, Andrew. "Mark Twain and Homosexuality." *American Literature* 67.1 (1995): 23–49.

Howard, John, ed. *Carryin' on in the Lesbian and Gay South.* New York: New York University Press, 1997.

———. *Men like That: A Southern Queer History.* Chicago: University of Chicago Press, 1999.

Howells, William Dean. *My Mark Twain: Reminiscences and Criticisms.* New York: Harper, 1910.

Huhndorf, Shari. *Going Native: Indians in the American Cultural Imagination.* Ithaca, NY: Cornell University Press, 2001.

Jameson, Frederick. "Marxism and Historicism." *New Literary History* 11 (1979): 41–73.

———. *The Political Unconscious: Narrative as a Socially Symbolic Act.* Ithaca, NY: Cornell University Press, 1982.

Jenkins, McKay. *The South in Black and White: Race, Sex, and Literature in the 1940s.* Chapel Hill: University of North Carolina Press, 1999.

Jones, Paul. *Unwelcome Voices: Subversive Fiction in the Antebellum South.* Knoxville: University of Tennessee Press, 2005.

Jung, Emma, and Marie-Louise von Franz. *The Grail Legend.* Trans. Andrea Dykes. London: Hodder & Stoughton, 1971.

Justice, Steven. *Writing and Rebellion: England in 1381.* Berkeley: University of California Press, 1994.

Kane, Harnett, ed. *The Romantic South.* New York: Coward-McCann, 1961.

Kaplan, Fred. *The Singular Mark Twain.* New York: Doubleday, 2003.

Kaplan, Justin. Introduction. *A Connecticut Yankee in King Arthur's Court.* By Mark Twain. 1889. London: Penguin, 1971. 9–23.

———. *Mr. Clemens and Mark Twain.* New York: Simon & Schuster, 1966.

Katz, Jonathan, ed. *Gay American History.* New York: Crowell, 1976.

———. *Love Stories: Sex between Men before Homosexuality.* Chicago: University of Chicago Press, 2001.

Kaylor, Noel. "Fortune's Wheel, *The Consolation of Philosophy,* Boethius, and Recent American and British Fiction." *Carmina Philosophiae* 10 (2001): 73–81.

Keen, Maurice. *Chivalry.* New Haven: Yale University Press, 1984.

Keller, James. "Tennessee Williams Doesn't Live Here Anymore: Hypocrisy, Paradox, and Homosexual Panic in the New/Old South." Dews and Law 144–56.

Kelly, Henry. *Chaucerian Tragedy.* Cambridge, UK: D. S. Brewer, 1997.

Kerrison, Catherine. *Claiming the Pen: Women and Intellectual Life in the Early American South.* Ithaca, NY: Cornell University Press, 2006.

King, Florence. *He: An Irreverent Look at the American Male*. New York: Stein & Day, 1978.

———. *Southern Ladies and Gentlemen*. New York: St. Martin's, 1975.

Kordecki, Lesley. "Twain's Critique of Malory's Romance: *Forma tractandi* and *A Connecticut Yankee*." *Nineteenth-Century Literature* 41 (1986): 329–48.

Kristeva, Julia. *Tales of Love*. Trans. Leon Roudiez. New York: Columbia University Press, 1987.

Krueger, Roberta, ed. *The Cambridge Companion to Medieval Romance*. Cambridge: Cambridge University Press, 2000.

Lacan, Jacques. *Feminine Sexuality: Jacques Lacan and the Ecole Freudienne*. Ed. Juliet Mitchell and Jacqueline Rose. New York: Norton, 1982.

Ladd, Barbara. *Resisting History: Gender, Modernity, and Authorship in William Faulkner, Zora Neale Hurston, and Eudora Welty*. Baton Rouge: Louisiana State University Press, 2007.

Lait, Jack, and Lee Mortimer. *U.S.A. Confidential*. New York: Crown, 1952.

Laqueur, Thomas. *Solitary Sex: A Cultural History of Masturbation*. New York: Zone, 2003.

Lawrence, D. H. *Lady Chatterley's Lover*. 1928. New York: Modern Library, 1959.

Lawson, Lewis. *Following Percy: Essays on Walker Percy's Work*. Troy, NY: Whitston, 1988.

Lawson, Lewis, and Victor Kramer, eds. *More Conversations with Walker Percy*. Jackson: University Press of Mississippi, 1993.

Lawson, Lewis, and Elzbieta Oleksy. *Walker Percy's Feminine Characters*. Troy, NY: Whitston, 1995.

Lévi-Strauss, Claude. *The Raw and the Cooked*. Trans. John Weightman and Doreen Weightman. 1964. New York: Harper & Row, 1969.

Lewis, Henry Clay. *Odd Leaves from the Life of a Louisiana Swamp Doctor*. 1850. Baton Rouge: Louisiana State University Press, 1997.

Magaw, Malcolm. "Pilgrimage to Ambivalence: A Reinterpretation of Robert Penn Warren's *A Place to Come To*." *Midwest Quarterly* 29 (1988): 469–86.

Mailer, Norman. "The Homosexual Villain." *Sexual Revolution*. Ed. Jeffery Escoffier. New York: Thunder's Mouth, 2003. 477–85.

McNeil, David. "*A Confederacy of Dunces* as Reverse Satire: The American Subgenre." *Mississippi Quarterly* 38.1 (1984–85): 33–47.

McPherson, Tara. *Reconstructing Dixie: Race, Gender, and Nostalgia in the Imagined South*. Durham, NC: Duke University Press, 2003.

Menon, Madhavi. *Wanton Words*. Toronto: University of Toronto Press, 2004.

Meyer, Robert. *St. Athanasius: The Life of St. Antony*. New York: Newman, 1978.

Michelson, Bruce. "Mark Twain, 'Foreigners,' and the American Self." *The Insular Dream: Obsession and Resistance.* Ed. Kristiaan Versluys. Amsterdam: VU University Press, 1995. 86–98.

———. *Printer's Devil: Mark Twain and the American Publishing Revolution.* Berkeley: University of California Press, 2006.

———. "Realism, Romance, and Dynamite: The Quarrel of *A Connecticut Yankee in King Arthur's Court.*" *New England Quarterly* 64 (1991): 609–32.

Midgley, Mary. *The Myths We Live By.* London: Routledge, 2003.

Miller, John, ed. *Vatican II: An Interfaith Appraisal.* Notre Dame, IN: University of Notre Dame Press, 1966.

Miller, Keith. "The Conservative Vision of John Kennedy Toole." *Conference of College Teachers of English Proceedings* 48 (1983): 30–34.

Millichap, Joseph. "Robert Penn Warren's Divine Comedy." *Kentucky Philological Review* 8 (1992): 34–40.

Mills, Jerry. "Equine Gothic: The Dead Mule as Generic Signifier in Southern Literature of the Twentieth Century." *Southern Literary Journal* 29 (1996): 2–17.

Mills, Robert. "'Whatever you do is a delight to me!' Masculinity, Masochism, and Queer Play in Representations of Male Martyrdom." *Exemplaria* 13 (2001): 1–37.

Mitchell, Jerome. *Scott, Chaucer, and Medieval Romance.* Lexington: University Press of Kentucky, 1987.

Mitchell, Margaret. *Gone with the Wind.* 1936. New York: Warner, 1993.

Montgomery, Marion. *Hillbilly Thomist: Flannery O'Connor, St. Thomas, and the Limits of Art.* Jefferson, NC: McFarland, 2006.

Moreland, Kim. *The Medievalist Impulse in American Literature.* Charlottesville: University Press of Virginia, 1996.

Morris, Linda. *Gender Play in Mark Twain.* Columbia: University of Missouri Press, 2007.

Morrison, Toni. *Playing in the Dark: Whiteness and the Literary Imagination.* Cambridge: Harvard University Press, 1992.

Moss, Elizabeth. *Domestic Novelists in the Old South: Defenders of Southern Culture.* Baton Rouge: Louisiana State University Press, 1992.

Muller, Gilbert. *Nightmares and Visions: Flannery O'Connor and the Catholic Grotesque.* Athens: University of Georgia Press, 1972.

Nelson, William. "The Comic Grotesque in Recent Fiction." *Thalia: Studies in Literary Humor* 5.2 (1982–83): 36–40.

Nevils, René Pol, and Deborah Hardy. *Ignatius Rising: The Life of John Kennedy Toole.* Baton Rouge: Louisiana State University Press, 2001.

Newton, Esther. *Cherry Grove, Fire Island: Sixty Years in America's First Gay and Lesbian Town.* Boston: Beacon, 1993.

Nissen, Axel. *The Romantic Friendship Reader: Love Stories between Men in Victorian America.* Boston: Northeastern University Press, 2003.

Nolan, Alan. "The Anatomy of the Myth." *The Myth of the Lost Cause and Civil War History.* Ed. Gary Gallagher and Alan Nolan. Bloomington: Indiana University Press, 2000. 11–34.

O'Brien, William. "Walker Percy's *Lancelot:* A Beatrician Visit to the Region of the Dead." *Southern Humanities Review* 15.2 (1981): 153–64.

O'Connor, Flannery. *The Complete Stories of Flannery O'Connor.* 1971. New York: Farrar, Straus & Giroux, 1988.

———. *The Habit of Being: Letters.* Ed. Sally Fitzgerald. New York: Farrar, Straus & Giroux, 1979.

———. *Mystery and Manners.* Ed. Sally Fitzgerald and Robert Fitzgerald. New York: Farrar, Straus & Giroux, 1969.

———. *Wise Blood.* 1949. New York: Farrar, Straus & Giroux, 2007.

O'Gorman, Farrell. *Peculiar Crossroads: Flannery O'Connor, Walker Percy, and Catholic Vision in Postwar Southern Fiction.* Baton Rouge: Louisiana State University Press, 2004.

Oliver, Nancy. "New Manifest Destiny in *A Connecticut Yankee in King Arthur's Court.*" *Mark Twain Journal* 21 (1983): 28–32.

Osterweis, Rollin. *Romanticism and Nationalism in the Old South.* New Haven: Yale University Press, 1949.

Oulton, Carolyn. *Romantic Friendship in Victorian Literature.* Aldershot, Eng.: Ashgate, 2007.

Owsley, Frank Lawrence. "The Irrepressible Conflict." Twelve Southerners 61–91.

Packard, Chris. *Queer Cowboys and Other Erotic Male Friendships in Nineteenth-Century American Literature.* New York: Palgrave Macmillan, 2005.

Palumbo, Carmine. "John Kennedy Toole and His *Confederacy of Dunces.*" *Louisiana Folklore Miscellany* 10 (1995): 59–77.

Patteson, Richard, and Thomas Sauret. "The Consolation of Illusion: John Kennedy Toole's *A Confederacy of Dunces.*" *Texas Review* 4.1–2 (1983): 77–87.

Pearsall, Derek. *Arthurian Romance: A Short Introduction.* Oxford: Blackwell, 2003.

Percy, Walker. Foreword. Toole vii–ix.

———. *Lancelot.* New York: Picador, 1977.

———. *The Last Gentleman.* New York: Picador, 1966.

———. *Lost in the Cosmos: The Last Self-Help Book.* New York: Noonday, 1983.

———. *Love in the Ruins.* New York: Picador, 1970.

———. *The Message in the Bottle: How Queer Man Is, How Queer Language Is, and What One Has to Do with the Other.* 1975. New York: Noonday, 1997.

———. *The Moviegoer.* 1960. New York: Vintage, 1998.

———. *The Second Coming.* New York: Picador, 1980.

———. *Signposts in a Strange Land.* Ed. Patrick Samway. New York: Farrar, Straus & Giroux, 1991.

———. *The Thanatos Syndrome.* New York: Picador, 1987.

———. "Why Are You a Catholic?" Percy, *Signposts in a Strange Land* 304–15.

Percy, William Alexander. *Lanterns on the Levee: Recollections of a Planter's Son.* 1941. Baton Rouge: Louisiana State University Press, 1996.

Porter, Cole. *The Complete Lyrics of Cole Porter.* Ed. Robert Kimball. New York: Da Capo, 1992.

Powers, Ron. *Mark Twain: A Life.* New York: Free Press, 2005.

Pressman, Richard. "A Connecticut Yankee in Merlin's Cave: The Role of Contradiction in Mark Twain's Novel." *American Literary Realism* 16 (1983): 58–72.

Prown, Katherine. *Revising Flannery O'Connor: Southern Literary Culture and the Problem of Female Authorship.* Charlottesville: University Press of Virginia, 2001.

Purcell, Mary. *The First Jesuit: St. Ignatius Loyola.* Chicago: Loyola University Press, 1981.

Quinlan, Kieran. *Walker Percy: The Last Catholic Novelist.* Baton Rouge: Louisiana State University Press, 1996.

Rath, Sura, and Mary Shaw, eds. *Flannery O'Connor: New Perspectives.* Athens: University of Georgia Press, 1996.

Regan, Robert. "The Return of *The Moviegoer:* Toole's *A Confederacy of Dunces.*" *Delta* 13 (1981): 169–76.

Reiss, Edmund. Afterword. *A Connecticut Yankee in King Arthur's Court.* By Mark Twain. New York: Signet, 1963. 321–31.

Richards, Gary. *Lovers and Beloveds: Sexual Otherness in Southern Fiction, 1936–1961.* Baton Rouge: Louisiana State University Press, 2005.

Robinson, Sally. *Marked Men: White Masculinity in Crisis.* New York: Columbia University Press, 2000.

Rotundo, Anthony. "Romantic Friendship: Male Intimacy and Middle-Class Youth in the Northern United States, 1800–1900." *Journal of Social History* 23 (1989): 1–25.

Runyon, Randolph. *Ghostly Parallels: Robert Penn Warren and the Lyric Poetic Sequence.* Knoxville: University of Tennessee Press, 2006.

Rupp, Leila. *A Desired Past: A Short History of Same-Sex Love in America.* Chicago: University of Chicago Press, 1999.

Ruppersburg, Hugh. "The South and John Kennedy Toole's *A Confederacy of Dunces*." *Studies in American Humor* 5.2–3 (1986): 118–26.

Salomon, Roger. *Twain and the Image of History*. New Haven: Yale University Press, 1961.

Samway, Patrick. *Walker Percy: A Life*. New York: Farrar, Straus & Giroux, 1997.

Scanlon, Larry. *Narrative, Authority, and Power: The Medieval Exemplum and the Chaucerian Tradition*. Cambridge: Cambridge University Press, 1994.

Schlesinger, Arthur. "The Crisis of American Masculinity (1958)." *The Politics of Hope*. Boston: Houghton Mifflin, 1962. 237–46.

Sedgwick, Eve. *Tendencies*. Durham, NC: Duke University Press, 1993.

Segal, Lynne. "Looking Back in Anger: Men in the Fifties." *Male Order: Unwrapping Masculinity*. Ed. R. Chapman and J. Rutherford. London: Lawrence & Wishart, 1988. 68–96.

Shanley, Mary, and Peter Stillman. "Mark Twain: Technology, Social Change, and Political Power." *The Artist and Political Vision*. Ed. Benjamin Barber and Michael McGrath. New Brunswick, NJ: Transactions, 1982. 267–89.

Silverman, Kaja. *Male Subjectivity on the Margins*. New York: Routledge, 1992.

Simms, William Gilmore. *Southward Ho! A Spell of Sunshine*. 1885. New York: AMS Press, 1970.

Smith, Henry. *Mark Twain's Fable of Progress*. New Brunswick, NJ: Rutgers University Press, 1964.

Spivey, Ted. *Flannery O'Connor: The Woman, the Thinker, the Visionary*. Macon, GA: Mercer University Press, 1995.

Srigley, Susan. *Flannery O'Connor's Sacramental Art*. Notre Dame, IN: University of Notre Dame Press, 2004.

Stokes, Mason. *The Color of Sex: Whiteness, Heterosexuality, and the Fictions of White Supremacy*. Durham, NC: Duke University Press, 2001.

Stoneley, Peter. *Mark Twain and the Feminine Aesthetic*. Cambridge: Cambridge University Press, 1992.

Stowe, Harriet Beecher. *Uncle Tom's Cabin*. 1852. New York: Modern Library, 1996.

Szczesiul, Anthony. *Racial Politics and Robert Penn Warren's Poetry*. Gainesville: University Press of Florida, 2002.

Tambling, Jeremy. *Allegory and the Work of Melancholy*. New York: Rodopi, 2004.

Tate, Allen. *The Man of Letters in the Modern World*. London: Thames, 1955.

Tate, J. O. "The Essential Essex." *Flannery O'Connor Bulletin* 12 (1983): 47–49.

Teskey, Gordon. *Allegory and Violence*. Ithaca, NY: Cornell University Press, 1996.

Thomas, Calvin. *Male Matters: Masculinity, Anxiety, and the Male Body on the Line*. Urbana: University of Illinois Press, 1996.

Thomas of Aquinas. *Summa Theologica*. Trans. Fathers of the English Dominican Province. 1912–36. Westminster, MD: Christian Classics, 1981.

Tindall, George. *Natives and Newcomers: Ethnic Southerners and Southern Ethnics.* Athens: University of Georgia Press, 1995.

Tolson, Jay. *Pilgrim in the Ruins: A Life of Walker Percy.* New York: Simon & Schuster, 1992.

Toole, John Kennedy. *A Confederacy of Dunces.* Foreword by Walker Percy. Baton Rouge: Louisiana State University Press, 1980. Reprint, New York: Wings Books, 1996.

Tracy, Susan. *In the Master's Eye: Representations of Women, Blacks, and Poor Whites in Antebellum Southern Literature.* Amherst: University of Massachusetts Press, 1995.

Twain, Mark. *A Connecticut Yankee in King Arthur's Court.* 1889. New York: Oxford University Press, 1996.

———. *How Nancy Jackson Married Kate Wilson and Other Tales of Rebellious Girls and Daring Women.* Ed. John Cooley. Lincoln: University of Nebraska Press, 2001.

———. *The Innocents Abroad.* 1869. New York: Oxford University Press, 1996.

———. *Life on the Mississippi.* 1883. New York: Oxford University Press, 1996.

———. *Mark Twain's Letters.* Ed. Albert Paine. 2 vols. New York: Harper, 1917.

———. *Mark Twain's Letters.* Vol. 1, *1853–1866.* Ed. Edgar Branch, Michael Frank, and Kenneth Sanderson. Berkeley: University of California Press, 1987.

———. *Mark Twain's Letters.* Vol. 3, *1869.* Ed. Victor Fischer and Michael Frank. Berkeley: University of California Press, 1992.

———. *Mark Twain's Letters.* Vol. 4, *1870–1871.* Ed. Victor Fischer and Michael Frank. Berkeley: University of California Press, 1995.

———. *Mark Twain's Letters.* Vol. 5, *1872–1873.* Ed. Lin Salamo and Harriet Smith. Berkeley: University of California Press, 1997.

———. *Mark Twain's Notebooks and Journals.* Vol. 3, *1883–1891.* Ed. Robert Pack Browning, Michael Frank, Lin Salamo, and Frederick Anderson. Berkeley: University of California Press, 1979.

———. "A Medieval Romance." *Sketches, New and Old.* 1875. New York: Oxford University Press, 1996. 171–79.

———. *Personal Recollections of Joan of Arc.* 1896. New York: Oxford University Press, 1996.

Twelve Southerners. *I'll Take My Stand.* Ed. Susan Donaldson. 1930. Baton Rouge: Louisiana State University Press, 2006.

Van Dyke, Carolynn. *The Fiction of Truth: Structures of Meaning in Narrative and Dramatic Allegory.* Ithaca, NY: Cornell University Press, 1985.

VanHoosier-Carey, Gregory. "Byrhtnoth in Dixie: The Emergence of Anglo-Saxon Studies in the Postbellum South." *Anglo-Saxonism and the Construction of Social Identity.* Ed. Allen Frantzen and John Niles. Gainesville: University Press of Florida, 1997. 157–72.

Warren, Robert Penn. *All the King's Men*. 1946. San Diego: Harcourt Brace, 1974.

———. "The Briar Patch." Twelve Southerners 246–64.

———. *Jefferson Davis Gets His Citizenship Back*. Lexington: University Press of Kentucky, 1980.

———. *The Legacy of the Civil War: Meditations on the Centennial*. New York: Random House, 1961.

———. "Mark Twain." *Southern Review* 8.3 (1972): 459–92.

———. *A Place to Come To*. New York: Random House, 1977.

———. "The Use of the Past." *New and Selected Essays: Robert Penn Warren*. New York: Random House, 1989. 29–53.

———. *Who Speaks for the Negro?* New York: Random House, 1965.

Watkins, Floyd, and John Hiers, eds. *Robert Penn Warren Talking: Interviews, 1950–1978*. New York: Random House, 1980.

Watson, Ritchie. *The Cavalier in Virginia Fiction*. Baton Rouge: Louisiana State University Press, 1985.

———. *Normans and Saxons: Southern Race Mythology and the Intellectual History of the American Civil War*. Baton Rouge: Louisiana State University Press, 2008.

Westervetl, Linda. "Robert Penn Warren's *A Place to Come To:* An *Altersroman* Inspired by Dante." *Genre* 34 (2001): 101–24.

Whatley, E. Gordon, ed. *Saints' Lives in Middle English Collections*. Kalamazoo, MI: Medieval Institute, 2004.

White, Hayden. *The Content of the Form*. Baltimore: Johns Hopkins University Press, 1987.

———. *Tropics of Discourse: Essays in Cultural Criticism*. Baltimore: Johns Hopkins University Press, 1978.

Whitman, Jon. *Allegory: The Dynamics of an Ancient and Medieval Technique*. Cambridge: Harvard University Press, 1987.

Wilmer, Richard H. *In Memoriam: A Sermon in Commemoration of the Life and Labors of the Rt. Rev. Stephen Elliott, D.D., Late Bishop of Georgia*. Mobile, AL: Farrow & Dennett, 1867.

Wilson, Charles. *Baptized in Blood: The Religion of the Lost Cause, 1865–1920*. Athens: University of Georgia Press, 1980.

Wilson, Katharina. "Hrotsvit and the Tube: John Kennedy Toole and the Problem of Bad TV Programming." *Germanic Notes* 15.1 (1984): 4–5.

Wimsatt, Mary Ann. *The Major Fiction of William Gilmore Simms: Cultural Traditions and Literary Form*. Baton Rouge: Louisiana State University Press, 1989.

Winchell, Mark. *Reinventing the South: Versions of a Literary Region*. Columbia: University of Missouri Press, 2006.

Wonk, Dalt. "John Kennedy Toole's Odyssey among the Dunces." *New Orleans Times-Picayune*, October 25, 1981, Dixie: 7+.

Wood, Ralph. *Flannery O'Connor and the Christ-Haunted South*. Grand Rapids: Eerdmans, 2004.

Woodward, C. Vann. *The Burden of Southern History*. 3rd ed. Baton Rouge: Louisiana State University Press, 1993.

———. *Origins of the New South, 1877–1913*. Baton Rouge: Louisiana State University Press, 1951.

Wyatt-Brown, Bertram. *Honor and Violence in the Old South*. New York: Oxford University Press, 1986.

———. *The Shaping of Southern Culture: Honor, Grace, and War, 1760s–1890s*. Chapel Hill: University of North Carolina Press, 2001.

———. *Southern Honor: Ethics and Behavior in the Old South*. New York: Oxford University Press, 1982.

Zaenker, Karl. "Hrotsvit and the Moderns: Her Impact on John Kennedy Toole and Peter Hacks." *Hrotsvit of Gandersheim*. Ed. Katharina Wilson. Ann Arbor, MI: Marc, 1987. 275–85.

Žižek, Slavoj. *The Puppet and the Dwarf: The Perverse Core of Christianity*. Cambridge: MIT Press, 2003.

Index